A CHILD OF GOD

To: Derek Family (handwritten)

Meant to Be

I would not be who I am today if I had not gone through what I did in my life - and today, I celebrate victory!

Becka L. Jones

Becka L. Jones (signature)

First Edition

The events and conversations in this book have been written in the best of the author's ability, although names and some details may have been changed to protect the privacy of individuals. Interaction, conversation, and any stories shared in this memoir is solely Becka L Jones perception of what happened.

ISBN 0692195114

ISBN 9780692195116

Library of Congress Control Number 2018960344

Cover Design by Becka L. Jones

Cover photo is Becka L. Jones dangling off a large rock shelf in Hawaii

Author Photo on back cover is Becka L. Jones and her dog Bella

Author email: bringingstoriestolife@yahoo.com

MEANT TO BE

CONTENTS

A Big Heartfelt Thank You to:

First and foremost: I want to thank God who stirred my heart years ago to write this memoir, and finally guided my every step through this process. God poured words into this book that made it successful for me personally, and I am so thankful.

I want to thank my high school teacher who believed in me and planted a seed to become an author, even though it took me many years to finally accomplish such a big feat of writing this memoir. I also want to thank my wonderful husband who has been my biggest support as I wrote my book at all hours of the day and night to finish. He has been my biggest advocate who has been such a loving husband through this whole process. For when I was writing the most difficult parts of this book, he has been there through it all. Without him, I wouldn't have been able to finish. I also want to thank my very good friend who not only edited my work, but also cheered me on when I wanted to give up. I would like to thank my mom who has been there through "thick and thin." I appreciate all she has done for me and all she does for me even to this day, and it means the world to me that she supports my writing career! She is not only my mom, she is my best friend! I love you all!

There are so many people I would like to thank who truly encouraged me through the process of writing this book. Those who were the stepping stones that helped bring me to where I am today, I want to thank you!

About my Memoir: Meant to Be

My life has been one big adventure. I didn't realize how much I had seen and how many things I had done until I wrote this book. Right after high school, I moved from cold Minnesota to sunny, warm Oahu, Hawaii and fell in love with paradise. I had many adventures, whether I was on an active volcano watching the lava flow just below my feet, swimming with the dolphins in the ocean, going on solo trips, hiking up gigantic mountains and waterfalls, or swimming at my favorite beaches. I enjoyed Hawaii and all it had to offer. It truly was paradise.

It may sound like a dream come true, but it wasn't always easy. I grew up in a single-parent home. During my childhood, my mom and I didn't seem to get along. My dad was not in my life, so I struggled with pain, insecurity, and feelings of rejection and abandonment. I had been sexually abused which messed me up, and then I met Jesus! I wouldn't say it was all happy times after I met Him, but Jesus saved me in so many ways!

I moved to Hawaii to run from my past, thinking that my future on an island in the south pacific would be perfect. I drifted from God and fell into a life of partying, depression, and self-pity. In this place, I met many people that tore me down in abusive ways, and eventually when I felt I was in a deep well of sorrow from pain and agony, I cried out to God who saved me! When God saved me, He brought loving and encouraging people into my life to help me along the way. By the grace of God, I was saved and even though everything wasn't perfect in my life, I had this intimate relationship with my Father God. I was on an amazing journey with Him, and He mattered the most in my life! God used me to touch many people's lives, and it blessed me much more than it blessed the people I met on this journey called life.

God called me to write my story which was a hard one to write, but I felt it needed to be told. I have gone through a great deal of healing by writing about what happened to me. God protected me throughout so many incidents that could have gone terribly wrong, but He saved me so that I would tell my story. I praise God I am still alive! I have a testimony to share, and I know some of you can relate to what I have gone through in life. If you are in that place where you see no way out, hang in there and call out to God. He can save you!

I wouldn't change my past for anything because I wouldn't be who I am today if I hadn't gone through the trials I did. God has brought me to a better place, and it is in Him that I lean on now! I love the woman God has molded me to be, I am now free, a woman living in victory.

Thank you for picking up my book. I hope it encourages and blesses you. This is my first book publication, and I plan on writing more books. Please watch for more to come. The names of people and pets have been changed in this book to protect their identity. I thank God for the people who have impacted my life in a positive way, because I would not be where I am today without them!

I also want to add that my story is not written in chronological order. When I was putting this book together, it fit perfectly because God was in the middle of it all. Praising God for all He has done and all He is doing for me.

My life verse: *"For I know the plans I have for you," said the Lord, "plans to prosper you and not to harm you, plans for a hope and a future." Jeremiah 29:11*

Jesus does not want your religion. He wants an intimate relationship with you!

Say "I love you" more times than you are used to. Everyone wants to hear it and you never know if you lose that chance to ever say it again.

Chapter 1

A New Beginning

Standing at the front door to my apartment, I swung the door open wide and stared into the dark, dismal, almost bare-naked apartment. The small living room looked drab and desolate, like a dark cave tucked snugly between four white walls. As I looked around, the room was almost completely empty, while boxes were piled in the hallway ready to be sent to the post office. No couch, no furniture, no lamps, no T.V. Hardly anything was left in this "hole in the wall" apartment except two suitcases of clothes, a few boxes, and a pile of papers. I had just a few more boxes in the bedroom to pack up to send away. Selling practically everything I owned had been a journey. It was a whirlwind. It felt surreal. A fast-paced stock market of selling just about everything and boxing up a minimum amount of clothes, papers, and beads for jewelry-making material to ship. I couldn't believe time went so quickly. It was just a month ago I had given my landlord a thirty-day notice and started selling things. How quickly everything spiraled into an almost empty apartment! "Am I making the right choice?" I asked aloud to myself.

I thought of what Jesus said, *"Leave it all behind and follow Me."* I felt God's message through His word applied to my life at this very moment. Jesus was calling me to something bigger, something I quite didn't understand myself, but I knew without a shadow of a doubt that God had called me into marriage. Not only marriage but moving from beautiful Hawaii back to cold Minnesota. I had lived in Oahu, Hawaii for almost seventeen years, and I was madly in love with the Hawaiian Islands. Hawaii was not only beautiful, but it felt like home, and

I had a church family and close friends that I loved. Hawaiians showed the true meaning of "Aloha" to me, and I had great memories of swimming, camping, hiking, walking on lava, and many other recollections of fun adventures in Hawaii.

I didn't intend to return to Minnesota where I was born; I would visit, but I had planned to never move back there. I felt I had more bad memories of my childhood than good ones. Now, God was leading me into marriage with this man He chose for me. God shared with me that I was to move to Minnesota to be with Lonnie and his two beautiful children. Even though I did not see the bigger picture yet of what was to come, I trusted and surrendered to God 100%. I knew He had His best for me and if I followed Him, He would take care of me. I sold things, I gave some away, I donated to shelters, and I thought of this verse:

Jesus said, *"You still lack one thing. Sell everything you have and give to the poor, and you will have treasure in heaven. Then come, follow Me" Luke 18:22.*

Still standing in the door frame, thinking about the past and my future, I looked toward the backward L-shaped hallway, and two upside down beady eyes looked back at me. My all-black cat Love lazily sprawled out with his tummy baring all with his four paws straight up in the air. As he stared wide eyed at me in the doorway, he yawned with a little "mew" hello and stretched out comfortably again.

"What am I doing!?" I suddenly screamed. However, the scream was all in my mind. All was still as I stood there. Doubt crept in just for a moment. "Is this the right thing, Lord?" I asked. I suddenly felt a blanket of peace rush over me. My cat Love still stared at me with expectant eyes, and then he sat up as if he heard my thoughts. His eyes looked longingly at me. I swear I think animals have a keen sense when it comes to their owner's feelings. When pets are connected to their owners, they can pick up when they are happy, sad, not feeling well, or moody. My cat was very sensitive to my feelings, though many times he just wanted to be fed.

Walking into my small dwelling, I looked around at the bare walls. The place looked so different. Eight years of my life had been spent in this small, dreary, old apartment, but I loved this place I called home. It wasn't much but I loved that it was right in Waikiki where there was endless shopping and I could walk just a few steps to the beach to go swimming. I met God here in this apartment in 2003. I had lost touch with Him for so many years. I walked away from God for so long that my life just fell apart, but when I called out to Him, He pulled me out of that deep, dark well and saved me.

Standing in my living room for the very last time, I was closing this chapter of my life for a better future with my soon-to-be-husband. Every step I took into the apartment was allowing me security in God as I took a chance on knowing Him more fully. My faith was growing, and God had picked this man for me, the man I am to spend the rest of my life with in marriage. I believe in God, not in religion. Religion is man-made, and God wants an intimate personal relationship with us, His beloved children. I had to overcome many obstacles before I realized I would be marrying the man of my dreams. I trusted God knowing He is the perfect match maker and He chose Lonnie especially for me.

I couldn't believe I was going to be married! I fell in love with this man, and I was excited to start this new chapter in my life with him and his two children living in Minnesota. Months before I had concluded, I would never marry. I had been hurt by men all my life and I gave up on the idea of ever marrying, but God had a bigger plan for my life. God showed me what my life would be like with this man of God and He told me He picked this man for me! I had a choice if I wanted to marry him or not. I chose to marry Lonnie.

As I pondered on my future, I sauntered into the bedroom, plopped down on the hardwood floor with a sigh, and looked around at the almost-empty room. There were tax papers and receipts, cards from family and friends, and pet-sitting contracts. Then there was a box of pictures, and I sucked in my breath as my eyes caught my favorite picture. I reminisced of the adventures I had with the many dogs I walked.

I picked up this particular photo of a dog I walked daily in mid to late afternoons as the Hawaiian sun would set beyond the ocean. Zumba was a big, white, fluffy Samoyed with a goofy, big grin and a happy prance that he did when he knew I was going to take him on a walk. As I stared at the picture, I remembered the day I took it. Zumba's black snout reached out to the lens of my camera and gently touched it. He sniffed as if the lens had a scent to it. I laughed as I took the picture. He always made me laugh and I would miss that!

Zumba had a long, white, fluffy coat of fur that would frequently be groomed and cut so that he would not be too hot in the summer months. The groomers always took special care to make Zumba look beautiful. They had a way of trimming down his long fur to make him look like a lion with a mane and short, soft bristly back hairs, shaved legs, and little white puffs escaping between his paws. He loved to be groomed. He would prance around me excitedly for his walk, showing off his special cut. It's as if Zumba knew he were the most handsome dog on the block.

He was always ready to go for his walk. He would smell my legs to see which dogs I had walked before him. He was a happy dog and one of my favorites. As we walked, Zumba would sniff and pee on everything he could, but he peed like a girl, squatting instead of lifting a leg! It was funny! He had a sweet nature and a curiosity for everything. If the wind blew leaves, he wanted to know what it was. He would hear a noise, stop to listen, look intently in that direction, and watch the neighbors as they went about their day. He made me look at life just a little differently and I liked that.

As I looked at the pile of dog pictures, I thought how I would miss all the dogs I walked, cats I pet sat, and all my wonderful clients I had grown close to over the years. I was moving from Hawaii to Minnesota to start a whole new life with my husband and his children, and I was excited for a new adventure with them.

Chapter 2

My Testimony

When I was younger, my mom and I did not get along well. She was having a rough time controlling me and my angry out-bursts, plus with financial burdens, there was a lot of stress on Mom. My dad was not in my life at all, and I think that had much to do with my anger issues. My mom reached out to a place called the Kinship program, which helped children from single-parent homes come together with a stable family that would help take some of the burden off the single parent. My mom wanted a family that could be loving, caring, and patient with someone like me. I know that God had picked this Christian family for me.

I met Jack and Sophia and their daughter Jasmine in 1983. I was a very shy kid, and I don't think I was on board with this program in the beginning. As time went on, I found that they were the kindest couple and their daughter Jasmine, who was a few years older than I, was very kind as well. I was a bratty kid, but Jasmine always let me hang out with her and her friends, and she treated me as if I were her little sister. We had a lot of fun together.

I was going through a tough time when I met this family. I was being sexually abused by a neighbor, and I didn't know how to deal with it. I pretended everything was fine, that I was a tough kid, and all was right in my world, but in reality, my world was all wrong. I hated my life, I hated my mom, I hated everyone and everything. I was angry at the world and out of control. My mom and I were fighting constantly, and most of our rocky relationship seemed to stem from her drinking.

I saw my kinship family as often as I could. I started looking forward to seeing them. It was my one outlet to do outside activities with a family, a dad, mom, and daughter. They were the perfect family to me. I looked up to them. We would go hiking, camping, ice skating, sledding - we did so many different things together. We made many memories as a family. They loved God, but I didn't know anything about God at that time.

I was raised Catholic. My mom didn't practice religion, so only when my mom and I would visit my grandma and grandpa is when we went to church. I didn't mind it. Stand, kneel, sit, stand, kneel, sit, and recite the "Hail Mary." It was an interesting way to worship a God I didn't know. My grandma was a devout Catholic who made sure all of us in the family knew we were raised Catholic and needed to stay Catholic. I loved the times with Grandma and Grandpa after church. We would go to their home in St. Peter, and Grandma would cook the most delicious foods for us to eat! She loved to cook, and she loved to bake. I loved spending time with her and Grandpa. It was nice to get away from the dirty, dark secrets that lay at home.

When I spent time with Jack and Sophia on the weekends, they started bringing me to their church on Sundays. It was nothing like the Catholic Church. They didn't stand, kneel, or sit throughout the service. They didn't have a confessional box where you had to say seven "Hail Mary's" before leaving. They did strange things like lift their hands in praise to the Lord and sing the songs in loud voices for everyone to hear. Some people would jump around or start praying out loud! It was a little much for me to take in the beginning.

I didn't know God, but I had heard of Him. He was this great big creator in the sky who made everyone and everything, and we could pray to the saints to have them relay a message to

Almighty God. At least that is what I was taught in the Catholic Church.

I asked Jack and Sophia questions about their church. It seemed so radical. People there seemed happy and genuinely caring and peaceful in their lives. I wanted peace. I didn't have peace I asked them how could I receive peace? They told me I needed to pray. I asked which saint do I pray to? Jack said, "No. You don't pray to the saints, you would pray to God Himself. We have a direct connection to our Creator and you can pray directly to Him." It sounded silly at first. I watched these people and studied them at each church service. Finally, one Sunday morning after service, I knelt in the corner of this small church and prayed. I cupped my hands together, closed my eyes, and spoke to God that day. I prayed to hear God's voice if He were real. I prayed to Him to forgive my many sins. I prayed He would cover me in love and peace, two things in my life I did not have and so desperately needed! I prayed for many things and then I waited to hear from Him. I didn't hear anything. I didn't feel much different at first. It wasn't like He struck me with lightning and I gave my life to Him. I stood up from praying, I felt a bit in a fog, and I went on with my day with this family who brought me to Christ.

A few days later, I was sitting at home and I decided to pray and ask God into my heart. I folded my hands together, bowed my head, closed my eyes, and started praying.

"Father God, If You are real, I want to hear from You. I want to hear Your voice. God, if You are with me, let me know."

I sat in the praying position for a few minutes. I just waited for Him to respond. A hundred thoughts were going through my mind. All these people at church were sure He was real, and I didn't want to miss out on what they had. I wanted the same thing. I wanted to feel the safety of God's arms around me. I wanted to hear His voice. I wanted "my Papa God" to take my fear, my sadness, and my anger away from me and replace them with this thing they called love.

Sitting there, I suddenly felt an overwhelming feeling of peace. It covered my whole body. It felt like someone put a soft blanket over me, so warm and fuzzy. I had never felt anything like it before then. I asked God if He had given me the peace I felt at that moment. I heard Him say audibly, "Yes, child, it is I." I stood up quickly and looked around. Who could have been talking? No one was there. It was just me. I wondered if it was really God. I again felt His peace come over me, and it's something I can't even describe. I just felt like a big weight fell off my back. Then I knew God was real and He had spoken to me!

God brought this family into my life at a time I needed them most, and my life was changed forever. I spent a great deal of time with them, and I won't lie, there were some challenging times. With patience, love, and prayer, they won me over. They didn't leave me when times were difficult. Many years later, Jack told me that there were times he wanted to give up on me as a child, but God told him not to do so! I am thankful they didn't give up on me! After I met God, my heart started healing, but I had a long way to go. Not only was I in the kinship program, but my mom found a class for me that helped sexually abused children. My mom also went to Al-Anon for help and I was in Alateen for children of alcoholics. She made good choices at that time to find the help we both needed.

This "Kinship" family became my second family. Both my mom and I can admit our lives were changed forever because of them. To this day, thirty-five years later, they are still family to me and I thank God for them. We stay in touch, and I feel so blessed to have them in my life! Praising God for the many blessings!

Chapter 3

Forever Friends

I have to say it, I love my mom. I don't just love my mom, I L-O-V-E her! I love love love her! She is not only the woman who gave birth to me, but she also is the one who raised me. She was there for me through thick and thin, and she never gave up on me... EVER. She is my best friend in the entire world. I ask her advice on everything. We bounce ideas off each other and ask what we would do in different scenarios. She is everything to me. I love my mom to the "moon and back," and she would say the same about me. I don't know what I would do without her.

She is beautiful, smart, witty, humorous, and fun to be around. When I was younger, wherever we would go, people would ask us if we were sisters. My mom would laugh and say we were, and she would soak in the compliment. One time we went to the mall where we planned a day of headshots. We put pretty fashion feathers and scarves around our neck to be silly and feel beautiful. We had our pictures taken. Twenty-four years later we took the same kind of professional pictures together. It was fun to replicate the photos. Thinking back to my early thirties, I am happy to say my mom and I became very close. It took many years for my mom and I to mend our relationship, but when we did, she became my best friend and we have had a lot of fun together ever since.

Once when my mom and Aunt Isabella came to visit me in Hawaii, we had a crazy idea to go skydiving together. It wasn't so bad since it was tandem with an instructor who had done more than one hundred jumps. We drove to the North Shore and with a small group of people, we piled into a little plane to fly up 13,000 feet. When it was time to jump, my mom was first. As the instructor walked with my mom to the open door of the plane, she looked back at me, and her face looked as white as a sheet. I gave her a thumbs-up to encourage her. As soon as my mom looked out that door, she must have had second thoughts about jumping. Her feet went up and her hands went out to catch the door frame, but by this time, it was too late. The instructor grabbed her hands, waddled with her to the very edge, and within seconds, they were gone! Then it was my turn to jump. I felt like a pro jumper since I had done it once before, but when I walked to the door, I forgot how high we were, and I suddenly felt dizzy. The guy I was strapped to asked if I was ready and I nodded. He pushed us off and I was falling, falling, falling, until the chute opened. Then we were lazily sailing through the air and I could see the brilliant sun over the horizon, the bright blue ocean below us, and the mountains in the distance! I caught my breath. It was a stunning view! When we landed and unstrapped, I ran to hug both my mom and Aunt Isabella. My mom, aunt, and I laughed and laughed because we couldn't believe we had just jumped out of an airplane and survived!

Good memories! But my mom and I didn't always get along. We used to fight like cats and dogs. Now I can call her anytime day or night and spill the beans about anything and everything, and she is always there for me and will give me her honest feedback. I am always there for her too, and I know she loves that we can call or text each other at any time. It took years to build our relationship, and I am glad we both worked at making it better. I figured someday she would be gone, and I could never take back the things I had said or done. I am happy that we made amends.

It was about fifteen years ago that we fixed our relationship. I thank God for patching things up between us. It is all I ever wanted, to be the daughter to this happy, fun, vibrant woman whom I could hang out with like a friend. She didn't judge me, she just loved me, and our relationship was and still is easy and fun. She doesn't have to worry about mothering me because I am all grown up, but deep down she will always see me as her little girl.

In 2003 when I was at my lowest point in life and needed help, I called out to God and He helped me. Not only did things just fall into place in my life in Hawaii, but God worked on my anger issues with my mom about her drinking and I was able to forgive her. I forgave her, and she forgave me. What a huge load off my back. Not only that, my mom became sober, and our relationship took a turn for the better. We began to mend our relationship and became friends. Praise God!

Our relationship was like a puzzle I had for years that sat on a table untouched. It had a few little pieces missing and it needed to be finished but it was just sitting there unfinished. When my relationship with my mom was fixed after so many years of brokenness, those missing puzzle pieces were added and my puzzle was just about complete. In the end, I was missing only one little piece from the corner of the puzzle, and that missing piece was my dad who had not been in my life as I was growing up. I have recently been working on that relationship as well.

Chapter 4

A Fabricated Childhood

At nine years old, I was a rough and tough, skinny, little kid who acted more like a tomboy than a delicate, fair-skinned girl with cute, colorful dresses, and blonde pigtails. I had done away with wearing girly clothes from earlier years. I wore boyish shirts with blah colors, ugly stripes, and shorts that were cut off and torn and not in style at all. I thought it was the perfect style for me. I stood out at school as the girl who was quiet and didn't fit in. I never seemed to fit in because I moved from school to school. I didn't dress up to look nice for school, and I didn't care what anyone thought of me. I was used to moving around a lot with my mom, and making friends was hard, so I gave up trying. I had a few friends, but I was always the new child on the block, the odd one out who hung with the "not so popular" children.

I had secrets which I never told anyone, not my friends, not even my mom. My mom raised me. My dad was not in the picture at all. My mom and dad divorced not long after mom gave birth to my brother, Matthew. He was sick and at fourteen days old, he passed away. It broke my mom's heart. I was one year old when my little brother died, and my dad left. My mom had a tough time being a single parent raising me on her own. Financially it was tough. She worked many hours to keep a roof over our heads and food on the table.

It wasn't always hard. There were good moments when I was young and growing up, but from what I can remember, I was almost always angry, and I didn't know why. My mom and I fought so much, especially in my teen years. Growing up without my father left me with a void in my heart. I became vulnerable and sought out love and attention. I didn't have a father to raise me and show me love. I didn't have a father to protect me from predators. I didn't have a father to show me how to respect others and make me feel like I was cherished. I grew up lonely and I felt like I had a hole in my heart because my father wasn't there. I was an angry child. I didn't know why I was so angry all the time, but I was angry. I always wanted to be by myself, hiding from others. I hated school and couldn't wait to come home and hide in my bedroom. I would pile my toys, clothes, books, and other items in my room almost up to the ceiling, "I kid you not!" I piled my toys so high as if I were hiding from something, and then no one would be able to find me in my room, and I felt safe. My heart hurt deeply, but out in the world I tried to smile and pretend it was all okay so that no one would ever know my secrets.

While other children had a mom and a dad, I felt uncomfortable telling my friends I only had a mom. They would ask me about my dad, and I would say, "I don't know anything about him." I was embarrassed not to know anything. I never heard from him growing up. My mom and I did not talk about my dad for many years. My mom and I didn't talk about much at all that I can remember.

At age nine, I felt lost and alone. Even with my mom around, I felt lonely. I know at that age, I was seeking love and attention, and I was vulnerable. I had a babysitter who was an older teenager that lived in the neighborhood. He was about fourteen years old. He would watch me while my mom would go out on a date or had a late night at work. My mom and I lived in a duplex apartment building in a low-income area in a neighborhood that was prominently black. There was a playground for kids to play in the back of the apartment complex. It had swings, a few slides, and hanging bars. I was at the playground often. One day, the babysitter and I went to the park and hung out on top of the slide together. I had a tan and white, long-haired teddy bear hamster that I brought with me. My hamster, Teddy, loved being outside when I would let him.

Usually there were a few kids playing at the park at any given time. On this particular day, the babysitter and I were the only ones there. As we sat at the top of the slide together and talked, this teen boy started petting my hamster Teddy who was sitting on my chest. At nine years old, it's not like I had a growing chest yet, but it was awkward that this boy was petting the hamster and his hand slid off Teddy and seemed almost like he tried to touch my boobs. Then his hand slowly moved down until it rested on the top of my jean shorts. I was stunned and didn't know what to do. I was naive and thought maybe the babysitter wasn't paying attention to where his hand went. He picked up his hand and again petted Teddy, and his hand would move off the hamster and down to touching my lower short's extremities. I didn't understand what he was trying to do. He told me to keep our little secret, and then he put his hand down my pants. I was scared. I told him I should get Teddy back home in his cage. I knew my mom was going to be home soon and hoped she was already there. Some kids started walking toward the park, and I was relieved that I wouldn't be alone with my babysitter any longer. He had touched my private parts and I was confused and wanted to run away. I was nine years old. I had never even thought about someone touching me in an uncomfortable way. When he saw the children coming toward us, he stopped, and I stood up and walked back down the steps of the slide to go home. Thankfully my mom was home, and the babysitter did not follow me.

I went up to my room and didn't say anything. My mom knew something was wrong. For the next few days she kept asking me if something happened. I wouldn't say anything but just went to my room and shut the door. The babysitter had told me this was our little secret and I couldn't tell anyone, but I felt dirty and I wanted to tell my mom. If I were going to tell her, it had to be before she started drinking for the night. I went downstairs and told her I needed to talk.

I thought this conversation could go one of two ways. She could either not believe me and we would start fighting and she would call me a liar, or she could believe me, and I would never have to see the babysitter again. I trusted my mom would keep me safe from him, so I sat with her and told her what happened. I was not good at sharing anything with my mom, and it was the hardest thing I ever did, but I did it. With my head down and feeling ashamed, I told her what happened and she "blew a gasket," not because I told her, but because her little girl was violated in a way she should never have been violated. She called the boy and told him she knew about the incident, and she better never see him around our place again. It felt good having her defend me. She threatened to call the police on him if she ever saw him again.

My mom worked during the day. She had a hard time finding me a new babysitter, so after I was finished with school, I would run throughout the neighborhood and get into trouble before my mom came home. A neighbor of mine, a kid who was a few years younger than I, liked to follow me around and annoy me.

One time I told this neighbor girl to stop following me, but she wouldn't. I then had an idea. I told her I had something for her. I went home, dug out crackers from the cupboard, put muddy dirt inside while a little cream cheese fell out the sides, and brought this yummy snack out for her. She was thrilled that I was being nice to her. She took the cracker sandwich and bit down hard, and as I heard it crunch loudly, the mud oozed out each side. I just cracked up laughing. I couldn't stop laughing! She threw down the cracker and with her head looking upward, she screamed! She screamed in such a high-pitched shrill that the whole neighborhood could hear her, including her overly protective brother who was a few years older than I. He ran to his sister who was bawling her eyes out and asked her what happened. He saw the cracker sandwich on the ground and as she pointed to me, he bolted right after me.

I turned around and jolting forward, I was a speed racer going toward a ten-foot fence trying to stay ahead of this lunatic chasing me. I thought of a gazelle being chased by a cheetah and how much faster the gazelle had to run to stay ahead of that cheetah. The teen used profanity saying all that was on his mind, and he sounded like he was right on my heels. I was scared to death and I raced ahead climbing up and over that ten-foot fence! I jumped down and kept running. I ran and ran until I could barely breathe, and I couldn't run anymore. I slowed down a quarter mile from the fence and looked back and he was long gone. I thought, note to self, I won't mess with his little sister again. One of my friends saw the whole incident, and she ran after me to see if I was okay. We walked toward a creek where I looked for gardener snakes, crayfish and little frogs to catch. My friend and I often walked down by the creek.

As we were playing by the rushing water, I heard something in the bushes and as I looked up, not ten-feet away, a man stood there in a police uniform. I had never been this close to a cop. He yelled at me, "Hey, what are you kids doing out here?" I felt like we were in trouble being on someone else's property. I was about to run when he said, "Freeze, I will arrest you." I didn't say anything, but just stared at him. I thought will he really arrest us, or should I tell him I was just running away from someone chasing me? Suddenly, he unbuckled his belt and dropped his pants to show his lower extremities. I had never seen a man's parts before. My friend grabbed my hand and yelled, "RUN!!" I dropped her hand, turned around, and "booked it" back to the fence leaving my friend behind. I climbed up the fence so fast and jumped over, but in the process of jumping over, I scratched my leg badly. Blood oozed out, but I didn't care. I was so scared, I raced back to my house and after opening the door, I slammed it shut. My mom was home and she asked, "What in the heck is going on?" I told her there was a policeman at the creek who dropped his pants and showed me his "thing." She picked up the phone and called the police. I said, "Mom, he IS the police!" She called anyway but the police didn't come. The cop on the phone said, "Since it happened earlier today, the guy probably flashed and fled. That's what flashers do." There was nothing the cops could do to find this guy. I went to the bathroom and cleaned up my scratch from the fence. I put band aid after band aid on it until it stopped bleeding. I went to my room, closed my door, and tried to forget what I had seen. I didn't go back to the creek for a very long time. I had believed that man had been a policeman and didn't realize he was just dressed up as one.

We had a next-door neighbor that was very nice. My mom talked to him occasionally. After school, I would say hi to him and my mom was fine with that. When I was with him, she knew I wasn't getting into any trouble. At his place he would let me watch TV, he would have candy for me to eat, and we would talk about nothing important. I didn't talk much, but I loved eating the snacks he would make for me and watching movies with him. My mom appreciated him since he looked out for me while she was at work. I went there only a few times before he started acting strangely. He asked me to sit on his lap to watch a movie, and I did, but I felt very uncomfortable. I didn't know him well enough to be this friendly.

He started making funny noises and breathing rather heavily and doing something funny to my back, under my shirt. He told me that what he was doing to me would be our little secret. Something was touching my back, and then suddenly I felt it touching the backside of my jean shorts! I had tight shorts on, so whatever was happening, he couldn't get it to happen. I remember my mom telling me never to keep secrets from her, and if anyone touched me and it felt funny, to tell her right away.

I jumped up and ran home. I called my mom at work and told her something funny happened with the neighbor. She took off work early and rushed home. She ran next door and wanted to pulverize the guy! He wouldn't open his door for her. She called the police but again the police wouldn't do anything. They said it was a little girl's word against the neighbor's word. My mom tried to get help, but it fell on deaf ears at the police station.

We packed up all our belongings and moved, again. Mom was going to do everything in her power to protect her little girl! I was sad to go because I had a few good friends and I liked the neighborhood, but I was used to moving, so it was nothing new. A new place, a new school, new friends, I was ready!

Chapter 5

Just Mom and I

When I was about five years old, my mom married a man named Gary who not only loved my mom, but also adored me. My stepdad wanted to adopt me, so my mom called my biological dad and asked if Gary could adopt me. If my biological dad said yes, it would take all rights away from him to see me or pay child support. He gave up the rights and a certificate had been written and notarized, and I took Gary's last name, Groves. I was officially adopted! I can't remember much about my stepdad, but Mom said he loved me very much.

One time, we were at a friend's farm and I was riding a horse that spooked over something and bucked me off. I fell and was knocked unconscious. I had hit my head and there was a great deal of blood. I don't remember that part, but I recall waking up in the car while my mom and stepdad were rushing me to the ER. It was a blur, but my stepdad was holding me and telling me it would be okay, just hang on. I was trying to sit up, but he was trying to keep me still and then I passed out. When my parents brought me to the hospital, the nurses wheeled me into a room to look me over. They had to pull tiny pebbles out of my head. Thankfully I didn't need stitches. That is the only recollection of my stepdad I had while they were married.

A year later, my mom and stepdad divorced, and I was stuck with his last name. I didn't hear from him again until I was nine years old. I was with Grandma and Grandpa at church when I noticed my stepdad a few pews ahead of us. He had a new family, a wife and child. After service, I pushed through the crowd of people to say "hi" to him, but he had rushed out of the church. It was almost my tenth birthday when Gary, my stepdad, called me out of the blue to tell me he had a birthday present for me. I was so excited to see him! I wanted a relationship with the only dad I knew. My stepdad and wife came to pick me up and we went to a restaurant to eat. They had a present on the table for me to unwrap after we ate lunch. I looked at the present. It was a medium-sized box. I wanted to open that present right then and there. I thought, "What could it be?" My mind raced to think if it were the newest toy on the market or maybe a Barbie doll. I loved Barbie dolls! Maybe it was a dress for me to wear to church. I was sure they had seen me at church and had to leave in a hurry for something important, so maybe it was a dress.

After eating lunch, I excitedly grabbed the present to see what it was. It was taped tightly, and I tore the box open and stared. I couldn't believe my eyes! I picked up the item and said, "Oh, thanks for the underwear, I guess." I stuffed the three pack of underwear back in the box and put it next to me on the seat. I was so embarrassed when I held it up in the restaurant for all the onlookers to see. I looked down and felt my face flush. How would my stepdad even think to give me something like this? It's such a private thing. I was very disappointed. That was the last time I ever saw him.

At this time in my life, my mom and I didn't get along, and it bothered me that she drank after work. We were always fighting with each other. Sometimes I would blurt out swear words, and she would give me "the bar of soap in my mouth." She said I had to think about what I was saying. Hey, it worked, a bar of soap for a filthy mouth! At least when I mouthed off, I knew what was coming! Whenever I was in trouble, my mom would spank me on the butt with a wooden spoon. Once she spanked me so hard that the wooden spoon broke, and she was irritated that she would have to buy a brand new one. I thought it was the funniest thing that she was so upset over having to buy another one that I couldn't stop laughing!

I believe a parent's discipline is good in certain situations, and I know that back then I deserved those spankings for being the bratty child I was. It was the only way she knew how to get my attention when I wasn't listening. I'm sure it was not easy for her to raise me without a father figure around.

Most nights after work, my mom would come home and drink excessively until she passed out. It made me so angry to see her drinking. I would always find fun activities to do in the neighborhood, so I wouldn't be home until dinner, and sometimes I would end up finding trouble with my friends.

One time I was hanging out in the school yard with my friend Natalie. We were running down the hill when I ran into metal bars used for pull-ups. I passed out and my friend went into the school to tell a teacher I was hurt. They called my mom who left work to rush to my school to pick me up, but I wasn't there. She finally found me at the school closest to our home. She was worried sick. I was in the nurse's office where they had patched up a small scratch on my face, and I had lost a part of my front tooth.

When my mom saw my friend Natalie, I knew I was in trouble. Mom had previously grounded me from seeing her for six months, and now she had caught us together again. I knew I would be grounded from seeing her forever. Mom always grounded me from seeing my two best friends, June and Natalie. For reasons I cannot explain, she didn't want me to hang out with either one of them, but it didn't stop me from seeing them. They were, after all, my best friends.

One evening June and I went to the Twins game in Minnesota. I have no idea how we were able to go to the game.

We were teenagers with no money. It was the World Series game and WE WON! It was the best time we ever had! When I arrived home late that night, my mom was worried sick. She said I smelled like beer and pot. I told her that I only drank pop and ate a hotdog. I promised her I did not and do not do drugs, but she didn't believe me. I was grounded for a long time from seeing June because of the assumptions. It was a bummer. I had to sneak around to see my best friend! It made me angry that my mom suspected me of drinking and smoking pot because I would never do that. My mom was an alcoholic, but at that time she had no control over it.

Being an alcoholic is a disease that can captivate the person's life in the beginning and entice them into a fun life of partying and feeling good. Drinking can make them feel unstoppable. It consumes them. Drinking heavily gives a false sense of confidence and an "I don't care" kind of attitude. Being an alcoholic creates a different part of the person, like a monster that comes out when they indulge in alcohol. It numbs the person to reality. When drinking, alcoholics can literally be on another plane in an abyss of self-pity, sorrow, and hiding behind a bottle that becomes their best friend. The person can end up losing control over everything in their life, including family and friends. It is a seductive lifestyle where they think they have confidence, total control, and the courage to do anything. Alcoholics truly believe they can stop drinking at any time, but it is deceptive. Alcoholism is a disease. It is an addiction that sneaks up and grabs the person before they realize it has a hold on their life. There is a difference between someone who has an occasional glass of wine or a beer and someone who constantly thinks about alcohol and feels it is necessary to survive in the world.

My family had been consumed in alcoholism for many years, a kind of curse that had stuck in our family's history for generations. Both Mom and Dad were sucked into alcoholism for many years as well. I know now the choices my mom and dad made would have been better ones if they had not been drinkers and maybe they would have stayed together while I was growing up. Thank goodness that years later, both my mom and dad sobered up and have been clean ever since!

During my childhood, my mother's drinking affected me in so many ways. I would sneak bottles of wine from her hiding place and dump the contents down the toilet, knowing full well that she would be angry at me when she found out. I was going to be whooped with a big wooden spoon on the bare butt, but I didn't care. I wanted her to stop drinking! I wanted her to realize how much it hurt me that she was drinking to the point of passing out. I wanted her to realize that the boyfriend she was with, was taking the place I wanted. I wanted her love and affection. I wanted her undivided attention. I wanted her to hear me crying myself to sleep at night, but I knew she was with her boyfriend or passed out and couldn't hear me crying in my bedroom. I wanted a mother back then, but all I saw was an alcoholic when I looked at her, drunk. I hated what it did to her. Deep down I am sure I loved her, she was after-all my mom, but from as young as I could remember, I felt her first love was that bottle and her second love was the boyfriend she was with at that particular time, and that made me angry.

My mom was so deep into her drinking that she couldn't have stopped even if she wanted to quit. It's the disease that consumed her. It made her think she was in control, when that was the farthest from the truth. My life felt like one big lie. When we would visit family, she would try to hide the fact that she was drinking, but during most visits, everyone knew that she was drunk. When I was younger, I was embarrassed, but as I grew up, I just became numb to it. I didn't care anymore.

Every night Mom would drink, and it made me so mad. She would come home from work and find her stash of wine or hard liquor. Whatever she was drinking, she would drink until she passed out or threw up. She would go into her bedroom and go to sleep, and I would stay up late and watch scary movies on the old 24-inch TV we had. It was the kind of TV that I had to get up and go change the channel. Early in the morning, I had to wake my mom up and make sure she would get off to work. The one thing I truly admired about my mom is no matter how bad it was, she always had a job to make ends meet and she made sure we always had a roof over our heads. After she was off to work, I would catch the bus in time for school. I never missed a day of school. It was the right thing to do. I know now that my mom did the best she could with what she had.

There was no support from my biological dad and Mom didn't have much money, but we managed. There were days she couldn't afford food to put on the table, and if our electricity went out, we would eat cold beans right out of the can. I liked those times with her the best! Our alone times together were special to me, and she would act goofy and make it fun eating cold hotdogs and beans right out of a can. Sometimes when she was driving the car, she would start dancing to a tune on the radio that she loved. She always tried getting me to join in, but I was so embarrassed that the people driving by would see her "bee-bopping" around in the car and wonder what was going on, but she always tried to make things fun.

Every so often we would go to the movies, just Mom and me. I loved those times together and always looked forward to it. On her way home from work, she would stop at the store and pick up a bunch of chocolates or candy bars that she would stuff in her purse. When we were in the movie theatre, she would magically pull out a candy bar, one for her and one for me. She would have this big, comical smile on her face as if sneaking in snacks was the greatest thing in the world, and to me, it was the greatest thing in the world. We would eat our chocolate bars, and after we finished, she would magically pull another few snacks from her purse for us! It always made me laugh. She had everything in her oversized purse - Snickers, Twizzlers, Milk Duds, and chocolate-covered raisins. It was like her purse was a bottomless pit of yummy snacks for us to eat at the movies. Good memories for me. Mom was sober, and these were moments I dearly treasured.

When Mom was driving, and we would enter a long tunnel, she would tell me to hold my breath and make a wish. I would hold my breath in the tunnel, make a wish, and let it out as my mom drove out the other end. Some of those tunnels were long and I would hold my breath until I felt like my chest would explode and then let it out as the tunnel ended. Each time I held my breath I wished for a puppy. I told her what I wished for and she said, "No way are we adopting a puppy!"

Another time, we were inside the tunnel when the traffic suddenly stopped. I refused to let my breath out because I was not going to let this "puppy-wish" go. I wanted a puppy so badly. Mom told me I had to breathe because my face was turning blue. I didn't care. I just shook my head "no" and kept holding my breath. I felt light-headed and Mom became panic-stricken, thinking I was going to pass out. She was honking her horn at the car in front of her, but it couldn't move an inch forward as the cars were packed like sardines in that tunnel.

After a few seconds, the cars started moving forward and we were out of that long tunnel. I just about blew out a lung that time, but my wish came true! We went to the Humane Society where I found a little black and white puppy - she was a Spitz breed. I sat on the floor of the shelter and held the puppy closely. I whispered in her ear that we were going to save her from this awful place. She was so sweet, and I loved her instantly. My mom wanted to hold her too. When Mom went to pick her up, the puppy was nervous and piddled on her. I thought it was the funniest thing and I laughed and laughed! I wanted to call her "Piddles," but I named her "Pebbles" instead.

I had a flawless facade to cover up the truth, so no one would know what was happening in my life at the time. I looked happy on the outside, but I was a great pretender. I was quiet. I was a shy kid. I was always wandering from the house and sometimes I would daydream about running away, but I never did. I lived in my own little world in my head. I had this imagination that would run wild and I could escape reality through it. It was easier to do that than coping with what was really going on in my life. I looked happy on the outside, but on the inside, my heart was hurting, and I wanted to die. It felt like someone had reached into my chest, squeezed my heart into a ball, threw it on the ground, stomped on it, and then put it back into my chest. Maybe it was loneliness, confusion, abandonment issues, and insecurities all tied up in a knot inside my stomach. To top it off, I was being sexually abused. I made sure I looked like I had it all together. I displayed a tough exterior to everyone around me; however, on the inside, I was a sappy mess, crying out for help and unable to say anything to anyone. I felt confused and angry. I hated everyone and everything. I felt numb and didn't want to live anymore. My heart was of no use. Things went on around me, but I didn't pay much attention to any of it.

It was from age nine to thirteen years old I was being sexually abused. Life went on. My friends didn't know, my family had no idea what was going on behind closed doors, and I pretended all was great in my life. Secretly, however, things went on in the background that terrified me. The fear of telling the truth scared me, but the repercussions of telling someone terrified me even more. Secrets are to be kept. Adults are to be respected. Adults know what they are doing. Kids don't know between right and wrong when it comes to abuse. I was very confused. I had mixed emotions and questions. Did I bring this on myself? I didn't know why adult men were touching me. I didn't know why anyone would touch me. I was a mess. I was a child who wanted to be left alone and didn't want anything to do with anyone. I was confused and ashamed. I didn't know if this happened in other families, but I was too scared to ask. I was a survivor who felt I needed no one.

As a young child, I yearned for love from someone, anyone, but when the sexual abuse started, I was so confused. My mind would shut down because I couldn't handle the sexual abuse. It happened so often that I was physically there, but my mind was somewhere else. Somewhere that was safer than where I was. I taught myself how to shut down, and I learned I could do this anywhere I needed to do so. At school, I would check out. I closed my eyes and I was in a large field with my imaginary horse, riding free with the wind blowing through my hair. It was just the horse and I until the teacher called on me to answer a question, which I couldn't answer. The kids would laugh. This happened often.

I loved contests, especially ones with cash prizes. When I was about eight years old, I entered a drawing contest and I wanted to win! I worked hard at my drawing. I had drawn a horse and a barn, with a dog and cat, and a house and a white picket fence in the background. A great big tree was in the middle of the yard. I had won the drawing contest and was awarded $10.00! I was so excited! $10.00 may not seem like much money, but to a young child like me, you would have thought I won a hundred dollars! I was on top of the world. The teacher asked how I thought of the drawing. I had opened a children's book to see a barn and horse, and I thought of other animals and different scenery for the picture and added it. That's it. They loved it!

One day, not long after winning the contest, I was sitting in the classroom and was happy to be in my favorite class. It was an art class, and that day we were going to draw. I was good at drawing. I could draw just about anything. I was sitting at the desk ready with my #2 pencil in hand. The teacher said, "This will be a unique assignment, there are pictures on the table from magazines, you will pick a picture off the table to draw, then cut the picture in half, glue it onto a piece of paper, and draw the other half. Be creative and have fun." I jumped up and I ran to find my picture. I picked a photo of a lady with olive eyes, the perfect nose, and curly brown hair. She looked lovely and I wanted to draw her.

I sat down, cut the face in half, glued it onto a sheet of paper, and started drawing. The teacher was walking around the room looking at everyone's drawing. She stopped at my drawing a few times and didn't say anything. The next time around when I was almost finished, I looked up at her expectantly, hoping for a compliment. I knew she would like my work. She said, "Becky, that's an awful drawing. You can do better than that." I looked at my drawing. I didn't think it was so bad. My excitement deflated like a helium-filled balloon that had a slow leak. I couldn't believe she didn't like my drawing. I didn't say anything to her, but I decided that I didn't want to draw anymore.

Things just spiraled out of control from there. The teachers at school started talking about how I didn't interact in class or do anything, so they decided I should be held back a grade. They talked to my mom and told her I should be in a Special Ed class for mentally retarded children. Mom trusted the teachers knew best, so the next year I was in a Special Ed class. I hated it. The whole year was a blur. It just made me angry that now everyone at the school thought I was mentally retarded. I knew I wasn't retarded. I just had issues in life.

There was a disabled student in my class who was a sweet boy. I remember he made me a ring. At first, I was appalled but I became friends with him, and my heart softened for all the children in the class. To this day, I have a soft spot for physically and mentally challenged children and adults. They have big hearts and are much smarter than people give them credit for!

That summer, my mom and I moved to a cute little house on the corner of Central Avenue. I loved this new house. It was perfect for us. It had a big fenced-in back yard where I started collecting a lot of stray animals. I would start with small creatures first. I collected a few painted turtles and numerous baby snappers. I named them all, and by the end of summer, I would let them all go back in the lake. I had a very big painted turtle I named Henry.

One day it was pouring rain, and there was a leak in the basement window where water was flooding the ground outside as well as pouring in and filling the carpeted basement floor. I took my turtle into the basement where he could swim in the water that was his little "pool." He loved swimming. When the rain stopped, I pulled the outside water hose into the basement filling up his "so-called pool" some more so he could swim farther and deeper in the water. Oh, I had a "licken of a lifetime" with the wooden spoon when my mom came home from work! She was not happy with that indoor pool I made.

I collected so many different animals. I had my Teddy Bear hamster, and I also found baby birds that had dropped out of their nests. I nursed them from an eye dropper until they were ready to fly. I found a puppy in the street, brought him home, and called my mom at work to tell her we now had two puppies! Mom wasn't happy with that, and as soon as she walked through that door, she had already found another home for that cute little guy. Whatever animals I could find, I would bring them home to love and nurture. I finally felt I could connect with something in my life, and with animals, I not only bonded with them, but I also felt a deep love for them! I loved these animals and made it my life mission to rescue any little creatures that needed help. I even had a deep connection with my dog Pebbles. I could look in her eyes and know exactly what she was thinking. She was my best buddy! I loved having such a deep bond with animals and loved them more than anything in life! Still to this day I have such a connection, especially with dogs and cats.

When my mom and I saved the puppy from the shelter, Pebbles became my best friend! She would follow me everywhere I went, especially when I rode my bicycle. We lived on the same block as a chain of auto part stores where our house was the only one on the whole block. After school and on weekends, I hung out with these old guys who ran the stores. They would tell me I could go through the old cars and whatever change I found, I could have. I would be there for hours scrounging around the junk cars for loose change! Then I would go to the 7-11 store on the corner and buy as much candy as the change could buy and I would eat it all in one sitting. One of the auto part stores had a big, mean Doberman Pinscher, and I would climb their eight-foot high fence, jump over, pet his sweet face, give him a kiss, and walk through the junk yard. Pebbles would squeeze through a part of the fence and follow me in. The men were shocked that the Doberman liked me, but I had a way with animals and no fear when it came to big dogs.

Pebbles thought the Doberman was very handsome, and she was knocked up by him fairly quickly after meeting him.

She soon had seven adorable puppies, but one died at birth. Pebbles gave birth to those puppies early in the morning, so I told my mom and Uncle Tyler, who was staying with us at the time, I wanted to bury the puppy when I came home from school.

When I arrived home that afternoon, I ran into the house and couldn't find the dead puppy anywhere. My mom was still working, and I asked my uncle what happened to the puppy. He said he threw him in the dumpster outside because the dead animal was stinking. I ran to look in the dumpster, but the garbage man had already taken the trash! I sat on the ground and bawled my eyes out. I was so angry at Uncle Tyler for disposing of the puppy. I had wanted to have a ceremony and bury the pup in the backyard.

I put that sad incident behind me as I fell in love with the rest of the little puppies that ran around the house. They followed me around everywhere. I told my mom I wanted to keep one of them, but she told me I could choose one of the puppies or keep Pebbles, but I would have to choose only one! I chose Pebbles, of course, because she was my best friend!

When the puppies were old enough, Mom told me to put them in a box, make a sign that said, "FREE PUPPIES," and sit on the side of the road to see if there was any interest. I had grown attached to them all, and it was hard to see them go, but in one day, all six puppies found good homes and it was fun to see children's smiling faces when they came to pick up the puppy they wanted to take home.

I also had goldfish in a ten-gallon tank, and one day I came home from school and there was a bar of soap floating on top of the water in the tank. All my fish were dead! I called my mom bawling my eyes out and told her what happened. I knew it was my uncle who had put the soap in the tank. My mom took me to the store to pick out more fish. I cleaned out the tank and started over. Not long after we had the new fish, I came home from school to find them all floating at the top of the tank, dead. I gave up on having fish. It was time to put the fish tank away.

After school was out for the year, I always found fun things to do. One thing I liked doing was visiting this guy who lived in an old, yellow school bus. He lived right across the street from me in an abandoned parking lot, and my dog and I would go hang out in his bus while he polished it up for his big road trip he had planned. He had gutted the school bus and fixed it up to live in. It was ready for full-time RV living! Every day I would visit him. He was so nice. My mom knew I was there and would walk over to tell me when it was time for dinner. One day this guy told me he was leaving for good. He was going to travel the whole US in his big bus. I remember being sad. He was my only friend in the neighborhood. He promised to come back and visit someday, but he never did.

When I was twelve years old, my mom dated an older gentleman who seemed nice. I liked the guy. My mom was "head over heels" for him. They both drank and smoked together, and they were with each other every moment they could be. They looked great together, and my mom seemed so happy. They were inseparable. He had a daughter named Lacey who was a few years younger than I. Most nights we would end up staying at his house, and my mom would make me sleep with Lacey in her bed! I hated it. She would touch me in places I didn't want to be touched and it grossed me out. I didn't understand what she was doing, but she would giggle and tickle me and touch me and I was mortified.

Every time my mom told me we were going to their house to stay overnight, I would plead with her to have me stay with a friend or a neighbor or anyone, but don't make me stay there. My mom couldn't figure out why I didn't want to go there, and I was too embarrassed to say this girl was touching me in my private parts. I especially remember my thirteenth birthday. My mom said we were going over to her boyfriend's house. I told her I did not want to go there for my birthday. I pleaded with her over and over. I asked if I could stay home. I didn't even care about my presents. Staying home would be the best present I could ever have. My mom assumed nothing and could not figure out why I hated going over there so badly. Mom won, and I had to stay in Lacey's room for my thirteenth birthday. I was so angry. When I was in Lacey's bedroom something cracked, and I checked out. Being abused in this way was a pivotal moment in my life where I just wanted to die. My mind went somewhere else and I blacked out from then on. I couldn't remember what happened when I stayed in her room on many overnights. To this day I have no recollection of what took place after my birthday. When the relationship between my mom and the boyfriend ended, I was so happy that I never had to see that girl again!

For years, I stuffed the memories away and pretended all was okay. I just wanted to forget, but the sexual abuse could not be forgotten. My innocence had been taken away. My mom put me in a group for sexually abused children, and I applaud her even to this day for taking the steps to help me. At the time though, I was numb to everything. In the sexual abuse class, all I could do was laugh uncomfortably at what the instructors said and did. They used dolls to portray what happened to us children and I didn't want to be in that class, remembering the abuse I had gone through. I would laugh at what the teachers did, but deep down I was just scared of opening that can of worms and delving into what really happened to me. The other children in the class were sharing their experiences. I just couldn't share emotion or say the right words about what really happened to me, so I laughed it off like it didn't bother me, but it did bother me. I was scared to death.

As a child, I not only had to worry about the abuse I was going through, but I also felt I needed to take care of my mom. I had to throw the booze away, rip up her cigarettes to help her quit, make sure she was awake to go to work in the mornings, and then I would go to school. I needed to act like I was okay so that no one would know my secret about the sexual abuse. I was terrified someone would find out, and yet I played it cool like I had it all together.

I felt my childhood was taken from me and I cried for that child who had her innocence stolen at such a young age. Those perverts, they have no control over me anymore. It has been thirty-four years since I stuffed away the pain, the fear, and the agony, pretending nothing happened. But no more! By the grace of God, I have broken the chains! Praise the Lord I am healed! God is my Rock and my Savior, and He takes care of me, Amen.

Chapter 6

It was Puppy Love

At the age of sixteen I was a very quiet and shy high school girl. I didn't have many friends, but I loved animals. LOVE is a mild word. I loved animals more than people! I didn't connect with many teens my age, I was kind of a loner. In school, I didn't pay much attention in any of my classes. My attention span was short, and my mind wandered constantly. School was boring for me and I wanted to be anywhere but there. I couldn't wait until the moment the bell would ring and I could leave for the day.

On warm days I would walk home from school since it was only a few blocks away from the apartment. In the cold winter months, I would take the bus which was always loud and rowdy. I did not like riding the bus. After the bus would drop me off at home, I ran into the house, threw my school books down on the counter, and then I would run outside to find something fun to do. I loved the outdoors and would bike around the streets for hours, or I would walk for miles and enjoy nature and being outside. I had two best friends from high school, Tiffany and Melanie, who were sisters that lived down the block from me. We would hang out most days after school and find fun things to do in the neighborhood.

I loved to hang out at the strip mall across the street from the apartment complex where we lived. I would sit outside the mall and people watch. The strip mall had a pet store, and my very favorite thing to do was visit the puppies and kittens in the store.

Every few days I would go to the pet store. It was fun to see all the new pets that arrived there almost daily. They had playpens set up in the back with puppies. The set-up made it easy for customers to interact with puppies and want to adopt them. The kittens were behind glass in the far back of the store. I always asked to hold the kitties. I'm sure it was annoying to the employees, but they were always so nice to me and would let me hold them. My very favorite pastime though was playing with the puppies that came in. Puppies were always the first to be adopted, and it was hard for the store to keep a supply of them, so when they brought new ones in, I made sure I visited them as much as possible. I had previously owned a dog. My mom gave my dog to Grandma and Grandpa to care for when we moved from a house into an apartment complex that didn't allow pets. I missed my dog very much.

One day I walked into the pet store and without looking at the front counter, I walked straight to the back where all the pets were. There were two very adorable and rambunctious black and white Siberian Huskies in the playpen, and they were all "fluff and fur." There was a small, wiry fenced-in pen that kept them from running all over the store. The pen was only a few feet high which made it easy enough for me to walk over and sit down in the midst of them. The two adorable puppies crawled all over me, and I squealed and giggled as they jumped on me to lick my face.

Suddenly, I heard a man clear his throat and my eyes gazed up from the puppy kisses. I hadn't noticed there was a man standing there. His arms were folded, and he had a scowl on his face. I put the puppy down that I was holding and stood up. I stepped out of the pen and asked, "Who are you?" The man replied, "I am the manager of this store." I smiled and said, "Oh, you are the new manager, nice to meet you, my name is Becky." He looked at me for a moment, then looked at the puppies, and finally back at me again. Then he asked, "Do you always go into a pet store and help yourself to the puppies without asking permission?" I laughed and replied, "I do! I have been coming in here just about every day playing with all the pets. I love the animals so much, I practically live here!" I laughed again and smiled really big at him.

I studied him closely. He was a handsome man who was tall and slender with wavy, shoulder-length bleach blonde hair. He had the kind of face that people would say he was a "pretty boy." He finally smiled at me, introduced himself as Ian, and we chit-chatted for a while. When I realized the time had flown by, I had to run home as my mom would be expecting me. I said my farewells and left. As I walked home, I had a funny feeling in my heart. It felt like a fluttering butterfly. I didn't know it at the time, but it was definitely love at first sight. Maybe not true love at that moment, but it was the start of something grand. I had never liked a boy before this. He was so much older, but it felt good to have feelings for this man. It made me happy.

Every day I came back to the pet store after school and played with the puppies until they were sold. I kept coming to see all the animals, but secretly I was coming to see the manager who paid me just a little bit of attention too. I really liked him. It wasn't two sided though. He would make jokes like, "You are here all the time. Why don't you just pitch a tent and live here!" or "Don't you have a home to go to?" I would smile and laugh. He could say, "The ice cubes are melting," and I would have thought it was the cutest comment he ever made. We talked just about every night while he worked. He was easy to talk to, he was smart, funny, passionate about life, and he loved animals more than anything. We had so much in common. I had never met a guy quite like him who I felt such a connection.

For me, it turned into love. I constantly laughed at everything Ian said, and it felt very good. Every so often a group of his friends would show up at the pet store to hang out with Ian. He seemed to be very popular with the ladies who were flirty with him. I liked his friends and thought they were funny. I wanted to be liked by them because if his friends liked me, hopefully he would become fonder of me as well. The ladies looked at me like I was just a child, but I learned from them how to flirt with him and after a few months, he confessed I was growing on him. His comment made my entire world! I was floating on cloud nine! He asked me out on a date and I said, "YES!" with exuberance.

I was a vulnerable teenager. I had grown up without a father in my life. I was yearning for attention from someone, and this man was more than willing to give it to me. I was getting ready for my date, and I wore my best outfit. The first time Ian pulled up in front of my home on a Yamaha motorcycle, my mom just about had a "conniption fit." She asked, "How old is he and what does he want?" She just about burst when I walked out the front door not answering her. I hopped on the back of Ian's bike to go on our first real date and we drove off. I could feel my mom's eyes like daggers in the back of my head. She was fuming, but I didn't care.

My mom didn't know how old Ian was at that time, but she knew he was over eighteen. He was actually twenty-one years old. He was five years older than I. When my mom found out Ian's age, she was so angry. Here is her innocent, little girl going out on a date with a man! She tried to call the police on him a few times, but they didn't show up at the apartment fast enough. Ian's bike was faster, and we would speed off before the police would arrive. My mom had my best interest at heart and she wanted to protect her baby girl the best way she could, but I was young and madly in love. I didn't care about anything but Ian. This was the first time a guy had ever paid attention to me and not just any guy, but a very handsome one!

I don't even remember where we went on that first date. The thing I remember is Ian told me to hold on tightly because his bike went fast. I was so shy, but so excited for our date. I held on as tightly as I could. It was my first motorcycle ride and I loved how it felt as the wind blew my hair, the sun hit my face, and the loud engine rumbled below the seat.

Ian and I hung out together every single day, and I was falling madly in love with him. He was romantic, writing me little notes, sometimes bringing me flowers, and devoted time to me. He was my first love and I wanted to spend the rest of my life with him. I wanted us to be married as soon as I graduated from high school which I thought would be my dream come true.

I was sixteen years old and had never been kissed. Ian said he would have to change that. When we kissed, I was hooked! I thought about him all the time. When I finished high school, I planned on marrying this man and having a bunch of babies. I wanted us to be like the *Brady Bunch.* When I thought things were becoming serious with us, I shared with Ian that I was a Christian who loved God. He thought that was cool. He came to a church play I was in, and he even came with me to church a few times. It made me very happy.

At the same time when I was sixteen years old, I met my biological dad for the first time. He had given his address to a family member who gave it to me. I wrote him a letter introducing myself. He wrote me right back. His letter stirred emotions in me about my childhood, feeling abandoned and rejected, yet I wanted to meet my dad so badly. I wanted to get to know him, learn more about him and be loved by him - all the things I had missed out on as a child; I stored that deep in my heart. He had three children who I had no idea they even existed! We all met not long after I received his letter, and it went well. I met my dad and half-brother and two half-sisters. I really loved meeting my siblings. I never had any brothers or sisters growing up as a child. I would have had a younger brother if Matthew had not passed away.

I kept in touch with my biological father because I wanted a relationship with him. I had missed out on so many years with him. I reached out to him from time to time, trying to keep some kind of relationship. He lived an hour-and-a-half from where my mom and I lived, so it wasn't like I could just run over to see him at any given time. I wanted so badly to spend more time with him.

During this time, my mom and I were fighting constantly, especially when she found out my grades were dropping because I wasn't focused on school. If I didn't raise my grades, I would flunk an entire year. I was receiving D's and F's in almost every class, except in English and Gym. I liked those classes! My mom came up with an idea to spark my interest. If I would work on my grades, she would pay me $5 for every A and $4 for every B. I loved that idea! The next semester, I was on the B honor roll with a few A's! Money talked, and I was motivated. She was surprised and ecstatic. I did well the rest of the school year and had made a little extra money.

My mom saw that money motivated me, and she told me if I didn't do any drugs, she would give me one hundred dollars when I turned eighteen years old. I also had never had a cavity, so Mom said if I didn't have any cavities when I turned eighteen years old, she would give me an additional one hundred dollars! I was ecstatic. When I turned eighteen, I received two hundred dollars!

My mom and I continued to have a rocky relationship, and it worsened after Ian and I were seriously dating. She did not like Ian at all. I finally finished my junior year of high school, and I was happy it was over. All summer long I spent time with my boyfriend. Things with my mom spiraled out of control and we fought constantly. She had recently married a guy I didn't like. It wasn't the guy she married that I didn't like; it would have been ANY guy she married that I wouldn't like. It was a mad house with my mom, her husband Jordan, and his overly excited three small children running around screaming and being annoying! The children would come over most weekends and I never had a quiet moment.

I didn't have a father figure growing up, so when Jordan married my mom and moved in, he acted like he was my new father trying to tell me what to do and when to do it. He tried putting his foot down and I couldn't stand it. Who did he think he was? It made me so mad. I was fighting all the time with both my mom and her new husband. In one fight with Jordan, I said, "I am not one of your kids; besides, how long will you be sticking around?" This was my mom's third husband and I felt father figures never stayed around for long.

During this time Ian and I continued to see each other and one night he and I were intimate. He had taken my virginity. I decided to move in with him. We were great together. I had this dream that we would marry and live "happily ever after." He lived in a cute, two-story, purple house in Minneapolis, Minnesota. He rented a room in the basement. There was also a lady named Henrietta who lived in another bedroom in the basement. Henrietta was good friends with Ian, but I sensed the feeling that she had a crush on him. I didn't let it bother me though. She was twice his age and acted more like a mother than a friend.

Ian continued to work at the pet store during the day. I didn't have a job, so I would wait for him to come home. One day I was picking up and cleaning the bedroom when I came across some pictures of him and a lady friend snuggling or whatever they were doing. The pictures were dated during the same time Ian and I were in a relationship! I was very upset! When I asked him about the pictures, he said it was a pose he did just for the camera. He made it sound so casual as if it were no big deal. I easily forgave him because I was so "in love" with him.

During the summer months, my best friend June would often drive over to pick me up, and we would check out the city life, and find fun things to do together. June was so excited to have her very own car! It was her first car and she wanted to drive it everywhere. She was boy crazy back then, so she would whoop and holler at cute boys as we drove by them and I would just laugh and laugh. We had such a good time together. We met many new friends that summer.

As the summer was coming to an end, Ian and I were starting to have some problems. He wanted to move to Hawaii in a few months and told me I would need to stay in Minnesota and finish my senior year of school. I was heartbroken that he would leave me. We had been together for 2 ½ wonderful years! Why would he not wait for me to finish school and then we could move to Hawaii together? He still wanted us to be a couple, just long distance; but I didn't want a long-distance relationship at all. I wanted him to stay for me.

I was saddened as I wrote this poem:

True Love needs effort to bloom:

Love is...

Very delicate

Very memorable for me.

Being in love is like the petals of a rose

So delicate, and yet so beautiful.

There are happy times

There are sad times too

In both situations, there is pain

With or without someone there beside you.

The rose is very much perfection

And doesn't lose its beauty

Until it starts to wilt and die

Then the love of it fades away into nothing.

Love between two people

If they don't get along

If they give up on their relationship

There is no hope to capture the beauty of love again

And soon, like the rose, the relationship wilts and dies.

It hurts so much when you lose the person you love

It's like the rose that withers

And never blooms again

Because it never even tried.

Love is soft, love is tender, love is what we make it.

-Poem written, age 18 years old

At this time, I badly wanted a relationship with my biological dad. I called and told him I couldn't get along with my mom. I shared with him that I didn't want to move in with her and her new husband for the school year. He said I could come live with him for my senior year. He lived in Kasota, a very small town close to St. Peter where I could go to St. Peter High School. I thought it was a great idea. I could get to know my dad and my little sister who didn't live far from him. I would have a fresh new start on life. I was very excited and optimistic.

Right before summer ended, Dad and my little sister Claire picked me up in Minneapolis. We drove the hour-and-a-half to Kasota, a town of only 600 people. The town was only a mile long. Dad had a cute, little two-story house with a small loft upstairs. The loft would be my room for the school year and I loved it. My sister Claire lived with her mom and came to visit us on the weekends. Dad had a nickname for my sister. Her name was "Binky." I was a little jealous that he had a special name for her. She was so lucky to have a dad to raise her. I missed out on a dad to protect me and love me as I was growing up. I yearned for that, wanting my daddy's love. I pushed the feelings aside about my childhood and started my new life with dad.

I loved my life. My dad and I were getting along great. He was like a big kid. He wasn't strict with me at all. He let me do what I wanted, and he was more like a friend than a dad. My little sister came over on the weekends and we were best friends! We became inseparable. We went everywhere together and had so much fun. I settled in well during my senior year of high school. I loved all the teachers I had, and even though there were clique groups in my new school, I found good friends with whom I hung around that year.

I started writing and my pen filled up over one thousand sheets of paper. Within a short time, I had eight folders and two notebooks full of stories! I was writing stories that I planned to publish someday. My dream was to be an author right out of high school. I had a teacher that would let me stay after school and use the new computers that had just come out in the 90's. They were big clunker computers that someone had donated to the school. I appreciated that the teacher let me stay after and lock up at night.

Every day after school, I would stay there and type on the keyboard for hours late into the night. I would type countless stories and poems I had written that I would end up saving to 3x5 floppy discs. I talked to a publishing company who said for $1,000.00 I could have my book published, and they would give me 200 copies of my book to pass out at $5.00 per book. That was a good deal! I was ecstatic! I had to make sure my book was finished before school was out for the summer. Every evening I worked hard to have this book completed by then. My friend Brian would come pick me up after a long night of writing at school. I was thankful I had good friends who supported me, a teacher that believed in me, and a publisher who was helping me with the financial aspects of it.

One day there was a call from the local newspaper that wanted to do a write up about me. They had heard from someone at my school that I was writing a book, and someone wanted to interview me! A few days later, a guy came to my house for the interview. He asked questions about how I started writing.

"...I think it all started when I was being sexually abused and needed an outlet, which I found writing to be the most freeing thing to do." Of course, I didn't SAY THAT! Instead, I said, "I love to write, and it is the most freeing feeling to put a pen to paper and just write an infinite amount of words that became my story. The guy who interviewed me took my picture and left. A week later, there I was, my picture taking up half the page in the local newspaper and my interview with an excerpt from one of my stories! I couldn't believe it! I was on cloud nine! It motivated me even more to write my book and have it published!

Because of this write-up in the paper, I was invited to a small group of writers in St. Peter that wanted me to speak at one of their engagements. They had read about me and were inspired by my writing at such a young age. It was a group of older ladies who loved fellow writers. I told them I would love to meet with them. I was excited, but as things turned out, I wished I had said no.

It was a month later that I showed up at the meeting. There were about forty women sitting in chairs. They had me walk up on stage to speak. I froze. I couldn't talk. I was scared to speak in front of these ladies. I had not even prepared a speech. I had something planned to say, but at that moment it all disappeared from my mind! I don't know what I was thinking. I said a little something and then wished it were over. They asked questions, I answered short "yes and no" answers, and then there was dead silence. It was a flop. Not something I could be proud of at all. After that, I promised myself never to do another speech in front of a group of people. I would rather die than speak in front of others.

At that point in my life, I was still in a long-distant relationship with Ian. I planned after graduation to move to Hawaii to be with him again. Ian hadn't come to see me before he left for Hawaii, because he was busy packing and getting ready to move. He had started his new life in Hawaii without me. He had a good friend there who had his own business and wanted Ian to help him. He took the offer. I was devastated and heartbroken. I really didn't think Ian would leave me in Minnesota. We talked on the phone all the time, and I used a calling card which cost twenty-five cents a minute. It wasn't cheap to talk to my boyfriend!

After months of school, prom was coming up, and I wanted my long-distant boyfriend to take me. I had missed prom my junior year which was no big deal, but this year I wanted to go. Ian promised me he would fly home just to take me to prom. It all sounded so romantic. I would finally see him again, and we would dance the night away on prom night! A few days before the dance, however, Ian called to tell me he couldn't fly home. He apologized, but it was a big let-down for me. My guy friends in school offered to take me, but I only wanted to go with my boyfriend.

Not long after I missed prom, Ian called to confess that he was at a party, met a woman, and she became pregnant with his baby! I almost dropped the phone! I was shocked! I didn't know what to say. There was dead silence on the phone for a few minutes. Thoughts were speeding through my mind. "He was going to be a daddy? What does this mean for us? Are we still together? Are they together? Will they marry now that they are having a baby together? How could this have happened?"

I asked him, "Are we still together or not?" He replied, "It wouldn't be fair for us to be together after what happened with her." He continued, "It was a one-night stand and she somehow got pregnant. She said I can be a part of the baby's life if I want but she is keeping it." I was naive and thought, "Can this even happen the first time?"

I just sat listening on the phone and didn't say anything for a long time. It was the longest phone conversation with the deadest air I had ever experienced. This was the end of our relationship. I just knew it. I had to let him go. We finally hung up the phone. My heart dropped. I cried and cried. I felt alone more than ever, and it was painful. I thought we would be married, but my dreams were crushed. Ian had left me. He not only left me in Minnesota, but he also left and went to another state, an island in the middle of the South Pacific, never to return. I already had huge abandonment issues, and now this!

From then on, I felt numb. Senior year was just a blur. I couldn't wait for it to be over! I focused hard on my book of short stories and finally finished it. I felt a great sense of accomplishment as I called the publishing company, but they had a change of management and the new manager would charge me three times the amount that the previous manager would have charged! I asked if he would reconsider. I was, after-all, just a high school student with not much money. The publisher said no. My heart was crushed again. I then put my dreams of publishing a book on the back burner and closed that chapter of my life.

I had close friends at my school, but after Ian and I broke up and my book dreams were crushed, my friendships just seemed to fall apart as well. I didn't tell my friends why I blew them off. I felt like my world had been torn apart and I just wanted to die.

At that point, I realized I had lost God somewhere along the way. When I had first met Ian, I loved God with all my heart and walked so closely with Him. At some point when Ian and I were together, I knew I was going in the wrong direction. When I prayed asking God's thoughts, God told me, "Do not be unequally yoked," but I didn't listen to Him. I believed I could change Ian. I thought maybe bringing him to church and praying for him would change his heart and that he would become a Christian, but that never happened. Instead, I strayed and then walked away from God. I can't even remember when it happened, but it did. I just remember after my boyfriend and I broke up, I felt lost and alone. I finally realized how far I had strayed from God, and I couldn't remember the last time we had talked.

Life went on. After high school ended, I left my dad's house and moved back in with my mom in the Twin Cities. She wanted me to find a job and start paying a little rent to live in the basement. I was fine with her request. Things started coming together for me. June, my best friend, was happy I had moved closer to her again. I had a good group of friends to hang out with, and I felt life was going well for me.

In the summer time, my mom took me on a fun boat ride on the St. Croix River. We had the greatest time looking at gigantic slabs of rock formations that went straight up on each side of the river. The boat ride was exciting as we rode peacefully on the water and looked at the spectacular views all around us. It was interesting to me how one side of the river was Minnesota, and the other side was Wisconsin.

Halfway through the boat ride, I saw cliff jumpers diving off the large rocks into the water, and I was fascinated by them. There were teens jumping off a large rock that was only fifteen feet high. Other people were diving off a rock that was sixty-five feet high, while one other person stood on a rock so high that I could barely see him. I found out later that the rock was ninety-two feet high. I didn't see that guy jump.

I was in awe as I watched these people diving from so high, then screaming with excitement, and "splash," hitting the water at full speed! My mom and I watched with anticipation as each person waited for their turn to jump off the sixty-five-foot drop. I turned to my mom and excitedly exclaimed, "That will be my new thing I am going to do!" Mom gave me an, "OH NO!" kind of look as she knew I was an adventurer who would do a crazy stunt like that. We enjoyed the boat ride, and when it was over, I had my mind set on finding the area where everyone was cliff jumping. I asked around and found it was at the State Park. It was illegal in Minnesota to cliff jump, but not in Wisconsin.

That next weekend, I drove to the Wisconsin State Park. Following the winding roads, I looked for the cliffs that I could jump into the river. I didn't have to look hard. There were cars in a small parking lot that gave it away. I parked my car and followed the trail to a huge rock that overlooked the St. Croix River. There were nine people standing around and talking. I saw a guy peek his head over a large rock ledge and pull himself up. He must have jumped once already and after climbing the rock, he was ready to go again. I walked to the edge of the rock, and as I looked down, I realized it was a huge drop to the water. To my right, there was a small trail to follow down to the fifteen-foot jump, and to my left there was another thin trail that climbed way up the side of the mountain. I guessed the trail went to the ninety-two-foot jump. I decided to try the sixty-five-foot drop.

I continued to watch the people dive off the rock with ease. After a few minutes, I was ready! I was warned there was a tree right below and a great big rock. I would need to avoid both, so I would not be injured. I ran straight off that rock, and suddenly I was in mid-air! It seemed like time stood still for a moment, then I was falling fast. I hit the water at full speed and sank down, down, down until my feet touched the sandy bottom. Then I pushed myself up and in a second's time, I was at the surface! I heard cheers from above. The crowd of people were so happy a newbie had survived! My adrenaline was pumping, and I was ready to go again!

There were huge slabs of flat rock I had to climb to reach the top of the cliff. I would need to grab a corner of one large rock, pull myself up, then grab another rock and pull myself up until my feet were safely grounded on the sandy trail. I loved hiking, so climbing these rocks was fun.

At the top of the trail, I was ready to jump again. I had a running start and flew over the edge. For a moment, I felt like I was flying. The wind in my hair, the air under my feet, "WHAT A RUSH!" I fell fast, hit the water and sank. Then I felt the sand touch my toes, and I pushed myself back up to the surface! Climbing up the rocks faster this time, I was careless, and I slipped off a rock, skinned my knee, and fell back into the water! I didn't let that stop me. I scurried up the rocks because I wanted that "RUSH" again! I didn't care that I had blood trickling down my leg. I was focused, and I wanted to feel like I was flying again! I was there all day, jumping for the rush. It was an addictive adventure, and I was sure I would be there every weekend from then on!

After a whole day of jumping and soaking in the sun, I was ready to go home, but I was curious to see the high jump. A few of the guys walked the trail up to the top, and I followed. One of them was planning to jump, which I thought was crazy. It was so high up! But I loved adventure, and if he were going to jump, I wanted to do so too! We were at the ledge, and as we looked down at the river, I became dizzy. This was nothing like the lower jump. We were so high the clouds were floating not far above where we stood! I started doubting if I wanted to do this. When I told the guys I wanted to jump, the "clear-headed" guy said, "If you jump, just be prepared to pay a $92.00 fine if you are caught! The State Park said it is illegal to jump at ninety-two feet high, but people do it all the time, like my friend here." He pointed at his friend and rolled his eyes. I couldn't afford the fine and decided against jumping at this altitude. His friend, without thinking, took a running leap and "flew-through-the-air" for just a second, and then dropped like a bowling ball, "FAST!" We again looked over the edge where he had hit a large tree hanging off the side of the cliff, and then made a huge splash in the water below, narrowly escaping a flat rock at the bottom. When I saw this guy could have died, that did it for me!

NO WAY would I ever jump off this rock! The guy came up for air, and he whooped and hollered and then yelled, "I cheated death once again!" Everyone laughed and cheered, but I just stood there thinking this was all fun and games until someone was hurt, but I was loving this kind of adventure! Every weekend that I had a chance, I would drive to the state park and cliff jump. It became my new favorite thing to do. It was quiet and peaceful in nature and I loved it. I tried to talk a few of my friends into coming with me, but they didn't want anything to do with it.

My mom continued to ask me about finding a job, and I finally did. I worked at a dry-cleaning business. I liked the ladies who worked there. They were very helpful training me and would chat with me like I was a part of their team. My friend June also started working there, and it was fun working together.

There was one guy who worked at the dry cleaners that was very good looking. After working there a few months, he and I started flirting back and forth. I had such a crush on him, and he knew it. He invited me out one night to a hotel, and Dominic and I had sex. It was a big mistake. I was still broken up over Ian. Maybe I was trying to make myself feel better. Maybe I just wanted to feel loved again. Dominic gave me attention and I fell for it, "hook, line, and sinker!"

When I went back to work that Monday, Dominic acted as if nothing had happened. I liked him, and I didn't realize he just wanted to get into my pants. What a jerk. He completely ignored me the whole day at work. I tried to talk to him after work, and he told me we needed to forget what happened. I was stunned! How could I forget what we did? I had never felt so used as I did that day!

A few days later, Dominic's girlfriend called my house and screamed that she had a shotgun and she was coming over to shoot me. I was shocked! I didn't even know he had a girlfriend and now this lady wanted to kill me? As she screamed obscenities at me, I held the ear piece away from my ear, and my mom stood near me and asked what was going on. I told her the story, and she grabbed the phone and yelled at the lady. Mom told her if she ever called again or came by, she would call the police and have her dragged off to jail. I had to laugh. My mom was great at defending me against this lunatic! I couldn't believe Dominic had a girlfriend! I was so mad and disgusted. It was too much to bear. I quit my job at the dry cleaners.

I called my ex-boyfriend Ian and shared what a big mistake I made with this guy Dominic. I was distraught and tearing up as I told him what happened. I waited on the phone to see what he would say. I was worried he would never want to talk to me again. It had been about a year since we had broken up, and we hadn't said much to each other since he told me about the baby. Both of us had gone our separate ways. He surprised me when he said I should come to Hawaii to visit him. I could see where he worked, and he would show me around the island. My mind wandered to a blue ocean, waves lapping at my feet, palm trees swaying, and a sandy white beach. I thought what a beautiful vacation this could be. Ian mentioned there was so much to see in Hawaii, and we would have a blast together! I said I would love to! I needed a vacation!

I had my first credit card right out of high school. It was one of those credit cards that you put money on it and could use it to build up your credit. I had the money to go, so I made reservations to fly to the island of Hawaii. I couldn't wait... I was off to Hawaii!!

Chapter 7

On My Way to Hawaii...

It was January 1993. I had a month to plan my trip to the Hawaiian Islands. I had always wanted to go to Hawaii. I imagined Hawaii was like *Gilligan's Island*, where they drive around in a Flintstone-style golf cart, sipping fresh coconut water from a straw in a real coconut. I also imagined tourists sitting on the beach under a grass hut to keep cool while the hot sun, reflecting off the water, beat their skin a bright red. Maybe I had watched too many episodes of *Gilligan's Island*, but that's how I envisioned it.

Things were good at this point in my life. I spent a great deal of time with my friends, and when I wasn't with them, I was on the phone talking to Ian long distance. I felt like we were "patching things up" and becoming friends again. It felt good. We talked about how wonderful Hawaii was. I could only imagine. I wanted to hear all about it. It sounded like such a romantic place to be. My mom and I were constantly fighting over the phone bill since I had been talking on the phone too much, and I was so ready to escape to paradise.

Finally, the time came. I flew to Oahu, Hawaii! As the plane landed, I noticed out the window that the airport was wide open to the outside and all the plants and trees were in full bloom. Then I walked right off the plane and into paradise. A light breeze hit my face, and I smelled a fresh scent of plumeria flowers. It was the most amazing smell. It was surreal that I was in Hawaii! I couldn't believe I had finally made it! I was so excited. Ian was at the gate to greet me. He was holding a beautiful purple-flowered lei and as soon as he saw me, he came over to give me a great big hug. It felt good to be close to him again. He put the lei made of real flowers around my neck. He said, "Now you can say you have been "laid" in Hawaii." I laughed. In Hawaii, putting Hawaiian flowers around the neck means you have been "leid."

Ian drove me around Oahu and showed me some old buildings in downtown Honolulu, and then we drove to beaches that showed the brilliant, bright blue water looking so tantalizing. The sun reflected off the water, and the beach looked so inviting. After touring around, I was tired from the long eleven-hour plane ride from Minnesota, so we went back to his apartment to rest. He lived in a quaint, two-bedroom, apartment complex in downtown Honolulu. Walking into his apartment, I was amazed that his entire living room wall was covered from top to bottom with an ocean-scene wallpaper. The wallpaper had sand at ground level, ocean waves in the middle, the sun in the top corner, some mountains on the side, and palm trees stuck in a knee-high pile of sand with their branches hanging low. I had never seen anything like it! It was so beachy. Ian had a big living room window that overlooked the busy street below, and a big park with a water fountain in the middle which sprayed water every which way. The trees in the park were huge and magnificent with large roots that hung down digging deep into the earth. It was very pretty! I would be staying in Hawaii for one week and I was so excited. I knew it wasn't possible, but I wanted to see and do everything!

Ian and his friend Shane had their own business with salt water aquariums, and they loved their work. They had a large clientele. Ian worked long hours and I was able to go to work with him a few times. Ian and Shane would go to the clients' homes to clean the tanks of algae and bring colorful large and small assorted fish to decorate the aquariums. The aquariums were full of fish and artificial coral. Some of the coral would be colored by Ian the creator. Each new fish added to the tank had a personality and were either aggressive or passive, and a person had to know which fish could live together in each aquarium. The salt water fish were so interesting and colorful. I learned so much about fish! Some of the calls from clients were an emergency like if the pump wasn't working properly or there was a leak or a dead fish; Ian or Shane would have to fish it out day or night at the client's home. They even had clientele on the outer islands. I was impressed with the company they had built from scratch.

Their biggest client was a well-known artist in Hawaii who loved the ocean and held a passion for marine life. He painted many murals on building walls to raise awareness about ocean life. He also had galleries all over the islands where he sold paintings of dolphins and whales or sculptures made of sea creatures like turtles, dolphins, whales, fish, or seals. He was an amazing artist! I met him once, and he signed a card that I still have to this day.

The days I could not go to work with Ian, I would walk the few blocks to the beach, sun myself, and swim all day long. I wanted to soak in the sun as much as possible and have a nice dark tan for when I went back home to Minnesota. The sun was so warm that I just soaked it in and loved every minute of it. At this time of year, Honolulu's weather was in the 80's which was strange to me since it was January when it should be cold and snowing like in Minnesota!

I met many people on the beach. I would talk to all sorts of guys that would come over to chat with me. There was one guy who was very nice. He talked me into riding around the island with him. I was so trusting and thank goodness, he was a good guy. He drove me around and showed me some amazing sights. We went to Sharks Cove where we snorkeled. It was a protective cove and just beyond the swimming area were huge fifteen or twenty-foot waves that would crash against the rocks.

I didn't ask why this place was named Sharks Cove. I would rather not know! I had fun snorkeling. There were pretty fish everywhere and they weren't scared of people at all. The waves inside the cove were only a few feet high, but they would push me around as if I were inside a washing machine! It was fun.

On a different day, I met another guy who brought me to a secluded beach which was on the east side of Hawaii in Hawaii Kai. There was a paved road that was winding and very steep as we drove downward. This ride was adventurous to say the least. I was thankful his car brakes were in working order, or we could have rolled right off the cliff and into the ocean! The road brought us to a clearing at the bottom of a mountain to a white sandy beach where we could swim with the fish at Hanauma Bay.

We swam for a while and then sun tanned on the beach. When the sun beat down, it was hot! We couldn't stand it for too long. There was a small stand with a big, grass hut where people would rent snorkel gear and buy food to feed the fish. I felt like a pro swimmer since I had swum with the fish at Sharks Cove. We filled a bag with fish food. As we went back into the water to cool down, fish swarmed all around us, not just a few fish but dozens of fish! I had food in my hand and I think they smelled it. I put my hand in the water and let some food go, and they attacked it like piranhas savagely eating everything in sight! There were small fish and big fish, and the big ones scared me! They were bumping into me trying to grab the food I held tightly in my hand. I was backing up a bit frightened as the water whirled around me due to the fish frenzy. I let all the food out of my hand when a big, two-foot, green parrot fish swooped up out of the water! I pulled my hand back and there was blood dripping off my thumb. I looked at my hand in shock. I thought, "Could there be piranhas in the water?" No, it was a parrot fish that had bit me trying to eat the food. My friend felt bad when he saw my bloodied thumb, but it didn't hurt, and I just laughed it off. As we walked up the beach, my friend took his shirt and wrapped it around my bloody thumb. I grinned big as I told him it would be fine. I was going home with a scar and would tell everyone I had been bitten by a big fish in Hawaii.

When Ian heard what happened, he felt bad that he couldn't be there for me since he was working so much. He confessed later that he was jealous this guy had been showing me around Hawaii, but it wasn't like Ian and I were together. We were just friends. This other guy was just a friend as well and a real gentleman.

Ian showed me many beautiful places while I visited. I not only fell in love with Hawaii, but also loved the ocean. I wanted to stay. The time went by too fast and before I knew it, I had to fly home. Ian and I had been intimate by the end of the trip. He romanced me and made me think maybe there was still a chance for us. Maybe if I moved to Hawaii like we originally planned, our relationship would blossom, and we would marry and be forever happy. It would be a dream come true for me.

I flew home and as soon as I settled in, my mom was "on my case" to find a job. She wrote me a long note about how I better find one in a month or I would have to move. I didn't have any motivation to work. All I thought about was how perfect Hawaii was.

I started feeling funny. I told my best friend June that I needed to take a pregnancy test. She came right over. I had one of those tests to pee on the strip and in a few moments, I would know if I would be a mom or not. A mom... or not... that was huge!

So many thoughts went through my mind. "How would Ian react if I were pregnant? Would I stay in my mediocre life, be kicked out of my mom's house, and fend for myself and my baby? Or maybe I am not pregnant, and all this worrying was for nothing." It seemed like I had to wait forever for the color strip to change. My friend June couldn't wait. She was hopping around, waiting impatiently for the test result. Finally, the minutes were up and we both looked and then stared.

Two pink strips. I was pregnant! We looked at each other. I was stunned. How could I let this happen? I stood there not saying anything, but June was ecstatic. She grabbed me and hugged me tightly saying she was going to be an "auntie." I didn't feel that kind of joy. I thought about all the responsibility a child brought. I would need to love and care for this child I would raise. I would have to nurture it, feed it, and clean diapers. How would I take care of a baby when I couldn't even take care of myself?! Would I care for this baby with or without Ian? Would he step up and take responsibility for this baby? I had so many unanswered questions.

I needed to call Ian. I had been back home only a few weeks and had chatted with him on the phone only once or twice. Would he be receptive? He would have to be. I was sure he still loved me. I called and called Ian but didn't hear from him. I left him various messages saying, "Call me, it's important. We need to talk." I was nineteen years old and scared to death. I had no idea what my future held. I felt like my world was crashing down all around me! Not hearing from Ian, I felt more alone than ever. I couldn't sleep, I had blood shot eyes, and had angry outbursts with my mom. I'm sure my mom suspected I was pregnant and could hear me crying at night.

Only a few people knew I was pregnant, and one person said, "Becky, the best thing you can do is to get rid of the baby. If you had an abortion, you could have a bright future ahead of you and unlimited possibilities." I just stared at this person, fuming inside. I felt like the cartoon character Popeye. When he was mad, smoke came out of his ears and his face was bright red from anger. That's how I felt at that very moment. I was so angry. I have never believed in abortion. To me, having an abortion would be murdering my baby. I couldn't do it. No matter what situation I was in, I would have to have this baby! I then waited on a call from Ian. No matter what his decision was, I would keep the baby and make it all work out.

After a week, I finally heard from Ian. He apologized profusely and said he was working crazy hours on Kauai, an outer island. He didn't receive the phone messages until he flew home to Oahu. He sounded sincere about his apology and asked me what the news was. I didn't skip a beat as I quickly blurted out, "I'm pregnant!" Ian didn't say anything for a moment and then asked what I wanted to do.

I went on to say, "I don't believe in abortion and I would like to keep the baby, but I don't know what to do." He was quiet for a moment while he let my words sink in. Then he said, "Well, come to Hawaii and we will figure it out together." That day, Ian was my hero. I was on cloud nine. I packed my bags, bought a ticket with my credit card, and in a week, I was back in Hawaii! It was February 1993. My mom did not think moving to Hawaii was the best decision I could make, and she was not happy with me. I just wanted to start a whole new life, and Hawaii sounded like the perfect place to do that. I knew things would be great with Ian. We would marry and be a family and live happily ever after.

In Hawaii, our relationship was great for a while, but Ian frequently flew to Kauai for work and we started fighting. I was eight weeks along in my pregnancy when I started experiencing stomach cramps and pain. Ian brought me to the doctor to check on the baby. The doctor said the baby was fine and as small as a peanut but instructed me to lean on the side of caution; if I were too stressed, I could lose the baby. I was very stressed at that time, and the doctor's words rang in my ears all that day and night. This baby was going to keep us together as a family, I just knew it. I had to find ways to de-stress and stay calm.

The next day, Ian flew to Kauai again for work. He had been away for two days when something happened. I was at Ala Moana Shopping Center where I was looking at a few tank tops, when suddenly I had an uneasy feeling in my stomach. I began cramping so I ran to the bathroom. Sharp pains shot through my abdomen. It felt like knives were jabbing my lower stomach. I sat on the toilet and blood came pouring out and I felt it and heard a plop - the baby came out. I had a miscarriage. I sat there on the toilet in horror. "This can't be happening!" I was too scared to move so I just sat there in pain for an endless amount of time. I knew I had passed the baby and I didn't know what to do.

The pain came in floods. At one moment when the pain subsided, I wiped, stood up, and looked in the toilet. There it was - a round, black, peanut-sized baby in a see-through, thin, layered sack. It was in the toilet mixed in blood and water. I was so scared! I pulled up my shorts, buttoned them, flung open the bathroom stall door, and cried! I tried to walk to the door to leave, but instead, another shot of pain went through my abdomen. I fell against the wall just a few feet from the door. Like a sack of potatoes, I hit the floor and curled my feet under me. With my face close to the floor, and my arms wrapped around my body, I cried so hard. I cried for losing my baby. I cried thinking the stress killed my baby. I cried knowing I couldn't reach Ian on the phone in Kauai. I cried for my relationship with my boyfriend, thinking the baby would have kept us together. I cried for our future together. I cried for so many unknowns in my life.

Suddenly, a lady and her five-year-old girl came out of a bathroom stall. The girl asked her mom why I was crying, and the mom said, "Never mind, let's get going." She hurried her daughter out the door. I wished she could have helped me, but I couldn't form any words to ask for help.

After the pain subsided and I calmed down, I stood up and walked to the nearest employee. I asked if I could use their phone to call my roommate to come pick me up. Kevin, Ian's roommate, came to pick me up. When I told him what happened, he talked me into going to the ER right away. He drove me to Kapiolani Women's Hospital where they rushed me in and checked me over. I think they were afraid I might lose too much blood from the miscarriage. A nurse settled me in a bed. She asked me if there was anyone who could be with me at this time. I said, "No, my boyfriend is working on Kauai." She asked if there was anyone else. I replied, "No." She asked if I wanted her to hold my hand. I was confused. I questioned, "Hold my hand for what?" She said they had to do a D&C right away, so I wouldn't develop an infection. I was in denial thinking maybe somehow my baby had survived. I asked her, "Will my baby be okay? This isn't an abortion is it because I don't believe in abortions." She held my hand and said, "I'm sorry but I am sure you have passed the baby, but we need to clean the remains from your uterus." Tears poured from my eyes and fell down my cheeks and I sat there in utter horror! My dreams were literally flushed down the toilet!

The nurse wheeled me into another room with a D&C machine. They hooked me up to a machine that monitored my heartbeat. I closed my eyes. Someone held my hand. The procedure was quick. I felt uncomfortable through the procedure, but it didn't hurt much. I felt so alone and scared.

Ian's roommate came to pick me up and I went home to rest. I tried calling Ian on the work phone, but I couldn't reach him. I slept for what seemed like days. When I woke up, I called Ian again and finally reached him. I told him I had lost the baby. I felt guilty as if it were my fault. I was sobbing uncontrollably. He apologized and consoled me; then he made plans to fly home. He felt bad this had happened.

My life spiraled out of control from there. I was falling into a deep depression from losing the baby. Ian and I went through a rough patch, we were constantly fighting, and I didn't know if our relationship would survive. It seemed like we couldn't resolve our issues. After losing the baby, I had so much fear just festering inside me about losing my boyfriend as well.

Not long after I lost the baby, Ian talked me into meeting the mother of his child and seeing their baby. This was the lady he had knocked up during a one-night stand while we were still together. It took a great deal of courage for me to meet her, but I felt it was important for him to be in his child's life and I wanted to be supportive. I won't lie that I had some jealousy. I wanted to have his baby, and mine had passed away. I was still heartbroken and reeling in pain from this awful experience.

Years later, I had a dream in which I was holding a little girl with bright blue eyes and blonde hair. She looked at me and smiled; then she touched my face and laughed. My heart just leaped for joy! When I woke up, I knew without a shadow of doubt that she was my baby girl that had died! She was in heaven with Jesus and was well taken care of. I wanted so badly to go back into my dream to be with her, but I knew someday I would meet her in heaven.

Ian's old roommate Henrietta from Minnesota who lived downstairs in the house where I had stayed for the summer, came to visit him in Hawaii. She said there was no way she would stay with us and be in the same apartment I was in, so she went to a hotel a few blocks from where we lived and stayed there. I didn't see her the entire trip because she told Ian she didn't want to see me at all. He would sneak out of the house at night to meet with her himself. That did not sit well with me, and we fought about it almost every night when he came home.

Ian's brothers from Minnesota also came to visit the same time as Henrietta was there. One evening, Ian sneaked out of the house again, and I followed him to the beach where I saw him meet up with his two brothers and Henrietta. They were at the Ilikai Hotel in the parking lot talking and laughing. I hid behind a large white pillar to watch them. I felt awful spying, but I didn't trust my boyfriend with this lady. I peeked around the corner and saw him pull her to him and kiss her! My breath caught in my throat and I felt like I had been punched in the stomach! The brothers cheered him on and my heart broke in a million pieces.

I didn't trust Ian, but I didn't think he would do something like that! Kissing another woman was "cheating" in my book. I couldn't watch anymore, and I ran home with tears streaming down my face. Everything was a blur. I couldn't stand the pain I was feeling. I went into the bedroom, closed the door, and bawled my eyes out. Ian didn't come home until late, but when he returned, I confronted him. He denied everything. He said that he saw me behind the pillar and pretended to kiss her just to tick me off. He denied that he kissed her at all, but I didn't believe him and somehow the conversation turned to a confession that he had walked with her down the beach holding hands a few times. I was blown away! Why would he walk hand in hand with her down the beach? To me, holding hands with the opposite sex was an intimate gesture, and why didn't he walk with me down the beach and hold my hand? I was jealous. I couldn't wait until this woman would leave and go home. She was staying for two whole weeks which were very rough for me, to say the least! I had to believe that they weren't doing anything wrong or I would have gone crazy. My boyfriend and I had been together six years. That was a long time. He was my first love and I thought we could endure anything. We had good times and bad times, but we always pulled through any crisis.

Finally, Ian's old roommate left Hawaii! I was so relieved. Not long after she left, however, Ian was tired of us fighting all the time, and he kicked me out of his apartment. I had nowhere to go, so I walked down to the boat harbor and just hung out with a few friends on their boat. I told my friends that my boyfriend kicked me out, and my friend Larry said I could stay with him for a while until I found a place to live. After a few weeks of staying with Larry, Ian found me hanging out at the harbor. Holding a dozen roses, Ian knelt in front of me and with tears in his eyes, he begged me to move back in with him. I thought it was all very romantic and so I did. However, my boat friends didn't think it was such a good idea.

Everything was great for a few weeks, but it all went downhill fast! I had a hard time keeping a job. Ian was dabbling in dark magic, and I wanted nothing to do with it! We fought all the time and were drifting apart quickly. We argued one night, and I screamed and cussed right in his face. Then he punched me in the face! I was shocked! I wanted to walk out right then, but I didn't have any money to leave. I was stuck in a bad situation.

Ian wanted me to take a weekend class to improve and work on myself. He even wanted me to pay for the class! I didn't have any money, but somehow, I was able to go to this weekend event anyway. I really liked the class because it showed me how to trust others and build friendships. It was a confidence-boosting kind of seminar. As the weekend was wrapping up, Ian told me I needed to move out in two days and find another place to live. I felt I had failed the relationship in every way. I was about to be homeless. I had no money and no job. My life was going downhill fast. I couldn't believe he would kick me out, but he was adamant to do so.

People were mingling on the last day of class when I met a guy named Dustin. He asked me where I lived just to strike up conversation. I answered, "Well, right now I live in Honolulu, but in a few days, I will officially be homeless." He asked, "Why?" and I told him, "My boyfriend and I aren't getting along, and he is going to kick me out." Dustin, being such a nice guy, offered to let me stay with him and his roommate. I told him I had no job or money, so I wouldn't be able to pay him rent. He said he trusted that I would find a job and pay rent, but not to worry about it right now. I was shocked. Why would this guy whom I didn't even know, so generously offer his place to me? I asked, "When can I move in?" He replied, "Tomorrow."

Ian came to pick me up from class, and I told him that I had found a place to live. He didn't say anything at first. I imagined that he would retract what he said, especially when I told him I would be moving in with two guys. I hoped he would tell me he loved me and wanted to make things work and that he had never wanted me to leave, but he didn't. Instead, he looked relieved, and with a sigh, he said it was great that I found a place to live. Then he asked when I could move out. I was shocked he would let me move in with two guys I didn't even know! They could be bad men wanting to hurt me in some way or even kill me, but Ian didn't seem to care. I couldn't believe it. I told him I would pack tonight and move out in the morning. I was certain in the morning he would change his mind.

When morning came, Ian helped pack my belongings in the car and drove me over to Dustin's apartment complex to drop me off. He had left me there, alone. I was so scared. I had no idea who these guys were, and I had never done anything like this before. It was very scary for me.

I phoned from a call box and Dustin came down to let me in. Right away, Dustin made me feel comfortable. He was a Canadian guy with a cute Canadian accent. He was so nice. He smiled often and was very proper. He was kind hearted and sweet. His roommate was very nice too. They both welcomed me in and made me feel at home. The apartment complex was across the street from the ilikai Hotel and the beach. I loved the beach, but it had been a long time since I had enjoyed swimming and catching some rays. I knew this move was good for me because I could do some "soul searching" while relaxing on the sandy beach.

Dustin's apartment complex was very fancy with a security gate, a nice pool, a barbecue area, elevators, and security guards 24/7. The apartment was on the seventh floor in the left wing of the complex. Our apartment was at the far end of an outside hallway showing an ocean view. How could I be so lucky? It was a one-bedroom apartment but had a private lanai that closed off as a bedroom. I crashed on the living room couch for a few days, and then Tim, the other roommate, let me have the lanai as my room because he was moving out. I had a great apartment to live in, and a clear view of the ocean, and I was loving it! After Tim left, it was just Dustin and I living in the apartment.

Dustin was easy to get along with and we became close friends. Within a month I was hired as a security guard at the apartment complex where I lived. I liked my job. Everyone was so friendly; tenants would bring the security guards food whenever we worked. There was an older gentleman in his sixties, Mack, who lived in the building. He always brought me a plate lunch when I worked. In fact, he would bring all the security guards food. Mack was one of the nicest guys I had ever met! He was an interesting person who loved to talk. He was half Hawaiian and half Portuguese and loved telling stories about his background and heritage. He had many interesting tales and I liked listening to him for hours on end. He had so much energy and positivity about him which amazed me for someone his age. We quickly became friends, and we often would go out and eat together. He would take me to different restaurants, any one I chose. Sometimes I brought my friends with me, and he liked the extra company. He would make us laugh! He was such a nice guy who reminded me of my grandpa who was my hero as I grew up. When my mom came to visit me in Hawaii, we went to dinner with Mack, and Mom had the greatest time listening to his many stories. When my grandma came to visit me one time, Mack took us both out for dinner! He was smitten by Grandma's beauty, of course! It was so sweet how he talked to her! He made her laugh and was certainly putting on the charm! Grandma had so much fun on her trip to Hawaii. (This was after Grandpa had passed away). We had such a nice time.

At that point in my life, I worked full-time at my security job. I made $9.00 an hour which wasn't much but it was the most money I had ever made, and it paid the bills. I worked with a good group of guys. I became friends with one of the security guards, Robert. He became one of my best friends even though we didn't have much in common. He didn't like the beach and he wasn't a free spirit like me, but he was the nicest guy, who had a huge heart and would give the shirt off his back for anyone! He always made me laugh and we always had fun together.

All my spare time was spent swimming and tanning at the beach. I was making new friends and loving my new life. I was finally happy and had found my peaceful bliss! After a few months had passed, however, Ian called out of the blue. He said he wanted to come by and give me something. I was a bit confused. I thought he had forgotten all about me. He stopped by and I met him at the front gate. I didn't want to let him in. I was still sore about him kicking me out and realizing he didn't care what happened to me.

In the foyer area, Ian was holding onto a small square box. He looked down, trying to find the right words as I walked toward him. Then he looked up at me. He just stood there with tears in his eyes. People walked by us while others chatted by the front gate. It was a busy, early evening at the apartment, but for the moment, time stood still. It was just the two of us staring at each other. In a moment's time, I didn't see or hear anything else around us. He looked handsome as ever, but I noticed pain in his bright blue eyes. I wondered why he was here.

Ian said he missed me much more than he thought he would. He had been keeping tabs on me and knew I was doing well. I had a job, I had friends, I had a place to live, and he was impressed. He opened the little box and there was a beautiful diamond ring! He took it out and pulled my left hand toward him and put the ring on my finger. It fit perfectly. He said he bought us two tickets for an Alaskan Cruise and he wanted to marry me. I looked at him in shock! I didn't say anything. I couldn't say anything. I just stared. He saw that I was taken aback. He said, "I will give you a few days to think about it, but I want to spend the rest of my life with you. Keep the ring and think about it, please." I wanted to take the ring off and throw it at him for all the hurt and pain he had caused, but in a split second, I found that tiny ray of hope that maybe it could work out for us after all.

Ian hugged me and took off in his jeep, and I just stood there for I don't know how long wondering if this was a dream or reality. I finally went inside the gate and still in a daze, I went by the pool side and sat in one of the comfy lawn chairs, just staring at my finger and the beautiful ring on it. I had never had an engagement ring before. The sky was darkening, the moon was out, and the pool lights reflected a beautiful, soft blue silhouette that made the patio look very pretty. I sat and stared at the lights for a moment.

One of the older ladies in the building who often swam in the pool came over and hung out at the poolside with me. We usually chit-chatted when I did my rounds at work as a security guard. She asked if I was okay. I told her my ex-boyfriend just asked me to marry him. She was quiet for a minute and then asked, "Do you see yourself marrying him?" I answered, "Yes, I want to be married." She looked me in the eyes and replied, "If you marry him, can you see yourself married to him the rest of your life?" I thought about that for a moment and said, "I used to, but not anymore." She said, "Then that's your answer." I had to laugh. She had a way with words that made sense.

I went up the elevator to the seventh floor to tell Dustin what had just happened. He blurted out his favorite saying, "Oh, for bloody hell!" It must be a Canadian thing. It always made me laugh. Dustin had to remind me what Ian had put me through and how he had thrown me out like a piece of trash, twice! I knew then, Ian could easily do it again. I was done! The next day I called my ex to come pick up his ring. I told him I couldn't marry him. I felt free that day. New beginnings.

A CHILD OF GOD

Chapter 8

Dolphin Encounter

Being on my own after the break up with Ian, I learned to become independent. I loved the feeling of being my own person. I fell in love with Hawaii and was enamored by the beauty of the islands. The people, the ALOHA spirit, the beaches, the bright blue ocean, the mountains, the sunrises and sunsets – I enjoyed everything about my life in Hawaii. I made friends easily and loved life with no drama. After the break up, there was a pivotal moment when I decided to change my nickname from Becky to Becka. The nickname Becka represented a new beginning for me, burying the past and looking forward to a brighter future. It was like an ugly caterpillar who emerges from a cocoon and transforms itself into a beautiful butterfly with new beginnings.

My roommate was fun to be around. Dustin was funny and easy going. He liked to swim and dive, and he showed me a place to swim with the dolphins. First thing in the morning, Dustin and I, sometimes with a group of friends, would drive over an hour to the west side of the island to jump in the water as soon as it was light out. It was 5:30 and the dolphins would feed soon. We had to swim out a half a mile to reach the dolphins, and then we would play with them. This was the life I fell in love with! I loved swimming and especially without the confinement of snorkel gear. I could swim further, faster, and longer without gear pulling me down.

I learned how to glide through the water. I would be like a mermaid, swimming fast and effortlessly. When I was in the deep ocean far from shore, the world just stood still for me. I would push myself to see how fast I could swim. I would glide along like a flying fish in a hurry. Less movement and smoother strokes helped make me a faster swimmer. I felt free in the water as if I were meant to be there. Within moments, I would be among the pod of dolphins.

I could look under the water about thirty feet down without using a mask. I would open my eyes under water and watch the fish and dolphins swimming around. I was used to swimming in the salty water with my eyes open which didn't bother me at all, unless the waves were choppy and slapping me in the face.

I loved watching a mother dolphin with her baby a distance away. It was fun watching the close interaction between the two. Dolphins will use their long snouts to push the sand around and make designs in it, or sometimes they just look for food under the sand. They are very playful and would swirl and twirl in the water and playfully interact with one another. It was a beautiful sight to watch. The teen dolphins were more mischievous than ever and would swim by the mom, bumping into them playfully, then swim off as if they were laughing and saying, "Ha-ha you can't catch me." I wish I could breathe under water, then I could watch and play with them all day.

When the dolphins wanted to impress the silly humans treading water and gawking at them, they would perform funny antics. A dolphin would swim fast, shooting forward toward the human like a torpedo, and then turn abruptly and shoot up to the surface. The dolphin would jump out of the water testing its limit of how high it could jump, and then fall back into the water, swim down toward the sand again, and peek out the corner of its eye to see if the human is still watching. Of course, we humans were loving the attention and were fascinated with their silly games. It was hard not to laugh at the dolphins and their funny antics but laughing took away air which took seconds away from enjoying the show they were performing for us. The dolphins grew used to our visits on the weekends, and I never saw aggression in any of them.

The more I swam with the dolphins, the better I was at holding my breath for longer periods of time. I only guessed I could stay under water a few minutes at a time, but I really challenged myself to hold my breath longer to stay in the moment with these amazing mammals.

Dolphins are curious creatures who are extremely intelligent. They like human interaction with the right people. The dolphins can feel energy from humans and if they trust you, they will come near. The mother dolphin will stay near her baby dolphin for years as it grows and matures. If the mother dolphin lets you near her young, you are special, and it is an exhilarating feeling to be accepted by her. I have been so very close to their young a few times, only a few feet away, but never have I touched a baby dolphin. It was fun watching the mother teach the baby "life lessons" right in front of me! Sometimes I would wonder if the mother was telling the baby, "Do not trust the humans, they will try to get near you," or was she saying, "This human is okay, but you must learn your senses to know the good humans from the bad ones." I had fun thinking of what the mom was saying to the baby. You could hear the dolphins communicating with each other under the water. The sound was a high-pitched squeal which would change to short chitter-chat between each other. Sometimes they would play and entertain each other, and when they laughed, it was a lower chatter sound, but all in all it was usually higher tones I could hear from a long distance under water.

Dolphins do not breathe through their mouths. You would think they do, but they don't. Dolphins breathe through their blowhole on the top of their head. They can immerse themselves under the water for long periods of time, and every so often they will go to the surface to breathe. If you were to see a dolphin come to the surface and push water up out of their blowhole, they are breathing.

I was close to touching a wild dolphin once. A group of friends and I were in a great big pod of about thirty dolphins that were surrounding us. The dolphin closest to me was big and bulky, but not fully grown. Sometimes I could see his stubbornness when I swam with this particular pod. He could be a bit rebellious which made me believe he was younger, a teen, maybe one or two years old. Sometimes he wouldn't stay close to the pod. He would swim along but do his own thing looking for food or playing in the sand by himself. Dolphins are family oriented and are very protective of each other from predators. They stay in close groups. I am sure they would knock a shark silly if he tampered with any of their family members! Even if there were a sick or dying dolphin in the pod, the dolphins would usually do their best to keep them close and protected. It has been known a dolphin will bring a sickly family member to a trusted human as if asking for help.

One time a large dolphin, about six feet long, swam toward me. He was so big, and I felt so small. His curiosity got the best of him and in an instant, he was only a few feet away from my face. I had to keep calm and not let my excitement get the best of me, but my heart beat so fast and so hard that I thought it would pop out of my chest. I really thought he could hear my heart beat as loudly as it was thumping. This teen stared me down for just a moment. He came closer still, and I thought, he must be testing me to see how I would react.

Would I swim away from him because I didn't trust his gesture, or would I stand my ground, be trusting, and accepted into his world? I stared deeply into his eyes that told a sad story about his life. I felt a connection with him. He inched slowly toward me. What a magnificent creature he was! I knew the protocol with these mammals. I was to never reach out to touch one unless it came to me first. Then that would give me permission to touch the dolphin, which builds trust.

In a moment's time, my excitement got the best of me and without thinking, my reaction was to touch his face right in front of me! All I wanted was to hug hi! My thoughts were racing, and I knew right then that I stepped over the line. He was so beautiful, so magnificent! I felt he knew my thoughts and picked up right away on my mixed emotions. In a split second, the dolphin used his big tail to swish water my way and he swam off. I belted out a nervous laugh and ran out of air. I had to swim quickly to the surface to fill my lungs once again. He could have hit me with his fin if he had wanted to, but he just gave me a quick warning by pushing me back in the water. I was reminded of the strength these mammals have and it amazed me! I knew I had expected too much. If I had stayed calm, I'm sure I would have been able to touch his face. Still, I was happy with how close I had been to him. Dolphins are very forgiving. I knew he was a gentle creature who knew my intentions were pure, and that is why he came so very close to me. I felt that day was the perfect day with my dolphin friends.

When the dolphins began swimming away, my friends and I all headed back to the beach to tell our dolphin stories. One lady said a dolphin pooped on her! She was horrified for a moment, but not totally grossed out since it happened in the water and the waste quickly floated away. We all "laughed our butts off" and I blurted out, "You are so lucky. That means he likes you!" We couldn't stop laughing. I didn't really know if the dolphin liked her or was playing with her or it could be that was a warning for her to stay away. All I know was that I was a little jealous that she was so close to the dolphin. She was the only one that was pooped on that day!

I shared with my friends about my interaction with the teen dolphin and how I was almost able to touch him. It was interesting how every one of us had a different experience while all of us were so close together surrounded by the dolphin pod. We all had our own dolphin interactions that came with life lessons taught in the deep blue ocean by our dolphin friends.

Shortly after this dolphin excursion, my cousin Sally and her friend Alyssa were coming to visit, and I wanted to share with them my dolphin adventures. We spent a weekend at the beach, but we didn't have a chance to swim with the dolphins. The water was mucky and cold, and the mammals were more interested in chasing their food rather than playing with humans. We still had a fun weekend watching the dolphins swim, catching sun rays, and having a great time together talking and laughing.

I had made friends with the homeless people that lived on one particular beach where I swam with the dolphins. On this beach where the sand was a pretty white color and the water was bright blue, the homeless could enjoy oceanfront property. Some of my homeless friends had lived there for fifteen years or more. They all had big hearts, every single one of them. Some of the men would dive deep and pick up huge conch shells off the bottom of the ocean floor. They would blow into the large shell and it made a noise that sounded like a trumpet. It was very surreal. Sometimes when diving, these guys would brush the sand away at the bottom of the ocean floor and find hidden large shells underneath. They would craft beautiful local Hawaiian jewelry from the shells they found to sell to locals and tourists alike who would stop by for a swim.

One of the homeless men was Kai, who was big and burly. He had such a passion and love for the Hawaiian Islands. Kai had lived on the beach for more than fifteen years. He was

born in Hawaii, and he loved anyone and everyone that set foot
on the beach. He was a happy guy who would joke and laugh
with anyone who would listen to him. He was easy to talk to
and had many Hawaiian stories to tell. His demeanor reminded
me of the singer "Brother IZ." Kai was soft spoken, loving, and
accepting of everyone, and he loved to sing.

Kai found shells with puka holes in the middle with
which he would string together to make Hawaiian jewelry. The
shells were usually white, sometimes yellow, brown, black, pink
or a mix of colors or even polka dot. Kai had a knack with color
and made authentic necklaces that people wanted. He would
use strong fishing line to string together shells of all kinds to
make the most beautiful necklaces. He made large-sized,
rugged-looking round shell necklaces for the men and more
dainty-shelled necklaces for the ladies. When I would visit Kai at
his tent, he always showed me the newest necklace he had
made and shared with me how he had been selling his creations
to people who had recently visited the beach.

One homeless lady named Trisha also lived on that
same beach. She was well known as the "dolphin whisperer." I
grew fond of her and we became friends. She was very good at
interacting with the dolphins, and every morning she was in the
water swimming with them. Trisha swam fast and she swam far!
The dolphins always swam to her because she was like a magnet
that drew them to her. She could touch them, coddle them,
cuddle them, and play with them. The dolphins loved to
socialize with her, and they acted as if she were part of their
dolphin family.

Trisha could stay under the water for a very long time. I
thought maybe she had gills because she could be under the
water for five minutes or more without a breath! I didn't think
anyone could do that free style. She would race the young
dolphins when they were playful and when she wanted to test

her human skills. Trisha had a beautiful relationship with them. I had never seen anything like it. I think she was a mermaid. She also sold Hawaiian jewelry just like Kai did, but her jewelry looked just a little different from his, as hers were daintier. Trisha made twist knots on the necklaces with small puka shells or tiny cone shells. She would make knots all through the cord and in between the shells and sometimes she added colored beads too. The necklaces were very intricate and unique in their own way. Trisha was even writing a book about her interaction with the dolphins. She said the money she made from selling the jewelry went toward her research of the dolphins.

Trisha also enjoyed overseeing everything on the beach. She wanted the beach safe, so she always watched what was going on. If out-of-town tourists came to swim with the dolphins, she would swim out with them to make sure no one was hurt or accidentally drowned. She didn't want anyone disrespecting any of the ocean creatures either. She was full of information about our ocean and narrated the best stories about sea life. Trisha was the funniest lady I had ever met and a fantastic story teller, talking about Hawaiian culture and the old folklore stories. I could listen to her for hours. We would make a camp fire in a pit and "talk story" all night. ("Talk story" is something Hawaiians would say).

This particular weekend was a pivotal moment for all of us because a big transition was taking place. The military had taken over the enormous mountains across the street from the beach to use for target practice! They would ignite bombs and use different artillery for testing. Now they wanted to kick all the homeless off the beach for safety reasons! These people had been living here ten or fifteen years! Where were they supposed to go? My heart broke for the people on the beach. This was their home. They had nowhere else to go. A lot of people showed up to support them. Sunday morning the police would come and arrest all the homeless and anyone else on the beach. It was a sad day for everyone.

I had come to know these people well and I loved them. They were good people with good intentions, but they had to leave. If they didn't, they would be arrested and sent to jail. Their tents, their beds, and other belongings would be dumped, and the "safe haven" would be destroyed. It would look as if no one had ever lived there. It was so unfair. I wanted to help, but there was nothing I could do. My cousin Sally, her friend Alyssa, and I decided to stay until late that night, spend some time with my beach friends, and go home so we would not be caught up in the early morning chaos.

Chapter 9

Playing Tour Guide

My cousin Sally and her friend Alyssa had visited me in 1996. They both had just graduated from high school and were very excited to see Hawaii. I had been living in Hawaii for a few years and loved my life. They came at a good time, visiting me when I was spending all my spare time at the beach, and swimming among wild dolphins. I normally worked non-stop just to make a living in Hawaii. I was a full-time security guard at my apartment building, and I also had clients that I walked dogs for in my new business. Yet, I took time off work for my cousin's visit. I was determined to show these girls how amazing life was in Hawaii! If I wasn't at work, I was at the beach with the girls every day.

I took Sally and Alyssa around the island to show them all the breathtaking views on Oahu. We drove only 2 ½ hours to see the entire island. I showed them my favorite beach called Sandy Beach. As we stopped there to take a dip in the ocean, I looked at all the beauty around us. The ocean was a bright blue color and beautiful with massive water as far as I could see! The gigantic mountains cascaded the landscape across from the beach, and it was incredibly breathtaking. I never tired of Hawaii, it truly was paradise!

Close to the beach we took pictures of an old building where the showers were outside, and the bathrooms were inside for the beach-goers. The outside brick walls were painted over with sea creatures, dolphins and ocean waves. Sally and Alyssa did some funny poses against the wall while I clicked away on the camera to capture some great poses. As we walked on the hot sand, we found the perfect spot to lay our towels to catch some rays. My cousin Sally lathered herself in sunscreen as she knew she could easily burn.

Back in Waikiki, the Hilton Hawaiian Village was across the street from my apartment building and I swam at that beach practically every day. If I couldn't find someone to swim with, I would swim solo, but most of the time I had someone with me. I was single and loving my life! The "beach boys" at the Hilton Hawaiian Village were the best guys in the world. They would rent out surfboards, canoes, big wheel water bikes, or any of the other fun water toys that people would want. These guys always looked out for me. I introduced Sally and Alyssa to the "beach boys" and told them to take good care of my cousin and her friend while I was at work. The girls had so much fun with the beach boys and made friends with practically everyone they met.

One day I was off work, and I asked Sally and Alyssa what was "one crazy thing" they wanted to do on their vacation. We all decided having our belly buttons pierced would be fun and crazy! I was excited because It was one thing I had always wanted to do! I didn't believe in tattoos or wild piercings for my body, but a belly ring, I was all for it!

It just so happened that across the street from where I lived was a piercing and tattoo shop. Honestly, it was a creepy place that looked run down and unsanitary, but we were young and thought this is a "once in a lifetime" opportunity. All three of us were excited to have our belly buttons pierced! We walked up the long flight of stairs to the tattoo shop. As we entered, we looked around at all the pictures on the wall of people with tattoos and piercings, some in very disturbing places. We walked to the desk and said we wanted to have our bellies pierced. The lady behind the counter looked us up and down and she asked, "Who first?" I said, "I will be first." I was adventurous and didn't want to "chicken out" if one of the girls was screaming in pain while having her piercing done. This tall, slender, tattooed gal had me pick out the gem I wanted and then brought me to the back where I would lie down on a "not-so-clean" chair. She pulled the chair back and was ready to insert the needle. She told me to hold my breath and I would feel a pinch. I held my breath and tried to think of nothing. I felt a pinch and within seconds the gem was in my belly! I looked down, and the blue gem sparkled! It looked so pretty! I went to the front and told the girls it was a "piece of cake" when the jewel was inserted but it had stung a little afterward. The girls picked their colored belly rings, had them put in, and now we were officially the belly-button sisters! We were so happy and ready to show our pretty belly gems to everyone!

We spent most of our time in Waikiki, a place to be continuously entertained. This place had everything - lovely beaches, stores to "shop 'til you drop," countless snack shops and other places to eat, and in the evening, plenty of free entertainment for everyone's enjoyment. Friday night at the Hilton Hawaiian Village there was a free luau on the beach and then a big display of fireworks over the water that lasted a solid fifteen minutes! That was a sight to see, and fun to have our toes in the sand while we watched the free entertainment! As we walked down the boardwalk, Sally, Alyssa, and I were listening to Hawaiian music played by a live band, and we were mesmerized by the big waves rolling in. Lucky we were in Hawaii!

I loved Waikiki! I would walk down the many streets where there was entertainment everywhere. Someone would be strumming a guitar, and another person would be playing chess on a picnic table. Another person would play drums, or there was one guy who was covered from head to toe in gold spray paint and stood completely still as if he were a statue. Only if someone put a dollar in his hat would he move. He would surprise all the people standing around because they thought he was not real. As I watched him, I couldn't even see him breathing. Then came the silver man who had to be in competition with the gold man. The two of them would see who could hold their breath longer and try not to move. The first one to move, loses. There was the singing choir, the man preaching from the Bible about the "end times," or an occasional violinist showing off her talent. I even saw a guy with his dog who had a pet mouse that sat on the dog's head all evening with onlookers just staring at the dog and mouse.

On one exceptionally hot day as I was tanning on the beach for Christmas, I saw a skinny Santa Claus, one who definitely needed to eat more cookies! He was walking on the sand wearing his big red suit and big black boots. He was telling everyone "Merry Christmas." He even had a violin which he played a tune for those sitting around him. There was so much entertainment to see in Waikiki and on the beach! There was never a dull moment. My cousin and her friend had so much fun on their trip, and we would stay up late and wake up very early in the morning to see and do as much as we could before they had to leave to go back home to Minnesota.

Time flew by fast and it was time for them to leave. Sally left to go home; however, Alyssa decided to stay with me another week. I asked if she wanted to skydive with me, which was also something I had always wanted to do. She said, "YES!" and we planned a day for skydiving.

Our day to skydive had come! We drove to the North Shore and talked about what it would be like to jump out of an airplane. We had no idea what to expect. We arrived at the site and we were so ready for this crazy jump. As we were signing our life away, (stipulation: If you die, we are not liable) I said, "Wait, I forgot something." I ran to the car, threw my flip flops on the floor, and sat on the seat. I opened my glove compartment to pull out my nail polish remover and a cotton ball and wiped off the nail polish that looked old and ragged. The guy that I was going to jump with was very cute, and I didn't want him staring at my tattered painted nails while we were falling out of the sky! I looked up to see Alyssa laughing at me. She motioned me over. We ran to the plane. We were so excited!

The crew had a group of us sit in a small six-person plane. When we were buckled up, Alyssa asked where my flip flops were. I responded, "I am doing this barefoot, baby!" She laughed. We had adrenaline running through our veins. As the plane took off, I looked over at Alyssa and gave her a look like "I can't believe we are actually doing this!" She smiled back, but I could tell she was as scared as I was! A few minutes later, the guys talked about the do's and don'ts of jumping, then the plane door opened and the guy with whom I was jumping tandem said, "Okay, let's get ready!" I started doubting this was such a good idea. I mean, why would I want to jump from a perfectly good airplane? The guy strapped himself to my back for the tandem jump. When we started walking toward the open door, I could see how massive the ocean was, the mountains so far away looked small from this angle, and I realized how insane this was! We were 13,000 feet high and we were going to jump! I must be crazy!

The guy I was strapped to asked if I was okay. I must have looked as white as a sheet. It finally sank in what I was doing, so I had to make things right with God very quickly in case I were to die that day! I forgot to tell the instructor I had a fear of heights, but I gave him a "thumbs up" that I was okay to jump. I tried to smile but I was terrified. Within seconds, we were at the open door and over the loud engine motor, he yelled, "Okay, I will count to three and together we will jump!" I nodded but I wasn't so sure. I looked down and felt queasy. I heard him count, "One... two..." then he pushed us out the door!

Suddenly, I was in midair and we were falling and falling fast! I couldn't believe it! This was surreal! He asked if I was okay and I nodded. He said he would pull the chord and the chute would come out and it would yank on my chest. It was a nice warning, but I wasn't prepared for how badly it hurt when he did pull the chute! It was just for a second, and then we slowed to a sweet, slow fall. That's when I had a good look at my surroundings. Everything was breathtaking - the water, the land, the "ginormous" mountains; it was all so beautiful! I really did live in paradise! I was so blessed!

As we neared the ground, he warned me to push forward and run when we landed. I bumped the ground and ran forward but it wasn't so bad. He unlatched us, and I turned around to see Alyssa running toward me. We hugged and laughed, and we couldn't believe we did this crazy skydiving and survived! Alyssa loved Hawaii and wanted to stay, but she knew she had to go home. Good memories.

Chapter 10

Beach Life

I walked out onto the beach and scanned the horizon. I gazed far out over the water, looking for any sign of dolphin fins skimming the top. I watched the ocean waves as they rose and fell. The sun was rising, and colors glimmered on top of the rippling water. It was 6am, the air was cool, and I was alone on the beach. I was ready for the shock of cold, crisp water to hit my skin. I loved that exhilarating moment where the chill of the water and swimming fast made my blood pump hard into my veins, and my adrenaline run high. As I scanned the horizon once again, I finally saw a fin just barely break the water surface. I waited a moment and saw more fins that breeched the surface as the dolphins came up for air.

I quickly pulled off my shirt and shorts, threw them on top of my towel, and in my brown striped two-piece swimsuit, I ran into the water, diving in at waist deep. I didn't use goggles or fins; I never used them. They made me feel confined and uncomfortable. I was used to opening my eyes under the salty water and I could see just fine when it was clear blue. When the water was murky though, I could barely see a few feet in front of me, and I would be much more aware of sharks lurking nearby.

On this beautiful day, I looked up into the cloudless sky, which was a baby blue color. Then staring at the ocean, it was a beautiful royal blue. The beauty of it all took my breath away. I dived into the ocean and swam down toward the sand. I swayed back and forth in the water as I imagined I was a mermaid going to my cute little cottage under the sea. I felt so happy! I swam above the sand into much deeper cold water. I held my breath for as long as I could. As my chest started to become tight, the pressure on my ears were too much, and with bubbles blowing from my mouth, I just couldn't hold my breath any longer! I felt like my lungs would burst at any second if I didn't get air! I put my feet down into the soft, white sand feeling it caress my toes, then I pushed myself upward to swim quickly to the surface. I took a deep breath as the pressure on my lungs relaxed. As I caught my breath, I looked back toward the beach and saw it was a bit far. I had drifted in the current. The beach looked desolate. I looked out towards the dolphins, and I knew I would be among them within a few minutes. Excitement washed over me as I thought of swimming with these large mammals once again.

I calmed myself down as the dolphins were very sensitive to emotion and not interested in overbearing human feelings. I looked under the water while I swam. I could see thirty feet down to the sandy bottom. I looked toward the dolphins and could see them swimming around. I swam. I swam hard. I felt like a flopping fish at first. I started concentrating on my breathing and my strokes. If I concentrated hard enough, I could make my body glide easily across the water which made me swim fast and smooth. I soon felt like a mermaid again, the ocean being my playground. My feet stuck together as they pushed me forward faster than ever before. Many of my friends had called me a mermaid and I loved the thought of being one.

In a moment's time, I was there among the dolphins. I floated in the water and looked at them swimming all around me. There were about twenty dolphins in this pod. They didn't even notice me at first. For a moment, I was just like them, swimming effortlessly under the water among their family. I was fascinated watching them play and swim.

There was a mother and baby dolphin about fifty feet from me. A mother dolphin will always protect her young from any predator in the ocean, including destructive human beings. This mother dolphin knew me, yet she was still wary and protective of her sweet, young baby. I understood completely. She would nuzzle her young and encourage him to swim to the bottom of the ocean floor to make artistic designs in the sand with his nose. Dolphins are very playful and have fun at whatever they do, and this baby dolphin was no different. He loved the art of sand drawing. I watched this young dolphin for a little while. He went to the surface with his mother to use his blowhole to take a quick breath before diving down a few feet. Then he did a few somersaults in the water and moved his tail vigorously to create mini-waves, while the mother dolphin lovingly watched him. It was a sweet moment.

As I continued to watch, my emotions overwhelmed me. My excitement of seeing these beautiful mammals swim so closely was an incredible experience, and my heart swelled with love. I was near a few dolphins that I could almost reach out and touch. I wanted so badly to grab ahold of a fin and go for a ride. I would jump on top of the dolphin, wrap my arms around his body, put my head on his shoulder, and go for a wild ride through the waves, swaying back and forth, feeling the water brush my face, tasting the saltiness on my lips, and watching marine life swim all around me. I would push my body as closely as I could to feel the rubber-like surface against my skin. I would pretend to be a baby on its mother's back going for a ride of its life. I quickly had to dismiss these thoughts though, as swimming on a dolphin would not be okay. I would never want to disrespect them in any way.

My thoughts were going wild. The pod picked up on my emotions, and I noticed the nearest dolphins starting to swim slowly away. I became more focused on my thoughts and kept my emotions intact. If I didn't do so, they would swim further, and my day would quickly come to an end.

I rose to the water's surface, took a deep breath, and then swam down toward the dolphins again. This time, fully focused, I watched the large, ten-foot spinner dolphins look me up and down, circle me a few times, and turn their focus back on playing with each other. I had been with this pod before, so they were familiar with my energy and the way I swam. Some days they would swim right up to me and just stare with a silly grin on their face and be playful. Other days the dolphins would rather play together and chase fish rather than swim with any observers. On those days I was completely ignored.

This very morning, the dolphins were curious and having fun swimming around me. One dolphin was a teen whom I had seen grow up from a small baby to a very spunky, curious, and mischievous young dolphin. His mother gave him his independence now that he was older. He loved to show off especially when others were watching him. He loved having an audience to chuckle at his goofiness. Dolphins love to laugh and entertain each other. I enjoyed spending this time with these beautiful mammals, and I would spend the whole morning in the ocean with them, if they would let me. I watched the dolphins swim, play, love on family, and just be who they are, free- spirited and pure-hearted mammals. I loved everything about them.

As I continued to swim along with the pod, this teen saw me out of the corner of his eye. He swam over to get my attention, flicked his tail at me, and then darted up toward the surface to take a breath and make a big splash. Then he came spiraling down to the sandy bottom like a torpedo whizzing through the water. He would swim across the sand, then shooting upward out of the water, do a few spins in the air, and again "splash," he would come swimming downward again. It looked like a "truth-or-dare" game among the young teens laughing at his silly antics. If his fellow dolphins could be judge for the day, they would probably have paper to write on and give him a ten! He looked my way just for a moment to see if I were still watching. When our eyes met I felt a connection, and I couldn't help but smile at the precious moment. He swam right to me and we stared at each other. He was only four feet away; it was a precious moment of connecting with him! He playfully rolled over and over in the water, blew bubbles, swam down toward the bottom, and propped up his tail fin in the sand as he twirled around and around and made pretty designs. I was amazed!

I imagined that I was right there with him, holding his fins and dancing to a song that we both knew very well. We would dance together in perfect harmony at the bottom of the ocean. I wished I could just swim over to him and bravely try dancing in front of him. Something like ballroom dancing or the waltz, but it was a fleeting thought as I knew this dolphin well. If I swam toward him too quickly, he would swim away, and it would break the trust we had built in the past few months.

For a moment, I wished to be a dolphin or a mermaid, so I could swim along with them, never to come back on land again. It was a fleeting thought, a silly one, but one I was lost in when I swam among these beautiful mammals! It was like I was lost in time. Time just stood still, and I didn't have to think about anything going on in my life. I could be free, swimming alongside these free-spirited dolphins who were in their own little world under the sea. I loved every minute I spent with them.

Suddenly, I needed air. I rose to the surface and breathed in the salty air, then I descended again into the water to watch them some more. The same dancing dolphin would look at me often and do a silly jig after our eyes met. I smiled. Dolphins are very smart, and they know how to entertain. After a few moments, the teen's mother swam to him to jolt him back to reality. I guessed that she told him to stop showing off to the human with her clicking mother-like tone. The teen dolphin looked at me one more time and I thought I saw him smile back. He swam off with his mother not far behind him.

I focused on the rest of the pod, who seemed to have been eating their morning fish. After a few minutes they looked full and happy. I had been swimming alongside them for quite some time. I swam to the surface and took a breath to see how far I had drifted from the beach. I wouldn't want to swim too far out and be swept away in a strong current!

Many people in Hawaii have been caught in a strong current that swept them away never to be seen again. They just disappear into the vast, wide ocean never to be found.

Every time I went swimming, I was aware of the dangers of the ocean tides, currents, and how the waves were when swimming long distance. Some days I wouldn't swim with the dolphins if the water was too choppy or the waves were massive. I cautioned more on being safe than adventurous.

As the dolphins swam farther and farther from me, I treaded water in the same place they had left me. I watched for a few moments as the dolphins swam off. I thought of what an amazing experience I just had! Memories would be etched in my mind and heart forever. I wanted to swim with the dolphins every weekend if I could. They made me so happy! As I started swimming toward the beach, I realized I had drifted far. As I treaded water, I started my long swim back.

I swam toward land in a lazy kind of way, treading water like a large sea turtle that had just eaten too much and was moving ever so slowly. I thought of my dolphin encounter the whole swim back. The time seemed to go by quickly since my thoughts were elsewhere. I missed a baby polka-dotted stingray gliding effortlessly across the sand below me. I only noticed it after I put my face in the water and looked around. I had swum right over the stingray with no idea that it was there.

As I reached the shoreline and my feet touched the soft sand, I steadied myself. Small waves were hitting my calves. I looked around and saw a few people on the beach, but not many. My legs were shaky and felt like spaghetti as I ran up the embankment. I laid my towel down and collapsed onto it.

As I thought of the dolphin encounter I smiled as I drifted off to sleep in the sun. When I woke up, the sun was high in the sky and my body was soaked in sweat. I had been sleeping for hours! My skin was hot to the touch and had already started to darken. I knew I was sunburned but that my skin would change to a golden tan by nightfall. I loved when my white skin would change to a pretty brown color. I loved the sun and how it made me feel. The way it touched my face and skin, I was a "sun child" after all, just soaking in the rays that felt warm and comforting. What a perfect day. I was happy!

I scanned the ocean for any sign of dolphins swimming, but it was too late in the day to see them. I flipped over to tan my back side. I fell asleep again for another hour. When I woke up, it was time to go. I jumped into the ocean to cool off, I wiped off quickly, and then hopped in my car for the long drive home.

Almost every weekend, I would swim with the dolphins on the west side of Oahu. Sometimes I was just swimming alone with the dolphins, but I liked going with another person or group of friends. Swimming with a group of friends was entertaining, especially with a newbie, someone who had never swum more than a quarter mile out in the vast ocean before. I liked watching my friends have a half-hearted panic attack when looking down into thirty-foot-deep water, realizing how massive the ocean was, and then freaking out! It was very entertaining for me. I would swim up alongside my friend and tell him or her it would be okay and to breathe, tread water, rest a moment, and then follow us out toward the dolphins. It always turned out okay and everyone had a blast.

I have so many good memories of the west side! My dear friend Dawn and I would go to Waianae on the weekends where we would camp out on my favorite beach and swim with the dolphins the entire time. The thing about Waianae is it has a bad rap. Some people who live in Honolulu would say, "Never go to Waianae. First of all, it's too far, and second, it's too dangerous. People get killed there." I would disagree that it is dangerous, no more than any other part of the island, but then I am partial to the Waianae locals and my best friends that live in the area. I loved Waianae and especially loved Makaha, which is a smaller community of people on the cusp of Waianae. The people are amazing, and the beaches are stunning. I have to say, I think the beaches in Waianae are the most beautiful beaches on the entire island of Oahu.

Dawn and I had so much fun at the beach. What I liked most about my friend Dawn was that she lived a hippie lifestyle. She was so free and happy without a care in the world. When we would hang out, she was always unpredictable. She was a "free spirit" after all. We always had fun together no matter what we did. We would "fly by the seat of our pants" at every turn not planning anything which made our adventures exciting.

One time, Dawn and I planned a weekend of camping and swimming with the dolphins. We drove to the west side of the island where we saw a large group of Hawaiian locals camping on a popular beach and having fun. It was late afternoon and the family was eating while one guy was playing on a ukulele and some of the children were singing. It was an awesome sight! We stopped the car and stepped out onto the beach. Dawn was the outgoing type, so she went right up to the locals and introduced herself. "Hi, I am Dawn and we would love to join you," she said as she looked at me and then back at the locals.

The guy with the ukulele stopped playing. Everyone stared at my friend being so bold and so "white." I stood there watching to see what would happen next. One of the little Hawaiian girls came over to take Dawn's hand. Dawn smiled and asked, "What's your name?" The little girl said sweetly, "I'm Leilani." Leilani couldn't have been more than six years old, but she hollered over to her mom, "Put on some music, we are going to dance!"

Jack Johnson was on the radio and Dawn and the little girl started dancing together. All the other kids joined in and a few of the adults too. I just laughed. This would only happen with Dawn! We had a fun time with this beautiful family. We ate with them and stayed late into the night "talking story." ("Talking Story" is what Hawaiians say when they are all gathered around telling stories). Dawn and I thanked the family for being so kind and then headed to our favorite beach where we would camp for the night and wake up to dolphins feeding in the bay.

This story reminds me of another time when Dawn and I flew together to Maui, my favorite Hawaiian island. We were there for the Halloween festival in Lahaina. Every year thousands of people flocked to Lahaina, a little place in Maui to party for Halloween. We decided to rent a van to sleep in, since hotels were all booked up with the thousands of people who were visiting that weekend! The van was an old, white clunker, but it had plenty of room in it to crash for the night.

I loved Lahaina. It was a small town, only about a mile long. Lahaina was filled with shops and entertainment, as well as a great coffee shop where I liked to have my favorite chai latte. The town also had a harbor with charter boats for fishing, sail boats, or catamarans that people could pay a small fee and experience a great time on the water. Just about every weekend there were craft fairs in the big park and plenty of entertainment on the strip. It was similar to Waikiki's entertainment on the strip in Oahu. Guys with big red or blue parrots walked around, and they wanted to put the parrot on people's hand or shoulder and take pictures. They were lifetime memories for the tourists. A guy would play his ukulele or harmonica, while others would be chipping away at wood to make sculptures of turtles or dolphins. I especially liked to watch those who painted caricatures. I couldn't believe the talent that these people had. It was amazing!

Dawn and I dressed up for Halloween and walked around Lahaina lost in a crowd of 60,000 people. We met many people with whom we partied with that night, and we had so much fun. After the night came to an end, Dawn and I crashed in the van which we had parked in a small cul-de-sac on the outskirts of Lahaina. We felt relatively safe since we locked the van doors and kept the windows only slightly open for air. Early the next morning about 7 o'clock, however, there was a loud knock on the window. We both sat up. A guy was standing outside the van looking in. This strange guy was staring in at us while wearing a robe and holding a cup of coffee in his hand! As he pointed toward his house, his dog was sniffing around in the yard. He invited us in for bagels with cream cheese and orange juice. I was starving and as Dawn looked at me, I shrugged my shoulders and said, "Sure." Dawn looked unsure about this, but I whispered to her, "He has a dog, I think he is a good guy." We followed him and his dog into his beautiful home.

We sat down for breakfast at his kitchen table. The guy liked to talk, so he kept the conversation going with interesting stories about Maui. After breakfast, he said we could stay awhile and relax and take a shower if we wanted. We passed on the nice gesture. Then we drove around the island sight-seeing and meeting many great locals on the island.

Another time Dawn and I flew to Maui again and rented a car. We wanted to see and do everything on the island, but we especially looked forward to driving the adventurous road through Hana. Dawn and I were so excited to see this beautiful place. Hana is fantastic! For anyone who had taken this long road trip, they would know it is not for the weak-stomached. It was an eight-foot-wide winding road that led into the middle of nowhere! Whoever was brave enough to drive the Hana road knew it took half a day just to venture through it. There were large mountains on the right that seemed sky-high and endless as they rose into the clouds. On the left was a sharp cliff that went hundreds of feet straight down to the rocky coral beneath where the ocean waves crashed upon the rocks.

Anyone driving the road to Hana had to be careful not to drive off the cliff. There were barely any guardrails on this narrow winding road to protect tourists as they dangerously drove close to the edge. We would be driving along, and a car would come from the opposite direction, but the road was too narrow for both cars. One of the cars would have to pull up the side of the mountain, almost sideways, to make room for the other car to go by. Sometimes the car would drive too closely to the cliff, and it looked like it might go over. The whole experience driving the road to Hana was somewhat scary, but also exhilarating not knowing what was going to happen on this adventure. Anything could go wrong or right while driving on this road!

We drove for hours along the Hana road into the abyss of farm animals and houses spotted across the grassy farm land. We saw chickens crossing the road and cows grazing in the pasture. There was flat land for as far as the eyes could see, then straight up cliffs and cascading waterfalls at every turn.

At one point, there was a horse standing in the middle of the road. We couldn't drive around him because the road was too narrow. I dug in my bag and came up with some crackers. We could feed the horse crackers to make him move. Dawn stopped the car, took the crackers, and coaxed the horse to one side of the car so we could drive by. The horse came over and started eating a cracker, but he wanted more so he reached his whole head in the car looking for the bag of crackers! His head and neck hung over Dawn's body, and we both cracked up laughing. We laughed so hard and we couldn't stop! We both scrambled out of my side of the vehicle and tried to lure the horse onto the grassy area with the remaining crackers. The horse was eating all of them! As the horse continued to eat, Dawn and I talked as I moved my hand toward the horse's back end to pet him. I came too close to his tail, and suddenly the horse made a noise and kicked me in the thigh with such force I fell flat on the ground!

I stood up, shocked that he had kicked me, but I didn't know at the time never to pet a horse by the back end, as it can surprise them. Lesson learned. A big, round hoof-print bruised my leg for weeks! It hurt for a long time. Friends would ask what happened, and I would laugh as I told them I was kicked by a horse.

Dawn and I loved Hana because of its stunning beauty. We were having so much fun, and as we were driving in the middle of nowhere, there was a lady at a table on the side of the road, selling homemade banana bread. We stopped and bought some. It was delicious! There was also a guy selling coconuts to drink coconut juice. He had a big machete with which he chopped off the top of the coconut so easily, and then he gave us each a straw, and we drank fresh coconut water from it. Afterward, he gave us spoons to eat the sweet, white coconut meat off the sides. What a great experience! It was the perfect weekend in Maui.

Back in Oahu, I was coming off my "natural high" from a great adventure in Maui. I was at the grocery store shopping for a twenty-four pack of Ramen noodles for $5.00 and a few cans of Spam for $1.29 each. This was my favorite cheap meal that would last almost two weeks. As I looked for my favorite Spam in a can, I saw a man who was standing with his back to me and looking for Vienna sausages on the shelves across from the Spam. I noticed his can of sausages was a mere twenty-nine cents.

He started up a conversation with me, and I could tell from his energy that he was very much a free-spirited hippie. He talked to me about how he lived right on the ocean in Kaneohe Bay and how living in a beach house was the best thing that had ever happened to him. He said he watched this incredible house for a rich couple who traveled all over the world. He was the caretaker for their beautiful home on the beach, and I was intrigued.

He introduced himself as Walter. He mentioned he had a group of friends that showed up at his place almost every weekend. I wanted to know more, as it sounded surreal. Walter talked about the beautiful palm trees that stood forty-feet-high with gigantic palms that swayed in the light Hawaiian breeze. The palms made great shade for the hammock underneath that he would lie in as he listened to the ocean waves crashing on the beach. He would pick a fresh coconut off his palm tree and drink the coconut water from it as he relaxed in the hammock. It sounded so nice. It's something I could only dream of.

Walter didn't work, he ate food from the land he farmed, and he lived on this beautiful property on the beach. I wanted to see this for myself. I couldn't give him my number since he didn't have a phone. He gave me an address and directions on how to find it. The GPS Navigation had not been invented at this time, so I had to use landmarks to find someone's house. He told me to take a left at McDonalds, go around the bin until I see the bay, drive all the way to the end where it opens to the beach, and then I would see the house on the left. He said there was a surfboard leaning against the fence. "Got it," I thought. I was so excited to check this place out. I hoped the week of work would go fast so I could meet up with him and his friends.

That weekend, I drove out to Walter's place. I was worried I would be lost because in the past I've had difficulties following directions to someone's home. I would often find myself taking the wrong direction and end up on the other side of the island. It worried me because it was not like I could call him and ask for directions. I figured if I didn't find this place, then I would turn around and head to Makaha to swim with the dolphins. That was always my "go-to" thing to do.

I followed the directions Walter had given me and to my surprise, I found the place! There was a tall, brown, wooden six-foot gate that etched the whole front area to hide the homes and beach view. As he mentioned, there was a big, yellow surfboard leaning against a part of the gate. That made it easy to find. I drove through the open gate and as the driveway wrapped around large grassy areas and huge trees, the driveway finally ended in front of a two-car garage. This house looked like an old log cabin. I parked the car and stepped out. I noticed there were no cars around. I looked up at the house. It had stairs that went up to a one-story home on top of the garage. As I stared at the house, I noticed it was small but elegant. A log cabin beach house - I loved it already. I walked up the steps to the door and knocked. "Hello?" I said. It was silent.

I knocked again and looked around. The yard was so big. I had never seen a yard as large as this. Palm trees were everywhere, and they were huge and swaying in the Hawaiian breeze. I could smell the salty air and hear the waves crashing on the beach.

The driveway weaved around to a bigger house that sat right on the sandy beach. My jaw dropped open as I stared at this huge house right on the water. The house was stunning! It had stained-glass windows and a chandelier that hung in the front foyer. I stood at the door for another moment and knocked one more time, and then I walked down the steps and toward this other house. I just stared at the house in awe as I walked. If I hadn't kept my composure so well in case someone was watching, I would have been noticeably drooling. It could have been an embarrassing sight! I just couldn't believe this guy lived here... for free. I wished that I could find a client that I could watch their beach house!

As I stood at the front door, I had a fleeting thought. What if this guy didn't live here? What if he led me to a creeper's place and what if I were to be kidnapped, never to be found again? What if he were a creeper who was standing behind the bushes with a machete and wanting to chop me up into little pieces! Maybe this is how he eats meat! He chops up women in distress, freezes their body parts, and then cooks them up when he is hungry! I shut my eyes and took a deep breath. This is crazy! I needed to stop with the relentless murderous thoughts. Years of watching horror flicks and my mind goes wild! "Get a grip, Becka!" I thought.

I had to trust my gut instincts. I knew I was a good judge of character, and I had a feeling this guy would be okay. I took a deep breath and shut off my mind as I rolled up my fingers into a ball and knocked on the door. Nothing. I knocked again. Nothing. I looked around, but the place was quiet and empty. I felt a little creeped out and it bugged me that I drove all the way out here and no one was home. Walter had told me he was always home. I stood there for a moment trying to calm down, and I then decided to walk out to the beach. I would collect my thoughts and figure out what to do next.

Chapter 11

Hippie Life

I followed a small sidewalk around to the backside of the house that stopped right at the sandy beach. I looked out at the ocean and it took my breath away. There were waves lapping at the shore, and the water was a bright blue color. I took my flip flops off, left them in the grass, and walked toward the ocean. I let my feet sink into the white blanket of sand, and it felt good. Small waves pushed the sand toward me and tickled my feet. As I looked up, it felt good to have the sun beat down on my face. As I stared at the crystal-clear blue water, I sat down on a hump of dry sand and watched the waves push their way onto the beach and pull back out to the massive ocean again. I loved listening to the sound of the roaring waves. It was very relaxing.

I heard a sound behind me and I looked up to see Walter standing there. He smiled really big and said, "You made it." I stood up and smiled as I gave him a great big hug. I said, "I am so glad I found it. This place is incredible. Your own little oasis in the middle of nowhere." Walter's smile was plastered on his face as if it were glued there. It made me feel so good. He was a very happy guy.

We walked back toward the house as his friends drove in with a white van. They parked in the driveway, and as we walked over to the van, a group of women came piling out. I couldn't help but notice they were wearing beautiful, elegant, colorful tie dye dresses. As we made our way toward the van, I had a whiff of pakalolo (weed) pass by my nose. I was not too familiar with the smell since I had never smoked. As Walter introduced me to the ladies, I noticed they all had hippie names: Star, Melody, Love, Joy, and Blossom. I smiled as they each said hello. I had never met anyone like these unique ladies.

I was wowed by their sweet nature and quick acceptance of me. I couldn't believe how nice they were. I was actually in the midst of real hippies! They all hugged me, and Star grabbed my hand to show me around the place. She talked about the owners of the house that loved to travel the world. She said the front house was where Walter lived. The larger beach house was the main house for the owners. Sometimes on the weekends Walter would invite a bunch of friends and they would party hard in the large beach house. Then the group of friends would camp on the beach overnight and clean up the house in the morning. The owners only showed up a few times a year and always gave notice before they returned so Walter could make sure the house and yard were clean. The yard looked immaculate! Nothing was out of place. I was just amazed at the surroundings, the beach, and my new hippie friends.

Star showed me the hidden garden between a cluster of trees. There were rows and rows of vegetables. It was amazing to see! There were cabbage, carrots, tomatoes, cucumbers, celery, and different types of lettuce. I had never met anyone with their own self-sustaining garden before. Shoot, my idea of eating healthy was a can of V8 juice and a peanut butter sandwich. I would get my daily vegetables, and the peanuts in the peanut butter is good for you, right?

After Star showed me the garden, we walked toward Walter's house and up the stairs to the front door. Entering inside, the home felt peaceful. I smelled incense in the air. A wooden incense holder lay on the end table, and the smoke spiraled up as it danced in the air.

As I stood in the studio, I looked around. The walls had colorful paintings hanging every which way. The furniture had a shabby, well-worn feel with its futon couch, an end table, and a few comfy chairs to sit on. It was small but cozy. I stared at the floor for a few moments as I looked at the oversized brown and gray rug that took up most of the living room. Someone had draped a multi-color, blue, red, yellow, and green tie-dye sarong over the top of the rug. I noticed how small and quaint the kitchen looked. It had a regular-sized fridge and freezer, which made small noises like ice brewing. The cupboard space hung over the sink and stove, and there was a white dishwasher working at its max that hummed as if it were alive. The window overlooking the plumeria tree out front with its white flowers in full bloom made the air smell sweet with perfume. There were green vines and bushes that were running along the fence, overtaking everything in its path. Over the fence I could see cars driving by on the two-lane street. To the left of the kitchen was the bathroom that had blue and white wallpaper that looked old and faded; it probably was the original wallpaper. The bathroom had a few palm tree wall hangings that created the perfect "beachy" look. Everything in the bathroom was in such close quarters that I could walk only steps from the toilet to the sink or to the shower. I stepped out of the bathroom and looked around.

Walter watched me as I looked at everything. He said, "It's a small place but it is perfect for me." I didn't say anything, but I nodded and smiled as I thought, "Yes, what else would you need; you live right on the beach!" The ladies in the living room were all chatting up a storm as they caught up on what was happening in each other's lives. The couch and chairs were taken, so I sat on the floor where Love was sitting. She started to thread together a purse she was making. I watched her as she so elegantly threaded colors together. The design on the purse was a peace sign with blue and red woven through it. I sat and listened in on the conversations around me and took in the energy and feeling of calmness and peace.

Then Walter suddenly pulled out a joint. They started passing it around and asked if I wanted some. "No," I told them, "I don't smoke." They were fine with that. The aroma filled the air for a long time. They were deep into a conversation in which I listened in. My hippie friends were in support of not working at a dead-end job and to live off the land. Working too much makes a person dull with no time to enjoy life. I thought, in a perfect world that would be great! I would love that kind of life, but I had to work to live, to eat, and to keep a roof over my head. I had saved no money and was barely making it in Hawaii.

I was deep in thought about the conversation when Love stopped working on her purse and reached for my hand. She asked what my hippie name was. I was taken aback. I had never thought about what it would be. She looked directly at me and asked, "What do you want to be called?" I thought a moment and said, "I love butterflies, how about 'Butterfly'?" I explained my love of butterflies... when a caterpillar in a cocoon changes into a beautiful butterfly, it reminds me that the old is gone and there are new beginnings. A butterfly became a symbol of my past being done away with and having a fresh new start on life. They all nodded and agreed that was the perfect name for me. I felt like I was fitting in already. I loved my new friends. They were so loving and accepting.

We spent most of the day just talking about all sorts of things; then we decided to take a dip in the ocean. We all took turns going into the bathroom to put on our bathing suits. We walked toward the beach and then ran into the ocean. As I paddled around, I noticed the water felt warm like bath water. I dived down to the sand and opened my eyes under water. As I touched the sand and felt the coarseness of it in my hands, I twirled around thinking about what my dolphin friends would do. As I swam around looking at the beautiful live coral, I did a few somersaults in the water before I pushed myself back up to the surface. It had been a few minutes before I came up for air. I took a breath and pulled my very long hair back off my face.

As I paddled around my friends, they laughed and told me I swam like a mermaid. I smiled as I told them it's probably because I swim with the dolphins. They were intrigued. I told them they can come with me next time. They were excited to swim with the dolphins, and I was looking forward to spending more time with my new friends. If all went well, no one would drown or be bitten by a shark. That day, we sun tanned and relaxed on the beach until dark fell, then I left to return home.

The very next day, I called my friend, Jacob, to meet me at my favorite beach to swim. Sandy Beach was a local hangout that was always packed on the weekends, but not during the week. Jacob and I liked to meet there during the week to swim a few barrels, then resume work afterward. I drove to the beach and parked my car. I was deep in thought as I looked out at the ocean. The waves were large and unpredictable. Suddenly, I was startled by someone standing next to my Mazda Miata. Jacob had stooped to peer into my window and I laughed. He liked to mess with me. I grabbed my towel as I was leaving my car, and Jacob and I sat on the hot sand looking at the waves. I started telling him about my new hippie friends and how excited I was that they will be swimming with the dolphins and me the very next weekend. Jacob was a very down to earth kind of guy, and he always liked to know what was happening in my life. We chatted a bit, then with the sun beating down and sweat pouring off my face, I knew it was time to jump into the water.

This beach was very special to me. It was not only beautiful with its stunning bright blue water, but the ginormous mountains on the opposite side of the road were spectacular. It was heaven on earth! This beach had the biggest waves on the

east side of the island and had the most injuries as well. It was a
popular hang-out for locals and tourists alike. Tourists didn't
realize how dangerous the waves were, but the locals did.

I watched the waves push their way in. I counted three
sets of waves come in, then I dashed out into the water as fast
as I could until the water was waist deep. I knew if I was hit by
one of those billowing monster waves, it could push my whole
body twenty feet up on the sand and give me a great big sand
rash. That would hurt. I swam out and Jacob was right there
with me. He was a fast swimmer, and I liked that he could keep
up. I was having a blast. I would ride a few smaller waves in, but
I was waiting for the larger waves. Once a larger wave set was
barreling in, I would put my right arm straight out, left arm
back, straighten my whole body, and let the wave push my body
toward shore. WHAT A RUSH! I knew time was short and I had
to go back to work soon. I looked around for Jacob who was
about fifty yards from me. I swam over to him and we chatted a
bit.

I was looking at the shoreline and not thinking about
much of anything when I heard a low rumble. Jacob had a look
of shock on his face as he yelled, "INCOMING!" I barely had time
to hold my breath as the wave came crashing down on the both
of us. I spun around and around under the water. I knew being
caught off guard, that I needed to let my body relax or I could
seriously be injured. I went with the wave and it pushed and
pulled. I felt like I was stuck in a washing machine. I was running
out of air and wondering when I could swim up to the surface,
but the waves were huge and kept pushing and pulling me
every which way. It felt like the wave was alive and had a hand
pushing me deep into a water abyss. Air was escaping my lungs
and I knew I didn't have much time. Suddenly a wave pushed
me down so forcefully I did a face plant in the sandy bottom. I
heard my neck snap loudly and my face burned as if it was lit on

fire. My friend grabbed my arm and pulled me out of the billowing waves. I choked and sputtered as he pulled me up onto the sand. We laid there on the sand for a long time. When I was able to finally breathe normal again, I started laughing. Jacob was breathing heavy and started laughing too. He said, "Good thing you didn't see how big those waves were." I said, "So, same time tomorrow?" We both cracked up laughing even harder. I loved the rush from the unpredictable waves. My neck hurt but thankfully I didn't injure it, and Jacob messed up his shoulder from our swim, but no matter the injuries we may have endured, we always came back to swim again. I was such a beach girl! I loved that I could work whatever hours I wanted and get beach time in also.

That next weekend, my hippie friends met me on the west side of the island to swim with the dolphins. It was early in the morning, and the sky was a pretty blue. The whole gang showed up and piled out of the big white van. Walter was driving, and Star, Joy, Love, and Melody were there too. We all jumped into the cold water and started swimming. We swam far out into the vast ocean. A few of the gals took their time swimming as they lagged behind and chit chatted.

I was swimming in the lead with my adrenaline pumping and heart racing, and I was very excited about meeting up with the dolphins. It took more effort than usual to swim because the ocean was a bit turbulent, which in turn made it more difficult to stay above water. It was hard not drinking in the salt water while pushing through the waves. But in a moment's time my new friends and I were surrounded by a pod of dolphins. We gathered together and treaded water as we watched the large mammals. I loved the dolphins. It took my breath away every time I saw them. Their beautiful, sleek bodies were long and slender with a big slanted fin on top, and a tail that swished to move them forward. They were as graceful as ballerinas, spinning around and around, then up out of the water like dancers twirling close together. I never grew tired of watching them. They fascinated me every time I saw them. As we swam nearby, it was as if they were showing off. We swam alongside the dolphin pod for a while, and then trailed a little behind as we watched their beautiful serenade.

I reminded my friends not to become overly excited but to be calm, so we would be accepted into the dolphin pod. I shared that sending "good energy" toward the dolphins would make them feel more relaxed around us, especially being a new group of people. A few moments later, a large group of dolphins came near! We swam under the water, and a few of the larger male dolphins came closer and pushed water toward us with their tails. This is a sign that they are in charge as they protect their young. We humans can watch them but need to respect boundaries. I signed to the others under water that the dolphins would come to us. We waited a few moments and the smaller female adults swam closely. The dolphins were playful with each other as all of them finally surrounded us. We wanted to reach out and grab ahold of them but knew we better not.

We continued to swim with the dolphins and then would come up for air and dive back down again to watch these beautiful mammals swim. We had a great time, but we couldn't stay long because the water was chilly, and the waves were choppy. We decided to go back to shore. The swim back to the beach was harder because it was against the current with the wind against my face. I think everyone was struggling. When we finally reached the beach, we all collapsed on our towels and baked in the sun until we were golden brown. Later we dug a large hole into the sand and built a wall of rocks in a big circle. We found small, dead tree limbs to start a fire in our man-made fire pit. We had hung out all day on the beach and it was a great time talking and laughing. We talked about how fun it was to see the dolphins. I felt a sense of connection with my new friends as I let them into my world.

I always enjoyed sunsets on the west side and this night was no different. As the sun went down, it hit the water's edge, and the sky blew up into beautiful colors of red, blue, orange and pink. All the colors mixed and swirled among large, wispy clouds overhead. Every night the sunset colors were incredibly breathtaking!

The ocean lapped at the shore and we could hear the wind rustling through the trees. It was the perfect night. As the flames grew, it was as if small, red-flamed men were dancing all around in the fire. It was mesmerizing as the flames grew taller and taller. We just stared at it for hours, silent and content.

The moon came out, large and bright, and showed a silhouette on the water which gave a sense of security like a large nightlight that illuminated from above. Walter and a few of the ladies decided to go night swimming. They ran into the ocean, splashing around and giggling. It sounded like fun. They hollered for us to come swim with them, but we stayed put mesmerized by the fire. No one brought tents, but we had sleeping bags and blankets from the car and each of us found a place on the soft sand to prop our pillow. We all finally rested our heads and fell asleep to the sound of crashing waves and the crackling embers from the fire.

In the early morning, I woke up and walked to the water's edge to scan the horizon to see if the dolphins were swimming in the bay. I would look far out in the deep water for any fin that may pop up and then look for a pod that was swimming through the bay as they searched for fish to eat. At first, I didn't see anything, but I was not giving up. I scanned the ocean looking for any current, any white water, or anything else that could be the dolphins swimming. After a few moments, I saw a dolphin's fin skim the water. Then another dolphin jumped up out of the water and fell back in with ease. I looked around at everyone sleeping and said, "Time to get up and swim with the dolphins." The pod was about a half mile out, and my friends and I needed to swim quickly to reach them before they left the bay.

We had all slept in our swimsuits, and we ran into the cold water to swim as fast as we could to reach the dolphins swimming not so far from shore. As I swam, I looked down and saw a large sea turtle swimming by ever so slowly. It was oval-shaped with green and brown checkered designs on its back. It had green algae caked on parts of the shell that swayed in the water as he meandered along. I stopped to watch this turtle for a few moments and then started my swim again, getting into the "rhythm of things." When we finally reached the dolphins, we all spread out a little further from each other than the day before. It seemed this was a bigger pod of dolphins that separated into smaller groups to feed.

I found myself swimming close to a large bottle-nosed dolphin that had to be ten-feet long. He was shy but curious. He was stand-offish from the other dolphins as if he had been cast out. I had not seen this one before and thought maybe he wanted acceptance from this pod.

As I watched him float around near the sand, I dived down to have a better look at him. I noticed something strange about his neckline. A rope was lodged into his skin and looked like it had been there for years. The skin had grown around a portion of the rope, consuming it as part of the body. It shocked me to realize this could happen and the dolphin could do nothing!

It was heartbreaking for me to see this poor dolphin unable to loosen this rope that was tightly wound against his skin. He watched me closely. I felt a need to help him. I swam toward him and could almost reach out and touch him, but he would retreat a few feet away from me. I thought about the hard life he must have. How he would never trust another human because humans meant cruelty for him. This rope had been thrown into the water by a human, and somehow it had wrapped around his neck never to come off. He was slowly suffocating and there was no one who would be able to help him. He was watching me out of the corner of his eye when he picked up on my sadness and slowly floated away. I hoped he would realize I just wanted to help cut off that big piece of rope wrapped around his neck and fin. I rose to the surface to take a few breaths and came diving back down to see if I could get a better look at him. He didn't swim far.

As I watched the dolphin, I thought about the rope so tightly wound about his neck. I didn't have a knife or anything to cut the rope. I was so disheartened. I wanted to save him, but I couldn't. He looked so sad. I thought "How long would his life last?" Not very long with that rope wrapped around his neck. I thought about the people who litter with no concern about the mammals, fish, and little creatures living in the coral. Humans throw too much trash in the ocean without ever thinking of sea mammals and the living sea creatures that are all affected by litter and will eventually die. What a dismal thought. I was bothered by the pain this poor dolphin would have to go through. He was defenseless, hopeless, and would suffer a very slow painful death, suffocating from the rope that slowly consumed him. I was sad for him.

I swam up to the surface knowing there was nothing I could do for this lonely dolphin. I had drifted away in the current, so I swam hard toward my friends, then together we swam back to the beach. Our fun weekend had come to an end. We packed up our belongings and headed out. I planned on meeting with my new hippie friends again the very next weekend. I was looking forward to it.

Chapter 12

The Sacrifices I Made to Live in Hawaii

I worked day and night just to live in Hawaii. It took everything I had to survive and keep a roof over my head. Yes, I admit, it was financially hard to live in Hawaii. Gas was expensive and for good reason - it was shipped from the mainland. Rental apartments weren't cheap as well, and food was twice as expensive as any other place in the US. Every month I had to scrape together enough money to pay my rent first, then electricity, gas for the car and if I had money left over, I would buy food to eat. I worked at any job that would hire me so that I could live in paradise. I was definitely in survival mode. At one point in my life, I worked at a string of jobs just to make ends meet. I worked at Walgreen's during the day, I was a waitress at a few Waikiki bars, I had my own pet sitting business, and I sold healthy body products for a small company.

My favorite job was having my own pet sitting business, which didn't seem like a job at all. I loved watching dogs and cats and couldn't believe I was being paid for it. I didn't go to college or take business courses. I didn't have any marketing tips or teaching tools to start pet sitting, but I loved dogs and cats so much that I wanted to be around them all the time. I thought, what better way to do that than start my own pet sitting business! It had minimal startup costs, and soon by word of mouth, I was walking dogs for clients and pet sitting cats when the clients would leave for trips. Sometimes I would stay overnight at the client's home with the pets while the owners were gone, and during the day I would stay busy walking numerous dogs or cat sitting in the home for various clients. I loved it! I was slowly building a business, making my own hours, and striving to become successful! I would have loved to drop all the part-time jobs and pet sit full-time, but I had not built up enough clientele to do so, and I knew it would take time to build a successful business.

I didn't shop at the high-priced stores in the mall like the average person, but I learned from being broke to buy clothes from thrift stores and other shops that were cheap and affordable. My favorite place for shopping was the Swap Meet, which was a large empty parking lot that was once a drive-in movie theatre. They tore the theatre down and used the parking lot for the local Swap Meet. Over one hundred sellers would pay a small fee and set up tables in the parking lot with items to sell. Hundreds of shoppers would come from all over the island to see what treasures they could find. The Swap Meet was open Wednesdays, Saturdays, and Sundays, and I loved going there to find good deals. I could find brand name clothing, a variety of books, Bath and Body Works lotions, organic shampoos, and even brand-new packaged Christmas gifts. People would also sell jewelry, surfboards, scuba gear, tools, furniture, shoes, and toiletries. People would sell anything and everything. I couldn't believe I could find brand new items I needed for only $1.00 when in a store it would cost $5.00 or $10.00! For someone who was broke like me, it was such a deal! There was also an inexpensive farmer's market in one section of the lot with plenty of fruits and vegetables and even a food market with grilled chicken and hot plate lunches. The plate lunches were "ONO!" (Ono in Hawaiian means "delicious.")

The Swap Meet was my favorite past time, and I met many good friends there. I would even sell there myself when I was broke and needed to bring in a little income for rent or food. Sometimes, I would leave there making hundreds of dollars; other times, I would only make the money back that I paid to get in to sell. It was a gamble, but no matter what, I had fun and would talk with the people selling their items next to me as I browsed through their stuff. I always said, "one person's junk is another person's treasure." I was able to make ends meet from buying and selling at the swap meet. Years later in 2017, the local Swap Meet closed so the new owner could build a high-rise. So many displaced sellers!

When I first started selling households items at the Swap Meet, I met a Hawaiian guy named Allen who was homeless. He was the nicest guy who would give the shirt off his back for someone else in need. Every weekend he was at the Swap Meet selling items he made. For twenty years he made beautiful Koa wooden bowls and Hawaiian jewelry. He would sell his treasures right out of his van where he also slept at night.

At our first meet, he brought over a few boxes of goods I could sell of his, and he said I could keep the money I made. It was a nice gesture, and I was able to make money by selling the items he gave me. What a blessing! It had not been easy living in Hawaii, having to work so hard to survive in paradise, and his big heart giving me his items to sell really helped me.

Allen and I became close friends. Every time I went to the Swap Meet we would chat about life. I shopped for a variety of items and would sell at the Swap Meet from time to time and for seventeen years, I became a regular buyer and seller at the Swap Meet. It was amazing to me that Allen and I stayed friends for all those years. He became more like family to me.

One day Allen told me he was very sick. He wanted to share with me how to make Hawaiian jewelry. He said I was like family to him, and he wanted to pass on the art of jewelry-making. I was happy he wanted to teach me, but I was sad he was sick and wouldn't be around forever. I had collected thousands of sea shells from the beach, so I was ready to make Hawaiian jewelry from my favorite shells. I promised Allen that people would hear his name for years to come after his passing. He or his creations would NOT be forgotten!

Allen was so sick that he made an appointment with the doctor. He found out he had stage-four colon cancer, and he had only ten months to live. He knew for years he would not live a long life, how he knew, I don't know, but still, it came as a shock that he had less than a year. I was devastated! We were such good friends, and to realize he didn't have much time to enjoy life was shocking to say the least. I wanted to be a shining light in his life, so I talked to my landlord and Allen was able to move into one of the apartments in my apartment complex. It was wonderful to see Allen with a roof over his head, a mattress to sleep on, food in his fridge, and a private shower, not like the showers at the beach. I helped Allen as much as I could, but the best part was I prayed for his soul and that Allen would find God. I spent time with him, and we had many great conversations and laughs. Even knowing his fate, Allen was still positive in his life and caring for others. Before he passed, he made some funny and silly YouTube videos. YouTube had just come out on the internet and he wanted to be a "star" before he passed on. To this day, I still visit his YouTube channel once in a great while.

When Allen was in hospice at Tripler, a Veterans Hospital, I visited him every chance I could. My heart was heavy, and time was short. He gave me all his jewelry-making materials, beads and shells to make an assortment of beautiful jewelry. It meant so much to me. The first time I made a necklace, I brought it to the hospital. I was excited to show Allen what I made! All the red plastic beads were strung up on fishing wire to make a red necklace. I was so proud of myself because it was my very first one! I was beaming as I pulled the necklace from my purse and showed Allen my handcrafted piece.

Now, for anyone who knew Allen, not only would he be joking around and laughing about everything, but he was also very honest and blunt. I loved his unique personality. He sat up in the hospital bed, looked at the necklace for a moment, and trying to find the right words, he blurted out, "That's not a necklace, it's a bunch of beads on a string!" We were silent for a moment staring at each other, and then both of us burst out laughing.

Allen passed away not long after that, but his memory will be with me forever. He inspired me to pursue my dreams, including creating beautiful jewelry and blessing others with the jewelry I made. An endless amount of creativity has poured out of me, and I thank God for that. I also thank God for my friendship with Allen. I will never forget how he has changed my life. After Allen passed away, I had run a few online jewelry shops for years that kept me very busy. I have never forgotten how Allen blessed me and shared his creative jewelry-making with me. I will never forget Allen and our friendship.

As I worked hard in Hawaii and lived paycheck-to-paycheck just to survive, the struggle was real! The difficulties to make ends meet were challenging to say the least, but it was worthwhile as I was blessed with beautiful "heaven-like" surroundings. I was also blessed with fabulous friends and many wonderful adventures along the way.

Chapter 13

Adventures in Hawaii

I loved my life in Hawaii and I had a good group of friends. Everyone called me "Butterfly" because I was a social butterfly who loved meeting new people everywhere I went. I was a "hippie wannabe" who wished I had been born in the 50's so I would have been a hippie in the 70's. Instead, I was born in the 70's and grew up in the age of rock music, record players, and cassette tapes. I loved the idea of being a free spirit, happy all the time with no problems, no drama, just "No worries, man." I loved the tie dye colors on sarongs, blankets, and tank tops and even to this day, I love tie dye everything.

In 2004 my business in pet sitting started picking up. I loved my work and couldn't believe I was being paid to walk dogs and play with cats all day long while the owners were out of town. Occasionally, I needed a break from working so much, so I would save up money every few months to fly to the outer island for a mini-vacation on the weekends. I flew to the various islands of Maui, Kauai, Molokai, and the Big Island.

In Maui, I always stayed at a hostel instead of a hotel. A hostel is basically a house that the owner would rent out individual bedrooms to many travelers from around the world. It would cost $20.00 per person to share a co-ed room. There were usually six people to a room, sleeping in bunk beds supplied with sheets, blankets and pillows. Some hostels had a few private rooms that were $35 per night, but they were almost always taken. I didn't mind the cheaper price of the co-ed rooms. There were usually four to five rooms to a house, and many people would come and go during the day. I would meet many great travelers and the hostels were very safe. They had a relaxing atmosphere with a "fly by the seat of your pants" kind of feeling. Hostels were kept clean and had a nice kitchen with all the breakfast food amenities you could ever want, plus coffee brewing and orange juice ready to drink. The home would have free internet, a living room with comfortable couches, and morning conversation with travelers from all over the world. I not only saved money not staying in a hotel, but I also met great people on these trips to the outer islands.

Every now and then I would sleep on the beach instead of paying for a place to crash. I never had a problem doing that, but once on the Big Island of Hawaii, a friend and I were sleeping on a beach when in the middle of the night, a guy kicked my friend's feet and told us we couldn't sleep there. I woke up ready to tell him off when I realized he was a cop! My friend and I grabbed our belongings to go look for a more secluded beach to crash.

Maui was my favorite island. I flew there most often. Sometimes I would go with friends, and other times I needed a solo trip. Tickets to fly at that time were $75.00 one way, $150.00 round trip for a weekend get-away at any one of the different islands. At one point, there were ticket "wars." The tickets were only $35.00 each way, $70.00 round trip. I took advantage of the good deals and flew to the outer islands as often as I could. Ticket wars happened because the two airlines that were established in Hawaii had to lower their prices when a third airline came into Hawaii to fly people between the different islands. This new airline dropped to a ridiculously low price and the other two airlines had to match the price, so they wouldn't lose business. One of the main airlines eventually lost out and closed for business since they couldn't afford the low prices. Sad for me to see this happen. When the new airline was established in Hawaii, both airlines went up in price to a whopping $150.00 one-way, $300.00 round trip! A bit too expensive for me. I didn't go on many trips after that, but I stayed loyal to the one airline that had been in Hawaii for years. I wanted to support local.

Halloween in Maui:

I worked at a country bar in Waikiki where I talked fifteen of my friends into flying to Maui to party for Halloween. I loved Maui and I was excited to spend the weekend there with my friends. Every year for Halloween there was a huge block party in the small town of Lahaina. On average, 60,000 people would party within a one-mile radius during this holiday. All streets were closed off to traffic. There were food stands and bands displayed on the streets. There was entertainment everywhere and many happy, drunk people! My friends and I dressed up in costumes and we walked down Lahaina, drinking beers and meeting the most interesting people. Up on a restaurant rooftop, there were three men dressed up in one ginormous marshmallow-man costume. How they did that, I have no idea! We had so much fun sight-seeing and meeting people. We stayed up all night bar hopping and partying until early in the morning when we crashed in one big hotel room. There were people crashed on the bed, on the chairs, and the rest of my friends crashed on the floor wherever there was room to sleep. It was a fun night, but it was over too quickly and in the late morning we all flew back home to Oahu. I had been to Lahaina for Halloween at least half a dozen times, and I never tired of it.

The Big Island Lava Flow:

I had a roommate Dustin who planned to visit the Big Island to fill out a college application for schooling. I wanted to go as well. I heard there was an active volcano erupting on the island, and I wanted to see it. Samantha, a friend of Dustin's, wanted to come as well. We all hopped on a small plane that fit about seventy people, and we flew forty minutes to the Big Island from Oahu. Out of all the islands, only the Big Island had an active volcano.

The Big Island was the youngest of all the islands. The erupting volcano spewed lava over the open land, spilling onto the roads and finally would sink into the ocean, cooling down and then hardening. When the fiery glow of lava would cool, it turned a coal blackish gray color. The lava was forming the island and it grew more and more every single day. Even now, it is still growing. It is called the Big Island because it really is the "BIG" Island.

Presently on the Big Island, one volcano in particular is erupting and wreaking havoc on neighborhoods as it pushes hot rushing lava over trees, homes, and anything else that stands in its way.

When we arrived on the island, we rented a car and drove around. There was so much to see. There were big, black lava rocks everywhere from years of volcanoes erupting. The Big Island had flat land which had an endless amount of black lava rock as far as the eyes could see. We would be driving along and suddenly be in a lush forest with cascading waterfalls on one side of the road and beautiful beach views on the other. There were countless hiking trails, including my favorite one which was inside a lava tube. There were huge thirty-foot lava tubes that had been formed years ago from flowing lava that turned into hardened rock. This lava tube became an adventurous hiking trail for many travelers like us who wanted to see something new.

My friends and I drove to Hilo to the college to pick up papers for Dustin, and then we hit the open road for more adventure. We headed to Kona where we came across the active volcano, but it was blocked off with a wooden barricade, and there was no way to drive in. We parked the car and decided to hike in. All we could see for at least a mile was blackened lava rock. We were a little disheartened at first. We walked and walked, but the landscape was all the same - black rock everywhere. After a mile, we hiked over a rocky hill and saw the ocean another half mile away. We headed toward the ocean. If nothing else, we figured we could jump into the water and swim around looking at the coral and colorful fish.

There was a large sign as we neared the ocean that said, "Do Not Cross," but we just walked right past it. Suddenly, I began to hear a popping noise and my tennis shoes were starting to feel hot. I looked down at my feet, and at the same time, Samantha yelled, "Look at the lava flowing under our feet!" I just stared. Under the cracked, hard rock was steaming hot orange lava flowing a few feet under me! Dustin said, "Oh criminy, I think we are stuck in a lava field!" We laughed. I was in awe. It was fascinating to be standing right over flowing lava. What a rare sight.

The lava was flowing like a river spitting fire up through cracks and making a popping noise every time it shot up a few feet. Samantha and I found old dead twigs and held them over the fire that was spouting upward. "Click," a memory was made with the camera. We took pictures of each other roasting sticks over the fire that was shooting up from the lava. I wished we had marshmallows to roast. The lava flow had meandered over the paved road, forcing its hot embers over everything in its path, including a dangly, old thin tree that leaned over. Most of it was consumed by the hot lava. The tree had died long ago from the intense heat.

My feet were becoming hotter. I didn't know how hot the lava was and I wasn't about to feel the rocks, but my feet felt like they were burning. Dustin, Samantha, and I walked toward the ocean where there was a large, gray cloud of smoke rising from the water. We wanted to check it out. As we neared the ocean, I heard yelling and looked behind me. Two security guards ran after us, yelling for us to leave the area! They looked mad.

We ran over the hot lava rocks so fast that we were almost flying! We ditched the guards and somehow found our way back to the car. We were laughing so hard and couldn't believe how much fun our adventure had been. It was the most amazing day!

I Flew the Plane:

At one point in my life I was obsessed with hiking! I loved it! I had a good group of friends I would meet with, and we would venture out to a new hiking trail every single weekend. One of my friends was a pilot who owned a small six-seater plane. He bought this plane to fly tourists to the outer islands and was processing paperwork to do so. My friend Logan and I, avid hikers that we were, asked Tim if he would fly a group of us to Maui so we could do some "crazy fun" hikes. He agreed it was a great idea. That weekend six of us were headed to Maui in a tiny plane.

The thing about a small plane is that once it is soaring high in the sky, the wind can blow it around like a matchbox car "flying through the air." Having more turbulence than a heavier plane, it can be unpredictable if the small plane would make the long trip over the ocean without any problems.

I was sitting in the cockpit next to Tim while he flew the plane. I was able to see everything from the wide window that wrapped the whole front of the plane. It was all ocean, just a massive blue that blanketed the whole view below us. I was in awe.

We started nearing the island of Molokai, and Tim asked if I would take the control wheel (the yoke) while he told everyone a story about this particular island. I was elated! I had never flown a plane before. I reached over and held onto the wheel and he began telling everyone a story. He said, "Look at Molokai, the island to our right. There is some deep culture in that island."

As everyone looked out the window at the island, I wanted to see it too. I peered out my side of the window. Still holding onto the steering wheel, I pulled the wheel too sharply. In a few seconds time, the plane dipped down and veered to the right! Tim quickly pushed my hand off the wheel and righted the plane, but for a moment, it shook up the group that WE lost control over the plane. Okay, it was I who lost control of the plane! I had been captivated by all the beauty surrounding us! At that very moment looking out the window at the cascading mountains and beautiful ocean lapping at the beaches, I had forgotten I was even flying the plane. I immediately lost all privileges to fly the plane ever again, but I still had fun sight-seeing while Tim told us about history in the Hawaiian Islands.

When we landed in a small air-strip in Maui, we had adrenaline running through our veins, and with a hiking book in hand, we set off for some great adventures.

Crashing a Hotel:

One time my mom came to visit me in Oahu, and we decided to take a trip to the Big Island for the weekend. We flew to the island and found a hotel where we would stay. We mapped out what we wanted to do in the short time we had. We were excited about this trip! It was where we were going to swim with dolphins at the Hilton Waikoloa Village. We heard there was a great coffee shop in the hotel, so we went early for coffee before our fun adventure.

As we walked toward the coffee shop, we turned a corner and saw a river running right through the middle of the hotel and a boat motoring down the middle of it! I turned to my mom and said excitedly, "Mom, we have to go on the boat!" My eyes were glassed over as I thought how cool it would be to ride a boat through a huge, elegant hotel like this one. We bought our coffees and hopped on the boat to take a tour. The boat lazily meandered down the river, and that's when I realized there was so much more to this hotel. I saw so many different shops and places to eat. Not only that, we rode right by a train coming from the opposite end of the hotel. My jaw dropped open and my eyes lit up like burning embers. I was so excited! I turned to my mom and with exuberance I said, "We have to ride the train through the hotel!" My mom looked at her coffee as she said, "Let me drink my coffee before we do one more thing." We both laughed. There was so much going on in this hotel. I wanted to do it all!

The time to swim with the dolphins had come. We walked down to the large salt water pond where there were a few dolphins. It had been years since I swam with dolphins in Makaha, so seeing one up close brought back such good memories. I became a little emotional. The dolphin instructor had a person walk into the water one at a time to have their picture taken with a dolphin. I liked the fact they called the dolphins with a whistle and whichever dolphin wanted attention from the person standing there, that dolphin would swim up and let that person touch it and give it kisses as the camera clicked away. Granted, it was such a "touristy" thing to do, but one my mom and I would remember forever. We were enthusiastic about this whole experience. When the dolphin was tired of all the attention, he would swim away and another one would swim up for his turn.

When the instructor called me over, I was very excited! I would finally be close to a dolphin again! I walked into the water and knelt down waiting for a dolphin to swim over. I would be at the dolphin's level which would be great for picture taking. The instructor whistled for a dolphin and a large grey one swam to me. He was very happy and playful. He rolled over, so I could rub his pink belly. I rubbed his belly and gave him a big hug. The instructor told me to give him a kiss. I was going in to kiss him on the cheek, but the dolphin moved his face and I kissed his beak instead! I almost fell over laughing. It was the biggest surprise! This had to be planned! They took pictures and then it was my mom's turn with a dolphin. She was nervous but excited to be in the water with this big porpoise. Mom was all smiles, and as she stood there petting the dolphin's leathery skin, the photographer took pictures. She went in for a kiss but made sure it was on the cheek. She figured this dolphin was a troublemaker with the ladies. I had to laugh knowing dolphins were playful and liked to clown around. This was such a memorable time together. As Mom and I were leaving, I said, "Okay, Mom, time to ride the train around the hotel." My mom answered, "I thought you would forget about that." I replied, "No way, I'm ready for the train ride." We rode the train, and it was a slow, relaxing ride from one side of the hotel to the other. "Now it's time for shopping!" Mom exclaimed. I laughed. I should have known she wanted to shop! We checked out the different gift shops and even found lotion bottles filled with the best smelling coconut lotion. The smell was to die for, so we had to buy a few bottles. We did so many fun things on the Big Island and it was a great trip, but the highlight was definitely being kissed by a dolphin!

The Road to Hana:

Once in Maui on a solo trip, I rented a car and planned a day in Hana. I loved it there with its winding road into the middle of nowhere with cliffs that go straight down into the ocean and gigantic mountains with breathtaking views. I was thrilled to be on this adventure once again. Hana was one long stretch of road that a tourist could drive for hours with much to see! Usually I would need a half-day to drive the road through Hana.

I always loved to stop in this little trinket store that was at the beginning of Hana. This shop had many nick knacks, Hawaiian hand-made bowls, and hand-crafted items made from shells. After I went inside the shop, I stopped at the postcard stand close to the register. I liked to buy a postcard or two when I visited the outer islands to send to a few family members or friends.

As I looked at the postcards, an older gentleman stood next to me scoping out a Hana travel map that he was about to purchase. I asked, "Are you driving to Hana?" He said, "Yes, I am." I looked at his Hawaiian shirt which was a "dead give-away" that he was a tourist. I asked, "Where are you from?" He responded, "Minnesota." I was surprised. I told him. "I am originally from Minnesota too!" I asked, "Are you going to Hana alone?" He replied, "Yes." I thought since he was from Minnesota, he would have to be a good guy. I said, "I am traveling to Hana, why don't we go together?" He was all for that. I jumped in his car and we drove the road to Hana. We chit chatted a few minutes when he asked me to retrieve his Bible from under my seat. He wanted me to read a few chapters to him. I was surprised that he was a Christian.

Looking back, it's amazing how numerous times I could have been in a bad situation or even have died but how God had protected me. I imagine many times there were angels watching over me, and God would bring good people into my life for a reason. This was one of those times God intervened.

As I opened the Bible and read some verses out loud. He asked, "Are you a Christian?" I replied, "Yes." He asked, "Do you go to church?" I said, "Not at the moment." Then he pondered on a thought and replied, "Have you given your life to the Lord and asked Him into your heart?" I responded, "Yes, years ago when I was a child." He continued, "What does your daily walk with God look like?" I had to think about that. I didn't have a daily walk with God. I wondered if God brought this guy into my life to steer me back to my heavenly Father. I shrugged my shoulders. He asked, "Do you love God?" I firmly answered, "Yes, definitely." That I knew for sure. For a moment, I felt like I was back in Sunday School at church.

There was a beautiful scenic lookout, and he pulled his car over, so we could stretch our legs and take pictures. We stood and looked at the massive beautiful ocean. He asked, "Do you know who created all of this?" I replied, "Yes, God of course." He smiled. "Do you know that He cares for all this and even the small sparrows in the sky, but do you know He cares for you so much more?" I responded, "Yes." The idea of how endless God's love was for me was sinking in and I kept this treasure deep in my heart.

"So, let me ask you again, are you a Christian?" he asked. I had to think about this. When I first met God, I was so "on-fire" for Him. I loved Him and sought His face. I would share the joy of the Lord with others. I had a friend in high school whose nickname for me was "Holy Roller" because I was so into Jesus. God was my everything. I was in God's living word constantly, praying for all my family and friends and hearing from God in my life. I pondered the word "Christian" for a few minutes and looked at my new friend. "No, I guess by your standards I am not a Christian." He said, "That's right. When you love your boyfriend, for instance, you want to be with him, right? You want to spend time with him and learn more about him, you want to enjoy his presence and be with him all the time, right?" I said, "Yes, of course." He continued, "With God, it's the same thing. When we love God, we want to be in His word, we want to pray and hear from Him, we want to share about Jesus and have the Joy of the Lord in everything we do." Yes, I thought. It made perfect sense. "So, are you saved?" he asked. "Yes, I think so," I answered. "If you were to die right now, would you go to heaven or hell?" he asked. I replied, "I would hope to be in heaven with God." He was very passionate about what he was talking about, and I marveled at his thought process unraveling before me. I mulled over all he was saying.

He went on, "God so loved the world that He gave His only begotten Son, that whosoever believes in Him, will not perish but have everlasting life, that verse is John 3:16." I pondered on his words. I knew that verse well. I grew up as a teen saying that verse over and over to myself, knowing Jesus died for me so I could be with Him someday in heaven.

"If you want to be saved, Becka, then you need to confess with your mouth, Jesus as Lord, and believe in your heart that God raised Him from the dead, and you will be saved. That is Romans 10:9," he said. I thought about that verse.

We decided to jump back into the car and resume our adventure. We drove deeper into Hana and talked about God and His amazing grace. I saw so much beauty in this place, and I basked in the thoughts of God's creation. It was a beautiful time for the three-hour tour. At the end of Hana, he took me back to my rental car. He gave me a few Christian books to read, we hugged, and he left. What a thought-provoking time with a stranger! I had a choice to seek God, become a Christian, and walk closely with God once again, or decide to stay in my sinful lifestyle.

I didn't think much about the stranger's words. I took the easy road and moved on with my life with very little thought about God. I do admit I loved my sinful life at that time. If I had turned toward God, I could have chosen a better life with Him, but it didn't happen that way. I do believe God led this man into my life for a reason. He planted a seed in my heart about God's love and forgiveness that years later, would lead me back to my papa God. But at this time, I decided to put the man's books on my bookshelf and move on.

Chapter 14

The Charmer

I met a guy in Waikiki who was not only handsome and personable, but also had a great sense of humor. Richard and I started dating and I instantly felt a connection with him. We really hit it off well. We had so much fun for a few weeks until late one night, I ran into his girlfriend at his apartment! He didn't tell me he had a girlfriend. It was an awkward moment standing there while she screamed obscenities at me in Japanese. I wasn't about to fight a five-foot, skinny Japanese lady. I told her I was sorry because I had no idea they were together, and I walked out!

I didn't hear from Richard at all. I was hurt that he led me on, but I was glad I learned what a creep he was in the beginning stages of dating him. I went on with my life and kept busy with swimming and work. However, a few weeks later, Richard called me. He said he was no longer with his girlfriend. He told me he really liked me and wanted to be in a relationship with me. He apologized up and down for not telling me about his girlfriend. He told me their relationship was at its end, and it just so happened she was in town visiting from Japan and wanted to talk to him the same night I came over to his place. I knew from experience that relationships were hard enough, so I just let it go and accepted Richard's explanation.

Richard was such a charmer who would write me sweet notes or give me flowers for no reason at all, and he knew how to say "all the right things" to make me smile. We really clicked, and I thought we were great together.

He liked to go out to party and drink and I didn't, but since I wanted to be with him, we would end up partying all night together. Drinking alcohol made me feel good. I found confidence in it. When I was sober, I was reminded of my problems: I felt insecure around people and my life seemed more of a struggle. When I drank, it was like my problems all disappeared, but only until I sobered up.

I started really getting into the bar scene because of my new boyfriend. Bars were open until 4:00am, so we would go out when he didn't work and stay out all night long. When he was working the night shift at the strip bar, I would go out with my friends to the bars in Waikiki. I was a social drinker who only drank when I was around my friends. I went a bit overboard partying though because I was able to get into the bars for free. I didn't like beer, but I loved those sweet, sugary drinks. They tasted so good, like a sweet chocolaty candy bar in a drink! I WAS HOOKED! I was the type that would drink until I was drunk, and then laugh and laugh until tears streamed down my cheeks. Everything seemed funny when I would drink. My friends called me a "happy drunk."

When I drank too much, sometimes I would pass out, then wake up on someone's floor early the next morning. Every so often I would wake up at a stranger's home where my friends and I had crashed for the night. I would have no idea whose place it was. With my excruciating headache and huge hang over, I would run into the bathroom to throw up and then grab my keys to drive home (sober). I never drove when I was drunk. I would sleep it off first. I couldn't tolerate people who would drink and drive, because that's when innocent people die. Still to this day, I can't stand it when people tell me they drink and drive. (Even driving a little drunk is not okay).

Richard also loved parties, so we would go to one party after another. I must admit, I had fun, but sin is always fun. I was lost in the world and so far from God that I thought there was no turning back to Him.

Richard started trying to control me. He didn't want me having friends like Robert, who was my best friend that I hung out with all the time. He did not want me to hang around Katherine either who was my best friend. Her and I would swim together just about every day. Richard also told me not to hang out with Koa, another good friend of mine who I liked to be around. These three people were my biggest support in life, and I couldn't see life without them. Richard acted as if I were a wild horse that needed to be tamed. He attempted to distance me from my closest friends so that I would only hang out with him. But I missed my friends.

When Richard and I would fight, it was a screaming match. The first time he slapped me in the face, there was a ringing in my ear – it was so loud, and my cheek throbbed from the pain. I felt the palm of his hand still pressed up against my cheek even after he had pulled his hand away. I looked at him in shock. Tears welled up in my eyes. I couldn't believe he had slapped me! Granted, I said some awful things to him, but that didn't give him the right to hit me! I put my hand to my cheek, and as I held it there with a painful look on my face, I had to look away from him. I was so hurt. He rushed to me, wrapped his big arms around me, and said he was sorry over and over. I said I was sorry for what I had said too. I really meant it. I must have disrespected him in some way for him to slap me so hard. As the shock wore off from being hit, I tried to think what I said that made him so angry, but I couldn't think of anything. I would be more careful next time.

Richard promised he would never hurt me again, and I trusted him. Our life went great for a while. We had so much fun together. When we hung out, we would go to the beach and get sun, jump into the nice cool ocean, or float around in the water while relaxing on our days off work. At night we would go bar hopping, drinking, and partying. He lived in a little apartment in Waikiki that wasn't far from where I lived so we hung out all the time. I think he was just happy I wasn't seeing my friends as much because I was with him all the time. I had been lonely for a very long time, and it felt good that a man was finally giving me attention and telling me he loved me.

When Richard drank too much, his violence would escalate towards me. We were at a bar one night, and I told him I wanted to go home. It was 2:00am and I was tired. He was drunk as usual and asked if I was flirting with a guy. I told him I would never flirt with a guy because I loved him. Richard was adamant I was flirting with this guy at the bar. He was so angry. He kept antagonizing me about the situation, so I just walked out. I didn't want him making a bigger scene than he already was. I was sick of his antics.

I didn't live far from the bar and I planned on walking home, but Richard followed me outside and grabbed my arm hard and pulled me down an alleyway. It really hurt when he grabbed my arm! He finally let go, and when I looked at my arm, there were red marks from his fingerprints. I was a little drunk so when I looked and saw the red marks, I thought it was the funniest thing and started laughing so hard. It didn't help that I was laughing because I was drunk, but he thought I was laughing at him.

Without a second thought, Richard slugged me in the mouth! Before I could react, he pushed me up against a car, then pulled me on the hood, and started punching me in the gut. It hurt, and I sobered up quickly when I realized what was happening. I lost my breath and couldn't scream. I felt like I was going to pass out from the pain. I couldn't believe he was hitting me on some stranger's car in the alley way! When he stopped punching me, I tried to scream, but he pushed his whole forearm across my mouth and his body weight on me. I could barely breathe. I was so scared I stopped fighting back. I went limp. He pulled me off the car and told me never to do that again. I didn't know what he was talking about. What did I do exactly? I didn't say a word. I was terrified. I just stared at him. He looked different to me now. This wasn't just a smack on the face. He just beat me up because he thought I was laughing at him, which I wasn't! He said he was sorry and that it wouldn't happen again. He had said that before and I didn't believe him.

Richard promised he wouldn't hurt me again and that things would get better. He moved from the apartment he rented with a roommate into a small one-bedroom place where he would live by himself. He still lived in Waikiki, not far from me. I liked his new apartment. When I walked in, it opened into the living room. The kitchen to the right was oddly on the backside of the living room. There was a tall, white book case, and the hall led to a small bathroom that had a tiny window that looked out over the businesses that flourished in the buildings off the main street. The bedroom to the left of the bathroom was small, but sufficient for one. We hung out at his place often. He lived close to the beach where we would go for sun and relaxation.

One night about 8 o'clock we were crossing the street going to the shopping mall. I said something to Richard maybe in a snotty manner and in the middle of the paved street, he grabbed my hair and pulled me down to the ground. As I fell, I skinned my elbow trying to balance myself. Atkinson Avenue was a very busy street, but at the time we were fighting, there was not one passing car.

A cop who was parked on the side street stepped out of his car and ran over to us. He saw the whole fight and he was so mad. He yelled at Richard to take his grubby hands off me. My boyfriend jumped back like someone had burnt him. He put his hands up like the cop was going to arrest him and I almost started laughing. Richard stuttered in nervousness as he said we were having a friendly discussion and just playing around. I stood there, brushing off the dirt from my shorts and looked at Richard and his silly charade. What a liar. I couldn't believe him.

The cop walked us over to the curb and told Richard to step back so he could talk to me privately. That made Richard so mad because he wasn't in control of the situation. The cop asked me what happened. Richard yelled over, "I told you, we were just playing!" The cop yelled back, "One more word out of you and I will haul you off to jail!" The cop was steaming mad at this point! Then he said loudly enough for Richard to hear, "I would love to put this guy in jail overnight if you tell me to arrest him. I saw how he pulled you to the ground, and that is enough for him to go to jail." I thought, "I would love to see him hauled off to jail." I was that mad, but I looked over the cop's shoulder at Richard and he had one balled up fist in his other hand. It looked like steam was literally coming out of his ears. He shook his head at me like, "Don't you dare tell him to put me in jail!" I was scared and told the officer that we were just playing around, and I was fine. Richard had the biggest smirk spreading across his face. He had won.

The cop looked me squarely in the eyes, handed me his card, and said, "Call me if you need anything." I think he knew there was abuse going on, more than just that one incident, but he couldn't do anything unless I wanted to press charges. I was so embarrassed about Richard making a spectacle of himself, so when the cop left, I just turned around and hightailed it back to Richard's place to pick up my keys and leave. He caught up to me apologizing for being such a jerk. I had nothing to say. He showed the whole world what a jerk he was when this incident happened in the middle of the street for everyone to see. I just wanted to leave. When I reached his doorstep, I grabbed my car keys from the table and I told him I was breaking up with him for good. In a tone that gave me chills, he whispered under his breath that he would kill me before I was able to leave him. I didn't know what to do. I left but I didn't know if that was the end of our relationship.

Richard started stalking me. I would run into him at my place when I came home from work. We would talk, but It was just small talk. At this point, I was walking on eggshells around him trying not to set him off. Anything I said or did could send him into a frenzy. No matter what I said, I would always make him mad. We would fight and breakup. He would threaten to kill me if I left him. I was sick and tired of hearing him say it and thought, "Hurry up and kill me already." I wanted this roller-coaster ride we were on to end. Our fights seemed to escalate every time we were together.

One day at Richard's apartment, it happened again. He was so angry at me that he punched me in the stomach, and when I pushed him away from me, he came at me again with his fist. I thought he was going to punch me in the face, so I turned my head to the side, but his hands went around my neck instead and he pushed me up against the wall, hard. I couldn't breathe. I was choking and trying to push him away when I realized my feet were off the ground and I was suspended in mid-air with his hands around my neck! He was so strong. I saw a flash of red and felt like I was going to pass out when he let go of me. I crumpled to the ground like a ragdoll. I pulled myself to the corner of the room and tucked my feet under me and cried. My throat felt like someone had scratched the inside of my esophagus. This man was a monster and I was terrified of him!

I looked at my "so called" boyfriend who had just assaulted me. I could have died. Reality hit me hard. I was done. He was insane. He stood over me and yelled at the top of his lungs. His face was beet red and I swear I saw steam come out of his ears. At that moment, I closed my eyes and I thought this was it. Richard was going to kill me! I waited for the blow to the head, but it didn't come. Instead, he said, "I want to kill you, but I won't because I love you too much." I opened my eyes and looked at him. A chill ran down my spine. If this was "love," I didn't want anything to do with it.

I was sobbing as I told him I was going home. I picked myself up, wiped tears from my eyes, and slowly and awkwardly walked past him hoping he would not touch me or say anything. He didn't move. It was like he was thinking of another apology, but even he knew he had gone too far. There was no turning back now. I knew he was a monster. Richard had choked me, and I knew I could have died. As I picked up my keys and walked out the door in hopes of never seeing him again, I heard him yell after me that he was "sorry."

For the next few days, Richard called and left messages apologizing. I didn't want to call him back, but when I finally did call him, he didn't answer his phone. I figured we both had some time to think and calm down, so I decided to drive to his place to talk. When I arrived at Richard's place, I walked up the steps to the second floor and counted each door I passed. I thought about how he had broken my heart into a million pieces. I was emotional thinking maybe this relationship could work out if I could trust him once again. I had high hopes by the time I finally knocked on Richard's door. He opened the door just a crack and told me it wasn't a good time.

Then his new girlfriend flung the door open and started screaming profanities at me! She told me I had to leave. I pushed my way past her into the apartment and told her that technically he was still my boyfriend. I looked at Richard who was quiet at that moment. How pathetic! He probably loved that two women were fighting over him. It reminded me of the same scenario when I was first dating him and met his girlfriend at the time. I turned and walked out. I was so mad! I wasn't going to play this game.

I saw Richard around my apartment a few more times. He and his new girlfriend would be holding hands as they walked down my street; for what purpose, I don't know. I hated my life. I wanted to move far, far away. I wanted a whole new life. I told a client of mine that I pet sat for that I needed to find a place to move quickly. My client said that she had a room in the lower-half of the home that she was not using, and I could move in there. The rent was affordable, and the owner was one of the nicest client's I had so I felt comfortable moving into the place. She helped me move my belongings over and as I settled into my quaint new place; it felt so peaceful.

Manoa Valley is a beautiful, lush garden area. Flowers were in full bloom in my large backyard, the smell of plumeria was in the air, and I had the best view of the mountains. I lived in a large room with my own bathroom and in the back side of the house, there was a laundry room to share with the owner who lived upstairs. I had my own entrance from the outside that opened into a luscious garden of flowering trees and plants everywhere. It was a serene place to live and the right choice for me. I loved my new place! My client loved it too because when she went away on trips, I would be there to watch her pets for free.

I had a pager I carried around with me. Richard would page me over and over and leave many messages on my voicemail. He was filling up my message box. It bugged me. He should have moved on already with his new girlfriend. I made plans for a TRO, hoping that would stop Richard from harassing me. (TRO: Temporary Restraining Order).

One day, Richard left me a message on my voicemail telling me he found where I lived, we needed to talk, and he was coming to see me soon. His voice sounded nonchalant, as if all was right in his world. Did he really know where I lived or was he just saying that to scare me? I locked all my windows and the front door in case he really did find where I lived. I hoped he was just trying to scare me. I tried to put the situation behind me. Richard was old news and I was now focused on my mom and Aunt Isabella's visit to see me. I kept busy planning their upcoming visit. I was so excited to spend time with family!

A few weeks later, I returned home from work, and as I walked the steps down to my front door, Richard stepped out of the bushes! What a creeper! At first, I was scared, but then I became angry that he had found me. I looked back to see if my client's car was in the driveway. If she were home, I could scream and have her call the police. She wasn't home, however. I asked Richard what he was doing here. He replied, "It took a while for me to track you down, but I finally found you." I tried to act like it didn't matter. He continued, "I know your mom is coming into town." A chill ran down my spine and I felt the little hairs on my neck rise. How could he know? I stood there in shock.

I quickly changed my mood as I went into survival mode. I smiled big and sweetly said, "I have missed you so much. I have been busy with work and just haven't had time to call." He stepped toward me and his face was inches from mine. I could smell his minty breath on me as he said, "I want to meet your mom when she visits." My blood ran cold. I knew he was trying to intimidate me. "How do you know my mom is coming to visit?" I asked. He grabbed a handful of my long hair and pulled me closer as he said, "I know a lot of what's going on in your life. I will spend time with you and your mom and if not, I will find you both and kill her right in front of you." I was weak in the knees and my legs started to shake. I was terrified that he would kill her. He had recently bragged how in the Navy, the guys in his unit would pepper spray each other's faces and choke one another just to see how close to death they would come. He was crazy!!

I told Richard I would give him a call for dinner plans. He then threatened me, "If you don't call me for dinner, I will show up at your place and make a scene in front of your mom." I looked in his eyes that were eerily dark. It scared me to think about what he was capable of doing if I did not comply. I agreed that I would make it happen. He smirked. He had won again. A few minutes after he left, I called the police to file a restraining order. While I was on the phone sobbing, I told the officer the whole story. I set a court date, but I would have to wait a whole month to go to court! The date seemed so far away.

Richard showed up at my house a few more times. I just played nice as if I still loved him even though deep down I was cringing at how much I hated him. I played the part so well that he truly believed I was falling for him all over again. I didn't ask about his girlfriend. I'm sure they weren't happy together, because he was fawning and kissing on me.

Richard again promised he wouldn't hurt me anymore. He wanted us to mend our relationship once again, but he sounded like a broken record. When we were together, I made sure I was careful with my words, so we didn't fight. I didn't want my client to hear us arguing and find out what a mess my life was! If our discussion became heated, I would say I was sorry and that he was right, and I was wrong. Those words would calm him right down every time. I truly saw how ugly his heart was. He was a pathetic control-freak! Everything had to be his own way. He had to be in control, and he was always right. I had never felt so much anger for anyone as I did for him. I lost all feelings I had for this shallow man, but I put on a good front.

Then the day came for my mom and aunt to visit. I was so excited! I had two flower leis in my hand as I waited at the airport. When I saw Mom and Aunt Isabella walking off the plane, I ran to hug them. I was so happy to see them! I put a pretty flower lei around both their necks. They were excited to be in Hawaii! We went to the baggage claim and waited. We chatted about all the fun things we wanted to do. When the bags arrived, we walked outside where all the cars come to pick people up. We were walking away from the parking lot when Aunt Isabella asked, "Where are we going?" I responded, "Just over here." I was trying to hurry us along because I had a big surprise for them. Isabella pointed in the opposite direction and said, "...but the parked cars are over there." As we walked closer to the surprise I had for them, a limo driver walked around to the passenger side of the limo, opened the back door, and greeted us, "Aloha, ladies. Welcome to Hawaii." Their jaws dropped open in shock. My mom laughed and asked, "Are we really riding in a limo or is this a joke?" I responded, "Yes, we are riding in a limo." I smiled big. Mom and Aunt Isabella were ecstatic! We sat in the back of the limo and had the best ride of our lives to Waikiki where they were staying at a hotel.

We planned a night out for dinner. I called Richard and told him our plans. We all met at the restaurant. My mom knew I had a boyfriend, but she didn't know details about our relationship and had no idea he was abusing me. We went to an ocean aquarium restaurant in Waikiki where there were plenty of fish and even a few sharks inside a 250,000-gallon aquarium. This restaurant had good food, and it was entertaining to watch all the fish swim around as we were eating.

I was a bit surprised when all went well, and we had a fun time. Richard was a perfect gentleman, and no one would have ever suspected he was abusing me. I was reminded of how charming and wonderful he had been in the beginning of our relationship. I pretended to like him, so I put on a good front. I thought I could be an actress. We held hands and looked like we were in love, but deep down I hated and despised this man. When my family left, I was relieved that no altercations happened while they were visiting.

That was the last time I saw Richard before going to court for the TRO. I worried about him going after my mom or trying to kill me, but all I could do was wait for this court date to obtain a piece of paper that said he couldn't come near me or he would go to jail.

As I waited for the court date, I asked three close friends to be witnesses for the TRO. They had seen the many bruises on my body time and time again, and they knew how Richard had beaten me down and broken my spirit. They were ready to put him in the ground for what he did. Katherine, my swimming buddy, was a great friend with whom I confided in a great deal. Robert was my best friend who was there through "thick and thin." He saw all the pain I went through with this guy. Koa was a good friend too. We had worked together at a fish store, and when the manager had made a pass at me, Koa stepped up and told him not to mess with me. I appreciated that since my boyfriend at the time didn't seem to care. Koa was a big, muscular Hawaiian dude with whom no one would fight since he could be very intimidating. The manager hardly looked at me after the altercation with Koa, so the manager never made another pass at me again. Koa and I became great friends, so when I asked him to be a witness for this court hearing, he was all for it. When court finally rolled around, my friends were there in support, and I was confident it would all work out.

As my friends and I walked into the courthouse, Koa suddenly saw Richard standing a few feet away. Then Koa grabbed Richard's t-shirt and twisted the cloth around as

Richard tried to pull away! It was comical to watch. I could see that he was deathly afraid. Koa pulled him closely and said, "You leave my girl alone, if you don't I will come after you!" Richard hightailed it away from us and into court so fast you would have thought a panther was chasing him! We laughed so hard and it lightened the mood of what was to come. I was thankful at that very moment for my wonderful friends.

Court was in session. The judge was a woman who listened to all three witnesses and was disgusted with Richard and all he did to me. She looked at me, and slamming the hammer down, she said, "It's a three-year TRO and if he even looks at you, he will go to jail." I was stunned. I couldn't believe it! The judge continued, "The TRO means he cannot come within three blocks of you or he will go to jail." She went on, "Do not call him or it will forfeit the TRO." I nodded. I was fine with that. I looked over at Richard who was so mad. His face was beet red. For a moment, I had a bit of satisfaction and an overwhelming sense of relief. My friends came through for me! They were so happy and ran over to hug me.

I moved again, this time into a cheap, ugly, two-story ghetto kind of apartment in Honolulu. The building itself was an ugly green color. I liked the apartment complex though because it had a security gate and made me feel safe. Everything I needed was within walking distance. I could walk across the street for groceries at any time or to a beautiful park or to the beach if I wanted to go for a swim. I knew the toxic relationship with Richard had messed with my head, but I was in a good place now and felt I was on the mend to a better life.

One day, my good friend Robert and I were hanging out at my new apartment. It just so happened I peered out my big living room window to see Richard, my ex, holding hands with a woman I had never seen before. I couldn't believe it! Here was my ex just below my window walking with another new girlfriend! This island was way too small for the both of us! I ripped myself away from the window and looking at my friend Robert, I whispered, "How did he find me?" I was so scared, my hands started to shake. I believed Richard could hear my voice from outside, even with all the traffic noise. All the old feelings came rushing back and I suddenly felt disgusted! I just wanted to run far away!

Robert thought it was just a coincidence that Richard was walking by the apartment, and he was probably right, but I was afraid Richard was still stalking me and had found me once again. I had lived in the new place for only a month, and I made a quick decision to move back to Minnesota where I could be safe and spend time with my family. I was sad to leave Hawaii, but it had to be done. I couldn't hide well enough from my crazy ex. Living on this small island, I was bound to run into people I knew; but this was too much, so I packed all my belongings and moved home to live with my mom.

Chapter 15

Road Trip

I was motivated to leave Hawaii for safety reasons. I didn't want to move, but I packed my bags, gave everything to the Goodwill, and used my credit card to fly home to Minnesota. I told my mom I was having problems with my ex-boyfriend, but I didn't tell her the whole story. My mom told me I could live at her place if I found a job and paid rent. That was fair.

My mom welcomed me home with open arms and had my room all ready for my stay. It was sweet. My mom had quit drinking many years before, and after she sobered up, we had been working on our relationship while I lived in Hawaii. I thought moving home was a great chance for Mom and me to make our relationship work.

I found a job fairly quickly. I worked at a warehouse that made pop machines for restaurants, and I worked on the assembly line, adding parts for the pop machines. I liked my job, but it was monotonous. I made a few friends quickly and one guy, Carter, who was especially nice to me, was very flirty. He gave me the attention that I craved. I felt I needed someone to love me, and soon after, we started dating. He was a sweet, soft-spoken man who had a very calm demeanor. He was easy to talk to and fun to be around. I spent a great deal of time with him.

After a few months living in Minnesota, my mom and I fell into our old habits, and we were fighting with each other again. We couldn't get along. Carter asked me to move in with him, and I jumped at the opportunity. Things were great! I loved how sweet he was and how he doted on me. I never had a guy dote on me like he did. My past relationships had been destructive and unhealthy, and I didn't know how to accept Carter's love well. I was so used to relationships where I would fight with my boyfriend, more like screaming matches, but with Carter, he was different. He didn't do any of that. Even if I tried to start a fight, he would sit there with a blank stare on his face and let me vent. I felt like I was yelling at a brick wall.

My new job went well until my back started giving me pain from lifting heavy boxes at work, so I had to quit working because I physically could not do my job anymore. Carter said he would take care of me, and I could stay home while resting to heal up. After a while though, I was bored out of my mind being home all the time. I wanted to go out to the bar every so often and do something fun with Carter after work, but he would be tired and wanted to stay home. Even on the weekends we didn't do much together. I was getting antsy. I wanted to spread my wings and fly! I wanted to go out on the town or see the big city lights. There were so many fun things to do in Minnesota. I asked him many times to take me out but to no avail. He was rarely interested in going anywhere with me. It made me feel insecure as if he was embarrassed to be seen with me.

There was a concert in Minneapolis, which I did talk Carter into going. I was so happy! I remember It was a chilly thirty degrees out. I was adamant about wearing a slimming, sparkly, pretty, blue dress out in the freezing, cold weather. I dressed up, put on makeup, did my hair, and was ready to go. I was freezing but the concert was awesome, and we had a fun night together.

Rarely did Carter and I go out to eat or venture out together anywhere. I was bored out of my mind. I met a guy named Damien who was very friendly. He wanted Carter and me to hang out with him, but Carter wasn't interested. He would rather tinker with his cars in the garage at home, then go out on the town. Carter assured me, though, that I could hang out with Damien without him, and he wouldn't mind it at all. I thought, well, if my boyfriend doesn't care, then I will hang out with my new friend. Damien became my best buddy! He liked adventure, just like me. We had so much in common. We would drive around town and go window shopping or end up at a poetry reading where someone stood on stage and shared with everyone a poem they wrote, or we would go out to eat someplace or end up drinking at the bar. We always had fun wherever we were, and it was nice meeting new people and making new friends. Damien had a knack for starting up conversation with anyone he met, and people just flocked to him. He was such a nice guy.

I remember one time, Damien and I were hanging out at the park and both of us were hungry, but we had no money for a meal. There was a wedding going on nearby. The bride and groom had just married, and the caterers had set up all the food on decorated tables. We walked through the park casually and acted as if we knew people from the wedding. Damien would greet people and thank them for coming. He found out the bride and groom's names from a distant relative of theirs and talked to the family members about how wonderful it was the groom found such a beautiful bride. I tried not to laugh. I was impressed he could put on such a good act. He was a natural at this facade, as if he had done it before. If someone asked who we were, he would say he was the uncle of the groom and I was a friend. I tried my hardest not to burst out laughing! We played this game for a short while as we meandered over to the delicious food and helped ourselves. When we finally left, we laughed and laughed and couldn't believe we had pulled it off! It was so much fun!

Living with Carter was not so easy. Things were not going as well as I had hoped. He wasn't doting on me like he did in the beginning, and after some time, I didn't really care. One time as I walked outside, I found Carter and his ex-girlfriend, who was eight months pregnant, talking behind the apartment building. I walked up to them both and asked what was going on. I knew about his ex-girlfriend. I knew there was nothing going on between them, but I didn't like the fact he was talking to her without letting me know she was there. She took a few steps toward me and standing just inches from my face, she calmly said that I had no part in the conversation between her and Carter since it was their baby together. I was so infuriated that I just about blew a gasket! I went from 0-60 in seconds! I had never met this lady before, and here she was trying to tell me this was none of my business? This was my business! He was my boyfriend!

Because of my last relationship with Richard, I was messed up in the head and so this little charade between Carter and his ex, set me off. I was so angry watching MY boyfriend talk to his ex while he completely disregarded my feelings trying to calm HER down! I was irate! It brought up memories of seeing my last ex Richard with his new girlfriend. I stared at both Carter and his ex for just a moment, then I whipped around, opened the apartment complex door, and slammed it shut. It was so loud that the sound echoed against the apartment building. The apartment manager was outside and watched the whole incident. He told Carter I had to move out.

I moved back in with my mom the very next day. I was already making plans to return to Hawaii. It had been one year since I had moved to Minnesota, but I was badly missing the Hawaiian Islands. I couldn't stay away from the place I called home. I didn't care that Richard lived there. The relationship was finished, and I was completely over him. If he messed with me, I would make sure to put him in jail as the TRO was still valid. Besides, my need for moving back to Hawaii far outweighed what Richard could ever do to me.

At my mom's house, I received a few sweet notes from Carter saying I could move back in with him. He said he still loved me, but I would have to control that hot temper of mine before I moved back to his place. I knew I couldn't control my temper. I couldn't help it. My life was a mess and I didn't need to pull Carter into it. He was better than I in so many ways. He did not know the baggage I had brought into the relationship. I never told him how I was beaten, battered, and bruised right before I met him. I never did talk to him about any of it. We didn't have that kind of relationship where I could communicate my deepest, darkest secrets. Instead, I tucked the notes away, not planning to talk to Carter ever again, and I then started to plan my trip back to Hawaii.

I told my friend Damien that I missed Hawaii and had to move back. One of my friends in California said if I would come visit him, he would give me a ticket from LA to Hawaii. I told Damien I was taking a road trip. He wanted to come along. We mapped out our drive from Minnesota to Texas to visit my aunt and cousins, and then drive from Texas to California to see my close friend Dawn. I would then visit my friend with the ticket to Hawaii and fly over the open sea into paradise. Damien planned on driving my car back to Minnesota to try to sell it for me. That was the plan anyway. It sounded like a fun road trip.

I packed my belongings and told my mom I was going on a road trip and will be moving back to Hawaii. She thought that was a bad idea. She was upset I was leaving, but I thought it was a great idea. I had never been on a road trip before. I was excited and couldn't wait for this adventure.

I had a few hundred dollars saved for the trip, and Damien had only a few dollars himself. We set out on an adventure of a lifetime. We were broke people on a mission - to have fun. We made some stops along the way to look for trinkets at tourist shops. While driving, we were enamored with the beautiful mountain views and rock formations along the way. It was fun just to fly by "the seat of our pants." We drove through quite a few states to reach Texas where my aunt lived. My aunt let us stay with her, and it was good to spend some time with my little cousins. Then Damien and I drove to California to see my hippie friend, Dawn. She took us to see a music festival with food and dancing. It was a great time!

After our visit with Dawn, we drove a few hours to see my friend who had the ticket for me. He was so nice, and I appreciated the fact he wanted to help me return to Hawaii. We had lunch with him, and then I was off to the airport. I said my goodbyes to my good friend Damien, and we went our separate ways.

Damien was driving my car back to Minnesota when he stopped in South Dakota to rest. He woke up to a cop tapping on his window. Because he had been drinking and the keys were in the ignition, the cop hauled him off to jail for a few years in South Dakota for that one little mistake! We corresponded back and forth while he was in jail. He was a good writer who would send me the sweetest poems and letters. I always looked forward to hearing from him.

For two years we kept in touch and the letters back and forth never stopped. Damien would even call me every so often to say hello. When I visited family in Minnesota, his parents drove me to South Dakota to see him in jail. It was hard to see him there. He had a heart of gold, and it was hard for me to see him behind bars. He said he wanted to start a relationship with me as soon as he was out of jail, but I didn't know if it was such a good idea. I lived in Hawaii, and he would be in Minnesota. I didn't want another long-distance relationship with someone.

After leaving Minnesota, I worked at a bar and started dating the bartender there. I decided to tell Damien about my new relationship as I knew I needed to be honest with him. It was only a few months later when Damien called to tell me that not only was he out of jail, but also that he had married! I was a bit shocked since I had never heard of this Lydia gal he married. He had never mentioned her to me before. He said they had been friends for a while, but Damien and Lydia realized they were soul mates destined for a lifetime of marriage. I was happy for him. I didn't want to reach out to him while he was married out of respect for his wife, but I wondered if he had been sending her poems as well as to me while he had been in jail.

I was happy for Damien but sad that I lost his friendship. He had been my best friend for a long time. So many questions swirled around in my head, but I thought maybe someday he would reach out to me and my questions would be answered. Within a year of marriage, they had a baby together. In my mind, our friendship was over. I would probably never hear from him again unless he and his wife were to divorce. Life went on, and I forgot about Damien for some time. Once in a great while I would write letters to Damien's parents, and they would write back. Their letters kept me in the loop about how their son was doing.

Ten years later, I heard from Damien's parents that he was having marital problems. I hate to say it, but secretly, I was happy. Maybe he would divorce and finally we could have a heart-to-heart talk and be friends again. We would pick up where we left off, talking on the phone for hours and hours. All the thoughts and questions in my mind years before would finally be answered, and we could meet up and our friendship would be renewed again. I had never forgotten about him. I waited for his call. I thought for sure his parents would give him my phone number.

One day his dad called out of the blue to tell me Damien died. He had committed suicide. My heart was broken into little pieces. Regret and guilt washed over me. All the "what ifs" came flooding into my head. I was lost for words on the phone. I would never hear his voice again. He would never again cheer me up when I was down and out. I would never be able to tell him that I loved him - the three magic words I had not said to him. He was such a big part of my life at one time, and it had meant so much to me.

I bawled my eyes out for days. I carried this pain in my heart for many years. A broken friendship never mended. So many unanswered questions just sat dormant forever in my mind. Even while he was married, I didn't forget about him. I still cared deeply for him. He was my best friend and now my best friend was gone forever. The sad thing was, his little boy would grow up without a dad, his wife was widowed and going through her own sorrow, and his parents would forever have a hole in their hearts that could never be mended because their son was gone. I finally gave it to God. My heart had to heal, and I hoped to see Damien in heaven someday.

MEANT TO BE

Dear Lord,

forgive Damien for what he did

I feel like taking his life was a selfish thing

I can't believe I will never see my best friend again

please take this pain from me.

He left his loved ones all behind

how unfair that he left without a good bye

Please mend my heart

and heal my pain

I miss my friend

Who I hope to see someday.

I pray that he is in heaven

And we will meet again one day

And then it will all be okay

I miss you my friend Damien

Thank You Lord, Amen.

-Prayer/poem I wrote in 2009

Chapter 16

Back to Hawaii

I flew from California to Hawaii, and I was so happy to be back in paradise. I could smell the aroma of plumeria flowers, and that's when I felt like I was home. I had missed this place. I had a friend pick me up at the airport, and as we drove toward Waikiki, I looked over at the ocean which was a bright, stunning blue color. I had almost forgotten how beautiful the water was. It looked so inviting and the beach seemed to call my name. After I dropped my bags off at my friend's place, I put my bikini on, and I was ready for a dip in the ocean. I went swimming the entire day!

A few days later, I went to the post office to purchase a post office box. With the many times in the past that I had moved, it was nice to have just one address for all my mail. The post office box was always my "go to."

As I was leaving the post office, happy that my errand was done for the day, I walked across the parking lot, and there stood Richard, my ex, just gawking at me. I stopped in my tracks and stared at him. I was no longer scared of this guy. I looked at him wondering what I had seen in him in the first place. I couldn't believe I had fallen for this crazy man's antics! Richard sauntered over to me with an "all-that" attitude. He chuckled as he said, "Well, it's Becka in Hawaii again. I heard you were moving back, and I figured I would see you."

We had mutual friends from the bar scene, and I am positive someone heard I was coming back and had to tell Richard the big news. I rolled my eyes. He had a big, ugly smirk on his face, like a monkey would have that was about to throw poop on someone walking by. I said, "You are not supposed to be within three blocks of me, and I suggest you walk away." He laughed as he said, "It's a small island. I was sure I would be running into you again, and here you are." I thought he looked pathetic. He had lost the game and didn't know what to do. He just stood there staring at me as I walked away.

As soon as I was back at the apartment, I called the police. I told them Richard broke the TRO by talking to me in the post office parking lot. The police said they would pick him up, and I could call back to confirm they had him in custody for breaking the restraining order. The next day I called the police station. They gave him a slap on the hand - he was jailed for twenty-four hours before they would release him. I won this time. He wouldn't be bothering me again.

I found a job and an apartment in Waikiki quickly. It was the era of email. Email had just been invented and it was the newest, crazed thing to do, connecting with friends and family over the internet. I had my favorite internet cafe to check emails. The internet cafe had big clunker computers to use since laptops were non-existent then. Near Manoa University, there were internet cafes popping up everywhere. It seemed like they were almost on every corner. My favorite cafe had food, snacks, and coffee. When I checked my email, I treated myself to a cold Starbucks mocha coffee and a hot "everything bagel" with cream cheese. It was the highlight of my day.

One day, I was hanging out in the cafe and sitting on one of their plush over-sized chairs drinking my Starbucks coffee, when I met a guy named Logan. He was the kind of guy that would travel all over the world and be paid for it because somehow, he talked the CEO into traveling write-offs that would save the company plenty of money. He loved to talk about his many adventures to exotic places and all the people he met along the way FOR FREE! I admired him for his courage to travel like he did. We started talking about our likes and dislikes, and I told him I would love to start up a hiking group and go hiking on the weekends. He wanted to do that also!

The first time, we rounded up a few friends and we all went hiking. It was so fun that we had to do it again. We invited more friends for hiking the very next weekend. It was so much fun, we decided to make it an "every weekend thing!" We kept inviting more and more people on the weekends, and our group was growing fast. At one point, we had thirty people hiking with us! We never asked for money. We just wanted to meet new people and have fun. It was an amazing time for me!

At the same time, my pet sitting business had taken off, so I was very busy. I was walking dogs all day long, so by the time the weekend came around and I was hiking up intense trails that challenged my strength and endurance, my legs sometimes felt like Jell-O. I was physically exhausted. My arms would shake from pulling myself up a side of a tree to resume a hiking trail or climb a rope to the top of a straight-up cliff. My legs, especially when running down a trail, would shake uncontrollably and almost give out from under me.

I loved the rush of hiking up dirt trails with large roots weaving in and out of the winding paths. I pushed myself at every step. I had to watch my footing as the trail would become steeper at every turn up this gigantic mountain. I loved how I pushed myself to the limits and kept going; even when my arms and legs would shake uncontrollably, and I would feel pain, I would push myself even more! My face would barely break a sweat, but my arms would glisten with perspiration. At the very top, I would see the most stunning view as the reward for all the hard work to climb to the peak. I loved these hard workouts, and it kept me in great shape.

One time I was following a group of hikers up the side of a massive waterfall. I was pulling myself up a long rope that hung 400-feet high. Making it to the top, I had to climb over a gigantic boulder. It was a ridiculous feat which I could not figure out how to conquer. I was so scared. One wrong move and I could slip off the boulder and fall to my death at the very bottom of the cavern! My friend Jason helped pull me over the side of the boulder. I was shaking uncontrollably and had to rest for a moment. With all the crazy hikes I had done, this one scared me the most. I couldn't believe it. Everyone had gone ahead except Jason and me. As I rested on a rock ledge, I noticed a wooden cross in the muddy mess that leaned against the large boulder I had just climbed over.

In Hawaii, if a cross was set somewhere with a lei on it, or flowers, that meant someone had died there. As I stared at the cross, that's when I realized someone must have fallen off right where we climbed up, and they had died. As I came to that realization, I chill ran down my spine. I promised myself I would never hike up another waterfall again, and I never did. Good thing this trail ended somewhere else. No way would I have gone back down this monstrous cavern!

Another time a group of friends and I drove to Waimanalo which was on the east side of the island. I was excited to conquer one of the biggest mountains in the area. Two avid hikers in front of us somehow scrambled up the steep side of a mountain to tie a rope to a puny palm tree for all of us to climb to the first rock ledge. I thought this was a crazy idea, but one by one, my friends were pulling themselves up this rope, and the tiny palm tree held on for dear life as we all put our trust in that little tree! I was the last to pull myself onto the ledge, and when I stood up and looked around, the view was so spectacular that it took my breath away! My friend Karen was on a rock ledge about 200 feet ahead of me and she hollered over and as I spread my arms out wide, "click," she took a great photo of me on this rock ledge I had just climbed. With cascading mountains all around and the ocean far below us, it was an incredible view! To this day, this photo is one of my favorite pictures. We hiked for most of the day and went deep into the mountains where it was so quiet I could hear a pin drop in the middle of nowhere. I loved hiking! To hike deep into the forest and be in nature where it was quiet and peaceful was quite the experience!

My very favorite hike was "Stairway to Heaven." At the start of the hike from the bottom of the stairs looking up at this ginormous mountain I would have to hike, it took my breath away. The stairs seemed to disappear into the clouds as if they went right into heaven. A group of us climbed more than four thousand rickety old steps that ended above the clouds. As we rested at the peak, I sat on a rock to take in the scenery. It was breathtaking! I thought of God, and how out of the deep ocean He created such a beautiful landscape. It was incredible! After lunch, my friends and I would run back down those rickety old steps on the side of the mountain. At one point there was a resting area and we stared at the gorgeous view of the ocean and the tiny little cars driving on the freeway far below. WHAT A RUSH!! I hiked "Stairway to Heaven" twice with a group of friends, and it will always be etched in my memory as spectacular.

Hiking trails are everywhere in Oahu and there was not enough time to do all of them, but we managed to explore just about every one of them. I will write a more in-depth book someday about adventures I've had in Hawaii including many of the other crazy fun hikes I had been on in the islands.

I had a few friends at the Ala Moana boat harbor who had their own boats. I would hang out with these guys, and sometimes I would go out with them on their fishing boats.

They were good guys, not like the grubby, dirty ones you would see hanging out on a boat being flirty with anything that had two legs. These guys were real "down to earth" fishermen who just loved to be on a boat out in the water. That was their life.

One time, Brayden, my friend who owned a fishing boat, was going to Maui and asked me and a few friends if we wanted to go for the weekend. I was ecstatic and jumped at the chance. I loved Maui and couldn't wait to be on the island again. I always wished to move there because it was a dream of mine; however, it was much more expensive to live there than Oahu, so I never had the chance.

The boat trip was fantastic! It was a thirteen-hour ride. Big waves in the channel rocked the boat back and forth, back and forth. It lulled me to sleep. I loved big waves and had always been fascinated by them, and this was no different.

Before I knew it, we were in the harbor and anchored out in the water. There were so many boats in the harbor that there were no slips for our boat, so we took a little dingy to the dock. We were thrilled to be there! We didn't need to rent a car. We were staying in Lahaina which is a busy little town with the most action going on in Maui. This little town is only a mile long, so we were able to walk everywhere to eat or find entertainment. There was so much to see and do. We walked down the boardwalk, checked out shops, and ate at Cheeseburger in Paradise which had great food. When dusk came, everyone wanted to go back to the boat, but I didn't want to leave. I wanted to stay. I told them to pick me up in the early morning, and we could head back to Oahu. I told them I would be fine for the night. I really didn't think it through. I had no money and nowhere to stay. I figured I could meet some people and crash at their place or sleep on the beach, but I was very naive.

After my friends returned to the boat, I walked around awhile and ended up at a bar where I had a root beer. It was late. I was sitting at the bar when a guy sat right next to me and started talking. He seemed like a nice guy, but I knew he was a smooth talker. I wasn't really into his game, a big macho guy with big muscles. It really wasn't my thing. I was tired and told him I wasn't interested in him. He bought me a drink anyway. I didn't even ask him for one. I drank it and he ordered another one for me which I drank. I was feeling a bit buzzed. I told him I was stuck with nowhere to go, and he said I could crash at his hotel right down the street. I was thankful and followed him to his hotel. When we arrived at the hotel, the guy had another drink for me. I was a "lightweight" who wasn't used to drinking so much. I said to the guy it was enough. I couldn't drink anymore. He talked me into having a few sips of the drink in his hand, and suddenly I felt woozy and fell back on the bed. I didn't know what was happening. Something was wrong. Warning bells went off in my head, and I knew there was something terribly wrong with me. When I tried to pull myself up, nothing happened. I lay there as if I were dead, but I was very much aware of my surroundings.

The guy pushed me as if he were testing how drunk I was. I just lay there. Suddenly, the guy pulled off my shorts and underwear, pulled me to the edge of the bed, and raped me! I tried to push him away, but my arms weren't moving. They felt like dead weight. My legs hung over the bed. I tried to kick him away, but my legs wouldn't work. I tried to say no. My words were slurred. I tried to get up and run, but my body wouldn't do what my mind was telling it to do. I tried to scream, but my voice was so garbled that nothing came out. I couldn't even move my head. I was so confused. It was dark, and the room was blurry.

What was this jerk trying to do? I knew exactly what he was doing. I screamed in my mind, but my body just lay there as if I were dead, and then I blacked out. I woke up groggy a little while later. The guy was on my phone talking to someone. I still couldn't move. I passed out again. In the middle of the night I woke up and found that my arms and legs were movable. I looked around the room, but I didn't see the guy.

I sat up, looked around for my shorts, dressed quickly, grabbed my phone and purse, and ran out of there. I didn't know if he was in the bathroom or if he had left or where he was, but I wasn't sticking around to find out. Later I received a $300.00 phone bill to Japan! The guy had used my phone to call his girlfriend and was on the phone with her for hours. It took some doing, but I worked with my phone company to take care of the charges so that I wouldn't have to pay.

I had been drugged and raped! I felt so dirty and alone. I didn't know what a date-rape drug was at the time. I had never heard of it before, but because I had no function of my arms or legs, I knew (years later) that the man must have drugged me.

I walked down Lahaina Street at 3:00am feeling dirty and disgusted. I just wanted to go home. I couldn't remember much about the night with the guy, but I knew he had violated me. I just wanted to take a shower and scrub my body everywhere he touched me. I walked to the boat harbor and looked out at my friend's boat. They had lights on and music blaring and I could hear them laughing. I wished I had gone with them. The boat was too far for them to see me or hear me if I hollered. I stood there for a moment, wondering where I was going to sleep.

I walked toward a restaurant near the harbor. The restaurant had a lanai that was somewhat covered, and a young gentleman was mopping the floor in the front area. They had just closed at 2:00am. I asked him if I could crash in the front area just to protect myself from people passing by and the cold wind. He told me it wasn't a good idea. He would be fired if the manager found out. I pleaded with him. I told him I had a terrible night and was scared to sleep in the park or on the beach. He then changed his mind and let me sleep there. I thanked him and lay down in the foyer, feeling safer than I had all night. After a few minutes, the employee brought me a few light blankets from the trunk of his car. I thanked him again and fell asleep for a few hours. At 5:30am, the same employee came to start the morning shift and woke me to tell me I should leave before anyone else showed up. I appreciated his kindness. I walked around the harbor and the park for a while until my friend started his boat and came for me.

When I boarded the boat, I gave Brayden the biggest hug. I told him I didn't plan well and that I ended up sleeping in the foyer of a restaurant. He felt bad, but it wasn't his fault. I never told him what really happened. He would have felt even worse. Brayden steered the boat toward Oahu, and I felt safe with my friends. I couldn't wait to get home.

Chapter 17

Lost in Sin

I lived in a small apartment in Waikiki with a roommate who was a young cop. We got along well. We both did our own thing and stayed out of each other's way. I started living the party scene, going out to have fun nightly with my friends, and my roommate lived the cop life, saving one life at a time. I admired him for all he had to go through in his profession. He would tell me stories of catching bad guys, and I couldn't believe what he had to go through in his line of work!

I couldn't find a job and struggled to make rent. I did some pet sitting, but it wasn't enough to live on. I continued looking for work, but it was a tough time to find anything. I knew a guy named Frank who said he would give me $1200.00 if I would spend time with him for the whole day and all we would do is talk. Frank promised he wouldn't touch me or say nasty things to me. He wouldn't do anything weird; he just needed a friend with whom to talk. He would also pay for my dinner.

At that time, I was so broke that I barely ate much. I didn't even make $500.00 a month, so $1200.00 in one day was a huge amount of money for me. I agreed to hang out with him. Frank was respectful and nice to me. He was twice my age and probably didn't date or spend much time with women. I figured he was just a lonely, old guy who wanted to be paid some attention. We talked awhile, but nothing serious. We went out to eat at a nice restaurant and when we went back to his place, he said I could go home. He wrote me a big, fat check for $1200.00. I had never in my life seen that much money at one time!

As I walked away, he asked if I wanted to come back later that week. He would pay me the same amount to accompany him again. I skipped home that day. I was so excited about the money! I kept staring at the check and couldn't believe I made all this money in only a few hours. I saw him again, and we talked for hours. He seemed a little more interested in me and asked a few questions about my life. I didn't say much. I was shy and private about my personal life. We went out to dinner again and had a nice time. I still couldn't believe I was being paid so much money and given a free meal! It couldn't get any better than this! We went back to his place and he wrote another $1200.00 check and said he would see me again. I was on cloud nine! This was the easiest money I had ever made! I just made $2400.00 in a few days just by hanging out with a lonely, old guy.

The next week he called and asked if I cleaned houses. I said that I had cleaned houses for past clients. He said he would pay me $5000.00, but only if I would clean in my bikini! I was downright disgusted. I told him I was running out the door and I had to get off the phone. I hung up and sat there. I didn't realize my roommate had come out of his bedroom, and he asked about the phone call I just received. I looked a bit flustered. I told him what Frank said and asked why he would ask me to wear my bikini while I worked for him. I was very naïve.

My roommate said Frank could be grooming me for a group of guys to come in later after I was comfortable making this kind of money, and then rape me. It was all part of a sex-trafficking ring! They drug the women, rape them, beat them, and then use them for sex trafficking or any other way they want. I laughed it off telling him there is no way this nice man would do such a thing, but he was adamant that Frank wasn't being a nice guy - he had bigger intentions for me. My roommate looked at me with concern. He went into great detail about how these pimps find nice girls who fall for easy money and then beat the women into submission, drug them, and control them into working on the streets in sex trafficking, sometimes shipping them overseas never to be found again. It happens all the time!

I knew I had a decision to make. I could earn $5000.00 in a few hours of cleaning in a bikini while I uncomfortably moved around the apartment with Frank's eyes on me the whole time or I could focus on finding a real job and work to live. I was so close to deciding to clean for him. The $5000.00 was a lot of money, and I could live a whole lot better if I had that kind of money. My roommate could be dead wrong about this guy, or I could be wrong. I had to decide. My roommate was insistent that I shouldn't do it. I decided not to call the guy back and instead go out to find a real job.

The next day, I walked around Waikiki applying for jobs and thinking I made the best decision. I collected four or five applications to fill out at home. I dropped off the applications that same week and heard nothing. I was in a slump, and I was becoming depressed. My roommate said I had to pay my rent, or I was out. I was looking hard for work, but nothing was turning up. The next week I ran into a guy at the beach in Waikiki, and we chatted awhile. He asked if I was looking for work. I said, "Desperately!" His girlfriend had been looking for a babysitter for her seven-year-old daughter while she worked the night shift. He said it paid well. $15.00 an hour, 10:00pm-5:00am, and the girl would be sleeping the whole night. I could sleep on the couch and be paid for it, and if the girl woke up, I would help her back to bed. I told him I would think about this job opportunity and call him back.

I went home and excitedly told my roommate I found a job. It was easy money for babysitting, but he didn't seem as happy for me. He said, "You are gullible." I just told him I have the best gig that pays big money and he called me gullible? He asked, "What's the name of the guy and his girlfriend?"

When I told him their names, he said, "The mom, Jill, is a hooker in Waikiki, who sells herself to make money for the pimp you met at the beach." I didn't know if he was just trying to scare me into not taking the job or if he was being truthful, but he had never lied to me before. I stood there with my mouth open. For a moment, I didn't know what to say. What a downer he was. I told him, "I'm going to take the babysitting job because I need the money for rent; besides, it's easy money and there is no way that guy is a pimp. He doesn't even look like one."

My roommate went on, "The first few nights they will have you babysit and then one night, a John will come in with a bunch of guys to rape you and beat you up, drug you, give you sexy clothes to wear, and be their hooker on the street corner just like Jill." I couldn't fathom it but thinking back to that guy in Maui who raped me, I never wanted to go through something like that ever again. It tore me up having been taken advantage of when I was raped.

I had so many thoughts racing through my head. I questioned him, "How could they take my innocence away and make me a hooker if I was against it?" He replied, "They prey on the weak and innocent women or girls with no confidence or those who feel worthless. They beat them into submission, so they will do anything they tell them to do. It happens all the time, more than you know." He had a painful look on his face. He looked down at the floor as he shuffled his feet and said, "I see this stuff every day, Becka, and I don't want to see you fall for it." I could tell he genuinely cared.

He looked up and asked, "How much would a parent normally pay you to babysit?" I said, "$5.00 an hour." He said,

"Exactly, and this guy would pay you $15.00 an hour to sleep at the woman's house and do nothing? Doesn't that seem a little suspicious?" I had to think about that. He could be wrong. It might just be the mom and this guy desperately needed a babysitter and would pay good money to have the daughter well taken care of by someone reliable. I called the man for a better feel of the situation. The man confirmed it was $15.00 an hour and I could sleep the whole night. He added that he would pay me an additional $10.00 an hour if I wanted to clean the apartment. $25.00 an hour for cleaning and babysitting? It sounded like an unreal gig, but as I talked to the man, I had an uneasy feeling. I didn't know where the feeling came from, but I thought if I did take the job and fall into sex trafficking, that would be a nightmare I couldn't even imagine.

My roommate said some of these women are sold overseas, never to be found again. After the women are all used up and discarded, they die a torturous death! The way my roommate was acting, you would think his best friend had died. This bothered me. I realized this is the most he had talked to me since I had moved in months ago. Could he be telling me the truth? Did he really care? Why would these men do such things? My head was spinning with questions.

My roommate had never raised his voice before because he was a quiet and mellow kind of guy, but tonight he was very upset about this situation. I decided against taking the job. It scared me to think I could be trapped in that kind of lifestyle with no way out. I had to trust my roommate knew what he was talking about when it came to such a situation. He had seen a great deal in the many years he had been a cop. I called the guy back and told him I found a fulltime job and needed to decline the offer but appreciated it.

I have no doubt in my mind the babysitting job was a set up that could have gone terribly wrong. My roommate saved my life, and to this day I am thankful for him and thankful to God for watching over me. I know God saved me and brought this guy into my life to make me aware of the dangers lurking nearby.

These men look for desperate boys and girls and women that want to get out of a complicated situation at home. Runaways often flee to an unsafe place and are many times pulled into sex trafficking or prostitution. Typically, there is no way out from this kind of life of abuse and torture.

Children are sold into slavery every single day, and it breaks my heart! I want the story told that it's not just in other countries! This happens in the US, and it's everywhere, in every state, in so many places you would never ever think of! It could be the unmarked semi-truck that drives down your quiet street or the storage shed at a neighbor's house or an old run-down building that looks vacant. Children are being preyed upon with no way out of hidden places. I just want people to be aware because I had almost fallen into that trap of sex trafficking, and my life today would be so different if God had not intervened and watched over me.

Parents: hug your children more tightly each night and be blessed that they are safe!

After my escape from a possible sex-trafficking ring, I was determined to find a job. A friend of mine told me there was a country bar in Waikiki that was hiring, so I thought I would take a chance and I applied. Within a few days the manager called me in for an interview. I didn't have any nice clothes to wear, but I did my best at an outfit that would pass as dressing up respectfully. The interview went well and as I was leaving, the owner who interviewed me said, "One more thing, do you like country music?" I turned around at the door and said, "No, but I can learn to like it." She responded, "Good enough for me. You got the job." I was elated!

I liked working at the country bar. The crew that worked there was amazing. I made instant friends with everyone. It was a fast-paced bar full of drinkers and partiers, especially after 10:00pm, and going into the wee hours of the morning 'til 4:00. The weekends were packed! On busy nights as a waitress, I pushed my way through the crowd to deliver drinks and be sure not to drop a beer on someone's head! I made great tips from waitressing and was finally able to pay my rent and other bills.

Not long after that, I moved from the apartment with my roommate into a cute, blue one-story house in Waikiki. It was a great location close to both the ocean and the Ala Wai Canal. Since I lived near my job, every evening I walked the few blocks to work. My new place was small. It had a kitchen and five bedrooms. My bedroom size was only a 10X10; in fact, all the rooms in the house were the same size. Each room was all set up for individual renters, and each bedroom had its own entrance. There was no living room area to hang out. It was a unique set-up, but I really liked it. I got along great with everyone that lived there. I felt like things were finally falling into place.

After working at the bar for a few months, I started liking country music. I really enjoyed my job and the people that worked there. I also worked hard to build up my pet sitting business on the side, but it was a struggle to make a living on pet sitting alone.

Working at the bar, I was wrapped up in the world. I had forgotten about God completely. I was living in a secular world where everything was about drinking, partying, and having fun, but I missed out on God's voice. I used to hear from Him all the time, and the further I walked away from God, the more I couldn't hear from Him at all! I didn't think much about it, but I now know that God was looking out for me, and like the story in the Bible of the prodigal son, God was waiting for me to return to Him again.

I wasn't much of a drinker before I started working at the bar but hanging out with this fun crowd of people at work, I really enjoyed the partying scene. I also had free drinks handed to me all the time. On my nights off, my friends and I would bar hop. My girlfriends and I would get into all the bars for free, a perk of working at a bar. We would party until 4:00am, and then go to Denny's for breakfast which was open twenty-four hours.

I met many guys working in the bar scene, and I always had a boyfriend. If it didn't work out with one guy, there were many others from whom to choose. Like my girlfriends said, *"There are plenty more fish in the sea."* I liked that saying. I made it okay in my mind to go from one guy to another because I wanted LOVE so badly, and I was willing to do anything to find the love of my life, my soul mate, with whom I would eventually settle down and marry.

At the bar, there was a guy named Parker who worked with me. He was the doorman who let all the pretty ladies in and looked at everyone's ID to make sure they were over twenty-one to drink. We were friends for a long time, and then we started dating. From the very beginning, I was sure he was my soulmate. We really connected. He was romantic, and I was so in love with him. I fell for him hard. I was in my early thirties at the time, I had never been married, but I wanted to be in the worst way! I wanted to settle down and have children and I had high hopes that Parker was "the one." He was a tall, handsome, "laid-back" military guy who was fun to be with, and always had a group of friends around him. He was the life of the party wherever we went. Ladies fawned over him.

When Parker and I were dating, I don't think he took the relationship seriously, but in my mind, I wanted to marry this guy. We dated awhile but because we were so much alike, both of us hard-headed and stubborn, it affected our relationship and we started fighting. I was brokenhearted when the relationship suddenly ended. I really thought Parker was the one. He always told me he would never cheat on me, so when I found out he had cheated on me before we broke up, that shattered me beyond repair. I was distraught and in so much pain, one bad relationship after another, and I was sick of it all. No more relationships for me!

I kept my mind busy and focused on working as many hours as I could. I had good friends who distracted me from thinking about the break up with Parker. One of my friends, Donny, was falling on hard times. He was a military guy who was one of my favorite patrons at the bar. Donny said his girlfriend kicked him out of her house, and he had been sleeping in his car. I told him he could stay with me for a few days while he looked for a place to live. I had a heart of gold after all and wouldn't want anything happening to him.

Donny came over that night after I was off work and moved in with one big duffle bag. I told him he could sleep on the floor. There was not much space in my little room, so I told him he would have to find another place soon. He stayed with me for a short while, and I felt a connection with him; he was becoming a good friend. He was easy to talk to, he respected my space, and I felt good that I was able to help him out.

One night we were drinking at the bar. I was feeling lonely, and Donny was there. We were talking and maybe I felt sorry for myself thinking about the awful break-up with my boyfriend. My "new roommate" and I went back to my place, made out, and had sex. I regretted it early the next morning. I was not the type of person to sleep with a guy I hardly knew or one that I wasn't in an exclusive relationship. Alcohol had consumed me, and I made a huge mistake. Donny wanted a relationship, but I did not. I wanted him to move out. Tension set in, making us both uncomfortable living in such close quarters in my little 10X10 room. Everything he did started to bug me. He drank my bottled water, ate my food, and had his stuff strewn all over my room. I think his intentions were to bug me and it worked!

One of the other roommates in the house moved out. I told Donny he should move into the empty room. He said he wanted to make things work with us, but honestly, I didn't want anything to do with him. He moved into the empty room the very next day. At least now I had my own space again! A few days later he had a girlfriend! He flaunted her around the bar on a night I was working. He looked very proud having her on his arm. I hoped now he would leave me alone, but he started doing childish things instead! He would stand in front of my bedroom with his girlfriend, talking loudly, and making out with her right in front of my window. I could hear sloppy kissing noises and I told him, "Go get a room!" He yelled out in a boisterous voice to the world, "I want to marry this woman!" I looked out my window and said, "I am happy for you." I closed my louvers. His girlfriend quickly found herself pregnant with his baby, and he was so proud to tell everyone. I was tired of all the drama not only in the house, but also at work too! I couldn't tolerate his childish behavior anymore. He disgusted me. I needed to move.

A month later, the house where I was renting sold to new owners. They sent all the tenants a letter in the mail stating that we could stay, but rent was going up $50.00 and we couldn't have any pets. I had my two cats that were my precious babies. I couldn't just get rid of them! I called the new owners to talk to them about my situation, and they were adamant, no pets allowed. I had thirty days either to find a home for my cats or move out. I didn't know what to do.

I had affordable rent where I lived, and no money to move. After receiving the notice, I went numb. I felt like a robot just doing what needed to be done. I worked, ate, and slept, but it seemed that everything I did was just a blur. I looked in the newspaper but couldn't find any place to move that was affordable. In the back of my mind I was wondering if I would be homeless with my two cats. For days, I just put my worries in the back of my mind and went on with life.

Not long after, a client of mine was leaving on a trip, and I would be watching her two cats. I met with Sandy for the contract and keys. She had been a client of mine for many years, so when she saw me, she knew something was terribly wrong. I had not said a thing to anyone, so when I told her I was being kicked out of my place, I just started crying. I was crying for so many things, not just for being kicked out. It was the move, the friend I helped, being broke, and worst of all, watching my ex-boyfriend whom I thought I would marry, move on with his life. On top of it all, I would be homeless within days! My life was falling apart.

I also didn't have any car insurance. I couldn't afford it. It was the first time in my life that I couldn't pay for my insurance. I was trying to sell my car, and the guy who test-drove it, did so erratically in Waikiki right in front of a cop! We were pulled over, and I tried to explain to the officer that the driver may buy my car. With no insurance, the cop threatened to put me in jail or pay a $250.00 fine. Jail for thirty days - that wasn't happening. I maxed out my credit card for a free "get out of jail" card.

As I sniffled and unraveled my story of what's been happening for the past month, my client, Sandy listened, and then hugged me tightly as my tears fell! I knew it was not the most professional thing to do. She had a wonderful nurturing nature about her and she wanted to help. She promised she would look in the newspaper and help me find a place to live. I thanked her, wiped my tears, grabbed her keys, and quickly left. I felt so emotional. My life was spiraling out of control. I knew I was falling down a deep well and felt there was no way out. I didn't know what to do. I took a deep breath and drove home to figure things out.

Cast your cares upon Him, for He careth for you. 1Peter 5:7

Chapter 18

My Sins Are Washed Away

I worked as many hours at the bar as I could to save up money. I heard from my client Sandy that she had a few leads for rentals. I called them, but the rentals were all taken. I had one week to move and no leads; I was going to be homeless if I didn't find a place soon. There were just no affordable apartments available. I was losing hope!

One night after work, around 3:00am, I walked home, exhausted. Feeling defeated, I opened my door and threw my keys on the table nearby as I looked around the room. I had not packed anything! Could I stay and hope the owners changed their minds? For a moment, I was hopeful, but reality set in, and it was painful. I knew they would kick me out. They didn't care about me. I walked into my room and closed the door as I pondered on what was to come.

My eyes welled up with tears. I didn't know what to do. I was at the end of my rope. My knees buckled under me, and I fell to the floor. I curled up in a ball and started bawling! I was crying a "waterfall" of tears! The tears were so big, and they wouldn't stop. It was like the river of life flowing. I just wanted God to wash away all my pain, all my worries, and all the sins I had committed!

A flood of thoughts poured into my head. It was like a movie screen of past events that had happened. I thought about my life. I thought about the bad decisions I had made. I thought about the rape, the beatings, the break ups, the pain - it was all too much to bear. All the times I thought I heard God telling me to come back to Him, I ignored Him thinking I was just hearing things. I started wailing. I couldn't handle the pain that washed over me, and I just wanted to die.

God seemed so far away. I intentionally pushed Him away to live my sinful lifestyle. I had walked away from God so many years ago and for what? To live in sin? So why now would He hear my cries if I called out to Him? What a mess I was in. How would I ever clean my life up?

Then I heard God say, *"Cast your cares onto me; you don't need to carry the burden yourself."* I knew it was God talking to me! He wanted me back in His arms. I had lost everything; I had nothing else to lose.

I cried out to God, *"God, HELP ME! I don't know what to do. I am in such a mess."* I started crying again. I heard God say, *"Child, surrender to Me, trust Me, and I will be by your side through everything."* God showed me the path I had taken and the choices I had made that brought me where I was at that very moment.

I was wailing as I realized how I had fallen into sin and how satan had made me think I was happy, but I was not. I finally understood I had been deceived and manipulated and my life was spiraling out of control. The devil had won, and I was a total mess! I had endured pain, loss, depression, and suffering for so many years. I had been duped by satan. God showed me at that very moment exactly how the devil had deceived me.

Be alert and of sober mind. Your enemy the devil prowls around like a roaring lion looking for someone to devour. 1Peter 5:8

I may have been lost, but I knew God could save me! I was broken enough to surrender it all to Him!

I prayed, *"Lord, please forgive me for walking away from You. Forgive all my sins, and everything I did against You. Lord, I surrender to You my life and everything I am. Make me clean again. Pick me up from this mess and help me. I need You. If You will fix my life, I will follow You all the days of my life."*

I cried some more. God said, "Promise Me you will follow Me all of your days." I said, "Yes, I promise." I felt a flush of peace come over me, and I felt renewed. I knew God was working in my life! I knew He gave me a clean slate with which to start over, because He loved me that much. I trusted He was going to fix my broken life, and I would follow Him for the rest of my days. I was saved and reborn again. I stood up, wiped my tears, took a shower, and fell asleep. That night, I slept better than I had in many months!

The next morning, I woke up and felt different. I knew God forgave my many sins, and I felt the old me was gone, and the new me was born. Like a fresh flower just blossoming after a pouring rain, I felt brand new. I said, "Good morning, Lord." I felt joy in my heart. I knew God was looking down on me with a smile on His face. He had been waiting a long time for me to come back to Him. As I thought of the story of the prodigal son, what a good reminder of a dark time in my life that I had to overcome. I was back in God's arms once again! I smiled for the first time in a long time. I went about my day without worry. Even though I didn't have any leads for a place to live, I felt peace and knew God would take care of me. It felt good not to have to worry about my problems. The verse that came to my mind was ***Romans 8:31 "If God is for us, who can be against us."***

One day I received a call from Sandy who told me an apartment had become available. She saw it in the newspaper that morning and said I should call them right away. I called the landlord to let him know I was interested in the apartment. He said I could come by and look at the place the next day along with anyone else who called about the ad. I would need to fill out an application, and he would pick who he wanted to live there. He was short and abrupt on the phone as he gave me the address. Then he hung up.

I knelt and prayed, *"Lord, I want this place so badly. Please help me! I can afford this place and it's not far from work. I only have a few days before I am homeless. Please take care of me. Lord, I pray no one else shows up so I will get the place. Be with me and bless me, Amen."*

I went to the bank and pulled out all the money I had. It just so happened it was the exact amount I needed for rent and deposit! I was ready to meet the landlord and see the apartment. I didn't care what it looked like. I just needed a roof over my head. I drove to Atkinson Drive and saw it was an apartment complex in a little cul-de-sac. The landlord was standing outside, writing something on a sheet of paper attached to a clipboard. I parked in the parking lot. I then walked up to him and introduced myself.

The landlord's name was Randy who was also the owner of the apartment complex. He told me he would wait a few more minutes in case someone else showed up to look at the place. I stood there quietly praying and asking God not to have anyone else come. We waited for five minutes, and I made small talk asking about the neighborhood and parking. He answered in short, abrupt sentences. He was not interested in small talk, but he told me the rental was a one-bedroom apartment, and rent was $625.00 a month paid by the 1st every month. There was one parking stall per unit. The manager lived below this unit. It sounded perfect.

After a few minutes, we walked up the stairs where he had me follow him on a walkway to the middle of the complex where there was a big, white door. We entered the apartment and walked into the living room. There was a kitchen on the backside of the living room. A small, narrow hall had a tall, white-painted book shelf from floor to ceiling. There was a small bathroom with shower, and the bedroom was to the left of that in the back of the apartment. I thought it would be perfect for me. I loved it. Randy quickly showed me around, and then he pulled out an application for me to fill out. I pulled out cash and waved it in front of him. I told him, "I have rent and deposit in cash, and since no one else has showed up I would like to rent this place!" Quietly, I was praying to God, pleading with Him for this apartment.

Randy mulled it over for a moment as he looked at the cash. He took the money and said, "Okay, it is yours. Fill out the application; you can move in tomorrow." I was elated, I wanted to hug him, but I held back. I thanked God quietly and shook Randy's hand as I excitedly replied, "Thank you."

My life was finally turning around! I felt God was lifting me out of the ruins. I called all my friends to come help me move. The next night, I couldn't believe how many people showed up to help! I was packing quickly, and I had trucks and cars parked all over the street to move my things. It only took a few hours to pile all my belongings into the vehicles. I was humbled by my many friends. When I needed them, they were there! After all my belongings were at the new place and I stood in my cute little apartment, I looked around and smiled. I loved this place, and I was so thankful. I knew I would finally have a good night's sleep.

As I unpacked and settled in, I suddenly had a feeling the apartment looked familiar. I thought, I must have been to this apartment complex before, but I couldn't remember whom I visited there. I put it in the back of my mind for the time being. I let my excitement of this new place set the tone as I unpacked.

I continued to focus on my new life with God. I started praying continually and having my devotion time to be closer to God. I had a good home church that I went to, making friends there, and things were going well. I worked long hours at Nashville's, and at the same time my pet sitting business started taking off. I was building my clientele for pet sitting, and I couldn't believe I was making money doing something I LOVED to do! It was a dream come true. However, I was over-worked and spread very thin. I would walk dogs starting in the early morning until mid-afternoon and then work at the bar from late-afternoon until 4:00am. Then I would start all over a few hours later, walking dogs throughout the day until I had to work at the bar again. I didn't sleep much, but in between walking dogs, I would lie under a tall, shady palm tree on the beach, listen to the waves lapping at the shore, and take a quick nap before my next dog walk. I was finally making money to pay the bills, and God was blessing me greatly. I kept my promise and followed God in everything in my life, and He was taking care of me.

One night I returned home late, just exhausted from working at the bar. I didn't feel like I was getting any rest. I prayed and asked God what I should do. God told me to let go of my job at the bar. I thought maybe I didn't hear Him right.

I loved working at the bar, but because I had found God, I had cleaned myself up and didn't drink or party at all, like I did in the past. I was walking the Christian life now and wanted to please God instead of myself. I prayed again, asking God what I should do. God said it again, *"Let your job go at the bar. It is not edifying Me in any way."* I knew I needed to obey God. I told Him, *"I don't know how to quit. I like my job and don't see how I can walk away from the money I make. If you want me to leave my job, Lord, You will have to do it for me!"* I prayed and left it at that.

On a Saturday morning, when I was swamped with pet sitting, there was a mandatory meeting at the bar for all the employees. I told the owner I would try to make it, but I had many clients that day and probably couldn't make the meeting. I didn't show up, so when I came to work that afternoon, the owner said, "You are fired. Leave now." I asked for my job back by explaining my packed schedule with pet sitting but to no avail. I had lost my job. I worked there for a long time and I loved working there, but it was finally time to move on.

A few weeks later, my pet sitting business took off, and I worked unbelievably long hours doing something I loved! I was so amazed by what God was doing in my life! I was also able to shine God's light to all my wonderful clients while taking care of their pets. Things were looking up. God kept His promise to me, and He was always faithful!

Cast your cares upon Him, for He careth for you.
1Peter 5:7

A CHILD OF GOD

Chapter 19

"I Would Do Anything for Love"

I had a few clients who wanted me to clean their homes on a regular basis, so I started cleaning for them as well as walking their dogs. It kept me busy. One client of mine lived on the east side of the island. She lived in the ritzier area of Hawaii Kai with its high-class people and expensive million-dollar homes. The houses were big and beautiful. I loved the twenty-minute drive from Kahala to Hawaii Kai. I would look at the beautiful ocean views on the right side of the road, and on the left I could see breathtaking mountains cascading above the many homes spread across the land. Hawaii Kai was not for the mere middle class. I had clients spread over half the island, from Hawaii Kai to Kahala and from Waikiki to Pearl City and Ewa. They were always nice to me even though they were in a different tax bracket than I. I loved their pets as if they were my own, and I enjoyed working for them.

My new client Tammy lived in Hawaii Kai and had a very large home. She had three small children, and the house was a mess of toys when I came to clean every few weeks. I didn't mind because that was my job, to clean up their house. It usually took six hours to clean for them. Tammy was one of my favorite clients, and it was good money.

I was very independent, and it felt good that I could build my own business without schooling. I was doing great. I thank my many wonderful clients for my growing business and thank God for the many blessings!

After cleaning for my client a few months, she hired a guy to fix the roof on her house. I came to work one morning and as I opened the trunk of my car to pull out my mop and cleaning supplies, I heard a guy on Tammy's roof singing a honky-tonk kind of country song along with the radio. I chuckled under my breath as I thought it was silly. This guy was nailing pieces to the roof and singing at the top of his lungs. At the very high notes, his voice cracked, and I couldn't help but laugh.

I walked inside the house and started my cleaning routine. After a few minutes this handy man would come through the room I was in to use an extension cord or retrieve more material. He surprised me as he bumped into me a few times. He kept apologizing, and then he finally introduced himself. His name was Blake, and he owned his own construction business. I continued cleaning the home and then as I packed up my supplies to leave, Blake caught me by the door and asked for my number. He wanted to go out on a date.

I stared at him; it was the first time I really noticed his looks. He was a very attractive, tall, six-foot, slender Asian man with black short hair, big brown eyes, and thin lips. He was clean cut and neat, even after working on a hot roof all day. He could ask any woman out, so I was surprised when he asked me for a date, especially since my hair was in disarray and I had a mild arm-pit stench from cleaning all day. I had not dated in years, and since my early thirties, I wasn't in a big hurry to settle down; besides, I didn't have time to date a guy. I was a busy working woman. I handed Blake my business card as I was leaving and said, "Call me." He watched me walk away. I thought I would never hear from him again.

Four days later, Blake called and asked to see me. We met for dinner at a restaurant. He wanted to sit right next to me while we ate. He said he wanted to be close to me. I thought it was sweet. Honestly it felt uncomfortable since I wasn't used to this sort of seating arrangement in a restaurant, but I liked the attention. We had a very nice time together - we ate, joked, laughed, and I noticed we both held common interests. He was easy to talk to, and I took everything lightheartedly. After our dinner, which he so kindly paid for, I went home in a good mood. I expected I wouldn't hear from him ever again, and that was okay. I had been single for five years, and I was not used to attention from a guy. I was more focused on my business which was booming at this time which kept me preoccupied.

A few days later, I went to clean for Tammy again and there was Blake, working on the roof. We were cordial when I was cleaning, and he would bump into me again trying to find an extension cord or more material for the roof. I think he had been trying to flirt with me! I had not been flirted with in a very long time, and it felt good that a guy was interested in me. Before I packed up to leave, Blake said he would give me a call. I wasn't holding my breath. I was a busy woman who was not about to wait by the phone for his call.

Blake called me that very next night and asked when he could see me again. I told him that I was a busy woman. He said he was busy too but wanted to see me. It had been so long since a guy had liked me. It felt really good. I wanted to share something with him that would either peak his interest or would have him run for the hills. I didn't care either way. I was "sticking to my guns" on what I believed.

On the phone, I told Blake that in 2003 I re-gave my life to Christ, and I promised God that I would stay abstinent until I was married. Anyone I would date, I would not have sex with unless we were married. He was quiet a moment, then said he had to think about it and hung up the phone. I didn't think I would hear from him ever again. He was a guy, after all, and guys mainly think with one thing when they live in the secular world. I didn't hear from him for a week, but then he called and said he wanted to give it a shot with me, so we started dating.

We saw each other almost daily, and he was so fun to be around. It seemed like we had a great deal in common, except that he liked country music, and I, not so much. Blake made me feel special, and I fell for him hard! I was madly in love with him. When I loved, I loved hard! We had a great deal of fun when we were together. He was nice and respectful, and I felt he must love me because he was saving himself for me. He was proud of the fact he wasn't having sex with me until we marry. He brought it up repeatedly. He reminded me of it more times than he needed!

I noticed Blake had OCD issues but nothing I couldn't look past. In his bedroom closet, he would have his clothes hung a certain way, so if I were to move his shirts or wash them and they were wrinkled even a little, he would be very upset. He also had to have his shirts color coordinated in the closet. He had to look neat and clean before he would walk outside, which I assumed that most men were that way, but Blake would take extra care to look in the mirror time and time again before leaving the house. I do admit, he looked really good and he knew it! On his bed were satin sheets that had to be perfectly made with not a wrinkle. It was good housekeeping, not something I was good at in my apartment. I also noticed before going to sleep every night, he would put on the movie *Sleepless in Seattle*. It had to be playing every single night. I thought it was odd, but I didn't say anything to him. I loved him, and I looked past Blake's little quirks.

He lived in a three-bedroom apartment in Kapolei with a few friends. They were nice ladies and I really liked them. There was just one photo on the fridge that bugged me every time I saw it. It was a snap shot of all three of them mooning the camera. He finally moved the picture to the side of the fridge because I told him it bothered me to see that every time I came over to his place.

Blake came to church with me every Sunday. He even raised his hands in worship and praised God. He loved God. I couldn't believe I had become so lucky. He was handsome and smart, owned his own business, loved God, and loved me! I was happy. I wasn't taking on as many clients because I wanted to be with Blake all the time, and my work suffered because of it. I lived in Waikīkī, and he lived in Kapolei which was a minimum forty-five-minute drive each way if there were no traffic. Every day after work he had me drive to his place to hang out with him. I did so, but it was a lot of driving.

Blake loved to go out to eat, and we would do so all the time. Blake would order two plates of food and eat all of it himself! I couldn't believe how much he could scarf down. I could barely eat my cheeseburger and fries, while he would order three burgers and two baskets of fries, and eat it all, plus drink a super-sized soda! Yet, he was skinny as a rail. I always wondered how he stayed so thin. When we went out to a restaurant, most of the time Blake made an excuse that he had forgotten his wallet and asked if I could pick up the check. It started to become a problem. It just seemed like I was paying for most of our outings and I couldn't afford it. I started thinking it was much too expensive for me to have a boyfriend! I wanted to get rid of my debt, not accumulate it, but here I was using my credit card for nights out with Blake and digging myself deeper into a hole. I didn't ever say anything to him, but it was weighing heavily on me – the long drives, picking up food, expensive gas, and not working much. I had no money and I was exhausted from it all. After a few months together, we started arguing about money. In his construction business, he made thousands of dollars a month, yet I was spending the little money I had on our outings.

He told me he was helping a friend of his who lived in the mainland. He was paying her college tuition. I thought that was nice of him, but in the next sentence he told me he paid her the money, but then he didn't have enough rent and asked me to help him pay his rent! I was very frustrated from loaning Blake money and worrying about my own rent. One time after he paid his friend's school tuition, she came out to visit him! I thought it was funny that she thanked him for sending her money for her ticket! We all met at a Waikiki restaurant called Duke's. The restaurant had a great atmosphere along with a live band and good food. This place was right on the beach. It was a popular hangout for locals and tourists alike.

Blake's friend who flew out to see him was dressed up in a cowgirl outfit, all decked out in a pretty ranch style dress with tall boots and a cowgirl hat. She said to Blake right in front of me, "I know you love cowgirls," and she gave him a great big smile. He grinned, and I could tell he loved the attention she was giving him. I just looked on in shock. She was singing country songs along with the live band, and she intentionally directed her singing right to MY boyfriend! She was singing in a silly country accent, and I had a feeling she requested the songs he liked. She also ordered a triple burger with double fries, HIS favorite! Then she ate everything pig-like as she rolled her eyes and made silly chomping noises. Blake couldn't stop laughing at how goofy she was. He was soaking in all the attention she gave him. I just stood there looking in at this sick act between these two. To anyone around us, it probably looked like we were all having fun laughing together, but inside, my heart was breaking in two as Blake's focus was 100% on her. I could have walked away, and he wouldn't have even noticed.

She told Blake she wanted to see him alone next time. I wasn't having it! I knew those two were going to be trouble together, and I didn't trust him or her. She was a very pretty woman, and I do admit I was a bit jealous of the energy I felt between them. My heart hurt. It felt like someone had pushed their fist into my chest, pulled out my throbbing heart, and threw it on the ground to stomp on it! I loved this man, but at this point, I started questioning our relationship.

That night as Blake was dropping me off at home, I told him the situation made me feel awkward and uncomfortable, but he didn't understand why I was so upset. Maybe I was being a little over sensitive about the whole thing. I had been hurt in the past and probably read more into this situation than I needed. I pushed my feelings aside and focused on Blake and me and our relationship. His friend left a few days later; she took an earlier flight home since he wouldn't see her. Blake emphasized again that he loved me so much that he wouldn't go see his good friend. I was relieved. My thoughts were running wild, and I felt I just needed to grow up and be more mature.

After that situation, I noticed more strange behavior taking place with my boyfriend. When he would see big-breasted women, he would stare at them with his large round eyes and blurt out, "GOOD NIGHT!" I didn't quite get it at first. When it became a habit where big-breasted women were around, I started getting the feeling he was talking about their upper proportions, especially after a large breasted woman was jogging by us and he stared after her and said, "Good night!" It didn't make me feel good at all.

Many times, he would yell at me calling me "Sheniqua." One time I asked him what "Sheniqua" meant. He said he had a girlfriend whose friend Sheniqua would tag along with them. The friend was slow when they would walk, and she couldn't keep up with them. He told me I was slow too and had to keep up with him. I felt belittled, but I tried to step it up and walk faster when we were out on the town.

Blake liked to choose an outfit I would wear when we would go out. He would come pick me up to go eat at a restaurant, but if I came out of my place in an outfit he didn't like, he would tell me to go back in and change to a better outfit. Sometimes he would tell me exactly what to wear. I did what I was told. I was not into fashion clothes like him, and I didn't have money to buy expensive name brand outfits. I trusted that he knew what outfits on me looked good together. I think it bugged him that I didn't have the newest and most expensive brand of clothing. I loved to shop for discounted clothing at the thrift stores. I didn't want to pay full price for anything! Blake was the opposite. He would go to Banana Republic to pick out a $150.00 shirt. He had the right to do that because he made thousands of dollars more than I did a month, so he could spend what he wanted on clothes. For me, I didn't have a fashionable sense at all, and it agitated him. I think he wanted a certain facade being out on the town, and I didn't fit that "perfect-couple" description. After a short time together, I realized he wanted to change me and how I dressed myself, among other characteristics I had.

Blake let me know my apartment was a pigsty every time he came over, which was not very often. He didn't like spending any time at my apartment, so he would sit in the car and wait for me. He said my place was a gross and disgusting hole in the wall. I liked it. It was a cute little place with cheap rent, half a block from the ocean for $625.00 a month in Hawaii, not a bad deal for a one-bedroom apartment.

I loved Bath and Body Works lotions. After a hot shower, I would lather my body in scented lotions, but Blake didn't like the smelly lotions. Every time I saw him, he would tell me to wash off the stinky smell. I would have to go back inside my apartment and shower again, so the "stink" was gone. I also liked wearing colorful sparkles by my eyes because it made me feel pretty, but Blake said that it was too childish, and it wasn't something adult women do. I stopped wearing the pretty sparkles. In a way, Blake was molding and sculpting me into the woman he wanted me to be! He broke my confidence and my spirit. When we would be out eating, he sat next to me and would whisper in my ear not to eat too much because I was getting fat. He was right. I wasn't walking as many dogs anymore or cleaning as many houses because he always wanted to be with me, so I had gained a little weight. He was justified in saying I needed to lose some weight. He told me over and over that I was fat.

One day Blake and I were at the mall. He had started to buy me cute, sassy outfits because the clothes I had in my closet were considered ugly and were not brand names. On this particular day, I was shopping for board shorts and a tank top, and Blake was going to buy them for me. In the changing room, I tried on a small pair of board shorts which fit me perfectly. Over and over Blake would tell me I was fat. I believed every word he said, so even though these board shorts were a small size three, I looked in the mirror and still I saw a fat girl looking back at me. He bought me the shorts and a matching top for the beach, and we went on with our day.

One day as Blake was driving he said, "Women can't drive, and they are reckless!" I disagreed with him. I was a little bit offended because I was an excellent driver who had never been in an accident that I caused. As soon as I told him so, he went off like a monster, yelling and telling me I didn't know what I was talking about. I was stressed out that we were fighting, and suddenly I felt my throat close-up and something in my throat snap. I couldn't breathe. I started hyperventilating and tried to cry, but nothing came out. It felt like time was passing slowly. My chest hurt. I thought this must be a heart attack. I put my hands on my chest and held them close to my heart. Tears streamed down my cheeks. I still could barely breathe. I was trying hard to take a breath. I thought I was going to die right then and there. Blake just kept on yelling at me, even as I clutched my heart and coughed and sputtered trying to breathe. A lump in my throat felt like it was growing. I prayed, "Lord, I don't know what's going on, please take this from me." I felt I might pass out. Blake had to pull over and he asked me what was wrong. I must have been turning blue.

Finally, his anger dissipated and then he tried to calm me down. I wanted to go to the ER, but I didn't have any health insurance. I prayed I wouldn't pass out and that I would be okay. Finally, I felt the lump go away, and I could breathe again. I realized later I had my first panic attack. I had many more panic attacks since then. Never in my life had I had a panic attack until this one. Our fights escalated from then on. We would fight, and I would have panic attacks. Many times, I questioned myself. I wondered what I was doing wrong. I realized I could never do anything right with Blake.

This is an excerpt from my journal on an evening that Blake said we should take a break:

"Tonight, I can take a shower and use my scented body wash, why? Because you are not around to complain how it stinks. I can slather my favorite lotion on my body and add sparkles to my face and not worry about you saying I smell disgusting and look childish. I can wash my hair in any shampoo without a critic to criticize. Today I can bask in my favorite scent. I can relax in my messy room and not worry about you telling me it looks like a pigsty. I can trip over my own feet and not have you laugh hysterically at me and say I am "such a blonde." I can screw up royally tonight in everything I do and not have you look down on me saying, "Only you, Becka!" Tonight, I am free to do what I want to do, and I want to be me!"

Bigger things were happening in our relationship. A pain was festering deep in my heart and soul. Every time we were together, I was careful what I did and said. I stopped eating so I could be thin enough for Blake. I ate like a bird, picking at my food. Maybe that would make him happy. I tiptoed around him and hoped that I would be everything he wanted me to be. I loved him and wanted him to love me back. I was scared I was losing him. I dressed like he wanted, had my hair up as he liked, and stopped wearing lotions except for the one he bought for me. Yet, our relationship was still falling apart. I was never good enough for him. I felt like I was walking on egg shells every time we were together. Anything could set him off. I tried hard to fix our relationship, but it didn't work, and I had no idea how to make things better.

After some time, I needed space, so I took a few days apart from him. I was in my little one-bedroom apartment staring at the four white walls and I fell to my knees and started crying. Thoughts just poured from my head about this relationship I was in. Then I started to wail! I cried so loudly and for so long, that after a while, I couldn't believe tears were still pouring out of my eyes! When I finally calmed down, I prayed,

"Lord, please tell me what is going on. Are you blessing this relationship or not? Tell me what to do." I waited for God's response.

God spoke audibly to me. I heard His voice in my ear:

"Child, I will not bless this relationship."

I sat up and my eyes shot open! I couldn't believe God was not going to bless this relationship. I stayed in prayer. Closing my eyes again, I asked,

"Lord, I love this man. I thought he was the one for me, but if you are not going to bless this relationship, I don't know

how to break up with him. I love him too much. I don't think I could break up with him. If you want us to break up, then YOU break us up, Lord. I don't have the heart to do it myself."

God was quiet. I cried for a long time and then picked myself up off the floor and washed my face. I knew God's answer was *"No"* to this relationship which meant if I chose to stay with Blake, I would be disobeying God, but if I broke it off with Blake, God would bless me. What would be my decision? I loved God, I loved Blake, whom do I love more... God, of course! I knew what had to happen. God knew where I stood, and I would choose Him, my Heavenly Father. Still, I didn't have the strength to break up with my boyfriend.

God gave me a comforting verse: ***And we know that all things work together for good to them that love God, to them who are the called according to His purpose. Romans 8:28*** God also reminded me of this verse: ***I can do all things through Christ who strengthens me. Philippians 4:13***

I went to bed comforted by God's words and for the first time in many months, I slept well and felt a peace flood over me. The next day Blake called and asked me to come over after work. I said okay. I went through my work day trying not to think much about what might happen. I knew God "had my back" and He gave me another verse: ***If God is for us who can be against us. Romans 8:31***

It made me smile. I needed that encouragement. I knew God was with me throughout my day. After work, I went to see Blake. As soon as I arrived, Blake said I should sit down because we needed to talk. I sat in anticipation with my hands folded in my lap. He said, "Becka, we have been fighting a lot. We just can't seem to get along." I nodded. He added, "I don't know how to say this, but I think we should stop seeing each other." I looked at him in shock, not because he broke up with me but because it was actually happening, and I knew God had put it in Blake's heart to break us up. I sat there and blurted out, "I agree, we should break up!" He said, "So, that's it." I confirmed, "Yes, that's it." That was the end of the conversation. It was the easiest break up I ever had. Usually there would be screaming or fighting, but not this time. God intervened, and I couldn't believe the break up was that easy!

It may have seemed a simple break up for me, but what came next was not. I cried and cried for months. I was so broken after Blake was gone that I didn't know what to do. My boyfriend had showed me how to dress, how to act, how to look, how to smell, how to be ME! Now that he didn't tell me what to do, I didn't know how to be me!

I prayed constantly, and God was right there with me. When I cried, God held me closely. I could feel His arms wrapped around me, but I won't lie, the break up still hurt, and it was painful to walk away from someone I had loved so much.

After the break up, I was falling into a deep dark depression. I never wanted to go anywhere or do anything. I lost my ability as a "social butterfly." Instead, I felt like a hermit, hiding from the world. I slept a great deal and moped around my apartment. I didn't even have the energy to pull in new clients for my business. I felt I had been such a fun-loving person with many friends before I met Blake, and now I was like an empty shell of a human being. I had lost my spark, and I prayed God would give me my joy back. I was in constant fear of how people would judge me. My anxiety took hold and controlled me. I was so worried about what people thought of how I dressed and how I looked. My hair, was it in or out of place? Did lotions I wear stink? I could hear Blake's voice in my ear telling me I am fat, that I stink, that I am clumsy, that I'm so slow, that my hair is out of place, that my clothes are all outdated and not in style. I tried to fit in, but I didn't know how to act around people anymore. I couldn't be around more than a few people without having major anxiety. I became a loner. I prayed constantly. The upside to this situation was my relationship with God was slowly re-building and growing stronger every day.

After a few months, God opened my eyes to how the relationship had been so unhealthy. I couldn't believe how blind I was to Blake's belittling. God started revealing in my prayer time with Him that this had been a volatile and abusive relationship. I didn't see it when I was in the relationship. The panic attacks stayed with me for many years to come. Whenever I was extremely stressed or couldn't handle a situation well, I would have another panic attack. It was a long road to recovery.

I had two close friends who were twin sisters. They were very happy when I finally walked away from this volatile relationship. They had known all along that it was unhealthy. My girlfriends helped support me through this very hard time. Their friendship meant the world to me. I started to heal. I did not realize how toxic the relationship had been until I was far away from it for many months. There was finally a day when I woke up and didn't even think about Blake. That was the day I felt free to be me. I had some healing to do and God was my rock and I knew He was healing my wounds. It got better from that day on.

A year later, Blake showed up at my door, and we chatted a bit in the doorway. He told me he broke up with his girlfriend, and then right there on the spot, he proposed to me. I was surprised and stood in the doorway a bit shocked. After everything we had been through, why this? Why now? He said if I say no, he would ask his ex to marry him. I asked him, "So your girlfriend is second best?" I told Blake to go back to his girlfriend and said goodbye to him for good. Then I shut the door.

Chapter 20

God Heal Me!

(DISCRECTION ADVISED FOR MEN OR THE WEAK STOMACHED)

I went to the doctor about a problem I was having. The doctor diagnosed me with "menorrhagia." The name sounded bad, and to me, it meant many years of suffering. Menorrhagia meant abnormally heavy menstrual bleeding. I had to deal with eight-to-ten days a month of heavy bleeding since I was in my twenties. I had anemic issues, I was tired all the time, and I consistently had to take iron supplements plus liquid iron formula just to make it through the day.

At this time in my life, I was also donating blood to the Red Cross. They didn't pay me anything, but it saved three lives for every pint I donated, and they gave out delicious snacks before I would leave. I had a blood type that anyone could use, and they wanted it, so they would call me every six weeks and tell me it was time to donate blood. Sometimes my iron would be too low, and I couldn't give blood and would have to work on increasing my iron intake, which all depended on my cycle.

It was a Friday morning when I started my period. I thought it was a bit early but didn't think much about it. I went about my day, but there was so much excessive bleeding that I had to cancel my appointments with my clients. I couldn't go anywhere without using a bathroom every half hour or so. I went home to rest for the day. It worsened. By day two, it was even worse. I drank water and had soup. I thought maybe I was getting sick or my hormones were off. In any case, I slept on and off for sixteen hours. I was exhausted. Day three was even worse, and by day four I looked in the mirror, and I was so pale that I was white as a sheet! I drove myself to a little Waikiki clinic that took walk-in patients who had no insurance, which included me.

I sat and waited in a busy waiting room, then asked to sit in a private room because of my situation. They were helpful and found a place for me that was more private. When a female doctor was able to see me, I told her that in the one hour that I waited, I had gone through five super tampons and two large pads. She was alarmed. She asked me some questions as she checked my eyes, mouth, and nose. She took my vitals and blood pressure, then she said she was calling an ambulance to take me to the ER! I knew an ambulance would cost me $500.00 or more, so I told her I could drive myself to the hospital. She grabbed my hand, looked me in the eyes, and said, "Becka, you have lost too much blood, your vitals are lower than they should be, and you are white as a sheet. I am afraid you might pass out. You could die! Now either you find a ride to the ER, or I will call an ambulance." I decided to call my friend Ava, who came to pick me up and drive me to the hospital.

At the hospital the doctor said I had lost three pints of blood, so they started an IV drip. They were preparing to give me at least two pints of blood. I was so scared! I didn't want someone else's blood. Ava's twin sister Aria showed up and both stood by my side. Each sister took one of my hands as they began praying over me. I don't remember much of anything after that. I'm not sure if I passed out, but I remember sleeping for a few hours after the blood transfusion. When I awoke, the doctor said the transfusion went well and I could go home. They only had to give me one pint of blood because my vitals jumped back so quickly, praise God. I knew it was Ava's and Aria's prayers that helped. God was with me.

The doctor said I needed to make an appointment to find out what was going on with my uterus. I made an appointment with a female doctor who had me lie down on a bed, put my legs up, and she basically did a very uncomfortable pap smear - something all women could agree is not fun. The doctor found an unusually large polyp on my uterus and said I had endometriosis. I asked if she could take the polyp out. "No," she said, "It is fairly large, and it is attached to the uterus. For safely, it can only be surgically removed."

The only thing going through my mind was how much all this was going to cost. I had no health insurance. It had been over fifteen years since I had any health insurance. None of the doctor visits or any surgery would be covered. I left there feeling down. I prayed and asked God to walk through this with me in this very scary time. I felt His peace and knew He was there with me, which was a great comfort.

I made an appointment with another doctor who checked my condition and said she could not touch the polyp. It was on the uterus lining and in a spot that if it were burned off, it could injure the tissue and complications could arise. I could bleed to death! She gave me a number to call an ER doctor. At least if I were at the ER, they could rush me into surgery if they needed to do so. I called the ER, but they said they wouldn't touch it after I described what was going on. I felt like I was on a hamster wheel, just going around and around. My head was spinning. For months, I called around trying to find a doctor that could help me, but it was to no avail.

At the same time, I attended church every Sunday morning and diligently went to the prayer table to have the ladies pray about my health issue. They were so faithful to pray for me. I was bleeding constantly, and it just would not stop! I was taking large amounts of iron and still searching for a doctor that could help me. Bills were piling up in my mailbox. The one night at the hospital was $6,000. Luckily, because I was a blood donor, they had taken $2000.00 off my bill, but it was still

$6,000 plus all the extra bills for lab fees, doctor fees, and all the appointments I had made.

The good news was my relationship with God was strengthening, and I was walking so closely to Him that I could hear Him on everything in my life, except for this health issue, but I still had faith that He had this! I prayed to God and asked His will in my life. I asked that He use me through this hard time. I thought of the story in the Bible of the lady who bled consistently for twelve years straight. I felt like I was she! In the story, Jesus was walking by her when she reached out with her hand and touched the cloth on His robe and He felt power leave Him. He turned around and asked, "Who touched my clothes?" She replied, "I did." He responded, "You are healed."

This is the actual scripture:

Mark 5:25-34, "Now a certain woman had a flow of blood for twelve years and had suffered many things from many physicians. She had spent all that she had and was no better, but rather grew worse. When she heard about Jesus, she came behind Him in the crowd and touched His garment. For she said, "If only I may touch His clothes, I shall be made well." Immediately the fountain of her blood was dried up, and she felt in her body that she was healed of the affliction. And Jesus, immediately knowing in Himself that power had gone out of Him, turned around in the crowd and said, "Who touched my clothes?" But His disciples said to Him, "You see the multitude thronging you, and you say, 'Who touched me?' And He looked around to see her who had done this thing. But the woman, fearing and trembling, knowing what had happened to her, came and fell down before Him and told Him the whole truth. And He said to her, Daughter, your faith has made you well. Go in peace and be healed of your affliction."

I was inspired by the story and knew without a shadow of doubt that God would heal me, not in my time, but in His perfect timing. I waited patiently, but I never hesitated to ask for prayers from anyone. The more prayer warriors, the better! I went to Monday night prayer meetings, where I had a group of people pray over me. A woman praying God's healing over my health asked if I had received any gifts recently. I thought about it, and God brought to my mind a gift someone had made and given me. I told the prayer warrior about the gift I received, and she said I would need to break it. I felt God press on my heart the same thing, to break a curse that was attached to the gift. I went home, grabbed the material item and a hammer, walked down to the beach, and broke the item into a dozen pieces. I never even thought something evil could attach to material possessions, but spiritual warfare was strong, and I knew from then on to be more careful. I felt God press on my heart that this was the right thing to do, and after "the gift" was discarded, I felt much better. I prayed asking God to heal me.

A few days later, I was talking to a lady at the doctor's office who said she knew a doctor that could help me. He was always booked up, but maybe I could get in to see him. I called and made an appointment, but it was a two-month wait. I told them it was "urgent" to help with my bleeding disorder. I asked if they would call me if there was a cancellation for me to come in earlier. It was a few weeks later that the doctor had a cancellation, so I was able to see him sooner.

Here I was, in the doctor's office again. I was so tired of all the appointments I had made and doctors I had to see. It was another pap smear with the doctor and nurse in the room. The doctor told me that I would probably need a hysterectomy. I didn't want a hysterectomy, granted I may not want children, but a hysterectomy was a big decision. I panicked. I asked if I could think about it. He said the bleeding would not stop until they do surgery on me. I was disappointed. I went home crying and knelt down and asked God what was going on. God didn't say anything, but I felt His presence and He pressed on my heart that it would be okay. He would not leave my side.

I made plans to have a hysterectomy. They told me to take pain medication they prescribed the day of the appointment because at the pre-surgery visit they would take some uterus tissue for lab work before the actual surgery. I didn't have insurance, so it would cost me $35,000 cash for surgery. I had to take out a loan. My bank wrote me a check and had it ready for me. I told them I would pick it up after my pre-surgery appointment. I kept in prayer.

"Lord, if this is what You want for my life, that's okay, but it seems like a lot of money to throw at a doctor. If you heal me Lord, there is so much more I could do for Your kingdom than the doctors who receive the money." I felt a peace from God.

I kept asking for prayer at church. One lady, Tina, who had been praying for me since the beginning, sat me down away from the others and asked me, "Could you be living a sinful life that is bringing this on?" I was taken aback by her comment. I told her, "No, of course not. I have never been closer to God than I am now. God has been walking with me through this hard time." I left after prayer, but her comment bothered me greatly, and I went home to pray about it. God gave me much joy in my heart. I knew He was going to do something big. I just didn't know what it was or when it would happen, but I knew God would reveal it to me soon and it would be a witness to others, all for His glory. It had been ten months since the day I had almost died. I sensed the time was near.

I was back in the doctor's office. It was the pre-surgery date, and I was to have them take samples of my uterus. I was lying on the table as the doctor was checking me out, and he asked, "Did you take that pain pill this morning?" I said, "I completely forgot. I am so sorry." He walked over to the papers he had on me. He was reading the previous doctor's notes when he said, "Well, then I have good news for you. I can go in and cut the polyp out with scissors. If you had taken the medication we prescribed, that would have made your blood thinner, and you could bleed too much. We wouldn't have been able to do it, but since you forgot the pill, we can go ahead and snip it off." "Wait, WHAT???" I said in shock. "You mean to tell me that you can just snip the polyp off and it will be gone forever, and the bleeding will finally stop?" He said, "That's what I'm saying." He smiled big as if he were my hero... he was my hero! I asked, "Will it hurt?" He laughed, "Not like the pain that comes with a hysterectomy. You will feel a tiny pinch and that is it."

He said, "Let me know when you are ready." I had to think a moment as so many thoughts were going through my head.

GOD HEALED ME! WOW!

I said, "Okay, I'm ready." He replied, "Already done." I was in shock! I didn't even feel it! I sat up on the clinic bed and asked, "But I don't get it, how come the nine doctors before you wouldn't touch it, but you went in and just snipped it off and it's done?" He responded, "Looking back on your records, it was a large polyp, but it has shrunk to such a small size that it was easy to just snip off." He went on, "I don't know how that happened." I replied, "I know how, God healed me!" I had the biggest smile on my face. He smiled too and said, "So I guess I can cancel your surgery. You won't be needing that anymore." I thanked him and left. I was "walking on cloud nine" all the way to my car! I was so happy! The first thing I did was to call my best friend Ava and tell her the good news that God had healed me! I was elated! I knew God was going to do something big, but not this big! God was so faithful!

I felt great and I went to the beach to get some sun. I was at peace. I called my bank and told them I didn't need the check. I shared with them how God healed me. That next Sunday at church, I thanked all the ladies for their prayers because God healed me! Everyone was overjoyed and praising God. Tina, who doubted, smiled, but had nothing to say to me. I prayed this was a testimony to her that God is faithful, and He heals! God always came through for me. All glory to God for perfect healing!

Be not conformed to this world, but be transformed by the renewing of your mind, that you may prove what is that good and acceptable and perfect will of God. Romans 12:2

Chapter 21

On the Right Road

After my relationship with Blake was over, I focused on rebuilding my life. I had friends, my business was going well, and I felt life was good. My pet sitting business became a full-time job, so I was very busy. It was my first year that I was in a different tax bracket than ever before, but when tax time came around, I realized the IRS took so much more in taxes for being in that bracket. Yet, it felt good to make a large income and I loved the work I did. I was piling up twenty-dollar bills in an envelope, and it felt good. I stuck the large envelope full of money under my mattress. God was blessing me.

My best friend Ava was the nicest girl I had ever met. She didn't judge me, never said a harsh word to anyone, and was always positive. Ava was single, and her twin sister Aria was married. I would have thought twins would be so much alike, but even though they were very close and lived together, they were still very different. Ava was a social butterfly who liked shopping and meeting people. She also loved the beach. She was fun to be around. Aria, her sister, was more on the shy side. The three of them lived in a townhome by the beach in Hawaii Kai. Sometimes between pet sitting jobs, I would stop by to say hi to the twins or Ava and I would meet at the mall to walk around and pick up a Starbucks coffee.

I started hanging out at the beach more often, and it felt great. There was something about swimming in the ocean that brought me peace. God told me once when I was swimming, that the water is where He would cleanse me and wash away my sins. When I was swimming, I would pray to God, singing and praising Him, thanking Him for everything in my life. I felt renewed and rejuvenated, ready for my day. It brought a whole new meaning to swimming in the ocean for me.

Ava loved meeting me at the beach, and we would chit chat about life while catching some rays and then jump into the water to cool off. She was my favorite person to talk to and I loved her. She was real, not like some women who talked a "good talk" but were as fake as they come. She loved the Lord with all her heart. Sometimes she would visit my church. Then after service, we would go to the Farmer's Market or drive around town to see what fun things there were to do.

Ava's favorite thing to do was shopping. I really wasn't into it, but I would go with her and help her pick out clothes or a gift for a friend. She had a heart of gold who always found trinkets to buy for her friends. I loved that she had such a big heart. Ava was a beautiful, tall, skinny, size-one blonde woman that everyone noticed when she would walk into a crowded room. The twins looked like the live version of a perfect Barbie doll, but Ava really put on the makeup, and it brought out her features even more. Whenever I was with Ava, guys would trip over themselves staring at her, fawning over her every move, and trying to get her number. I always thought it was the funniest thing. They never noticed me, but then I didn't wear make-up or look like her in the least. I would have my hair up in a pony tail and wear a ratty tank top with board shorts most of the time because I was always ready for the beach! I didn't care if guys looked at me or not. I wasn't interested in the dating scene at all. I loved my life and was content right where I was.

I had a client named Adam who I pet sat his two small dogs for many years. He was a nice guy, and we became good friends. He eventually moved to Kauai for work. One time, Ava and I decided to visit him. I loved Kauai with its cascading mountains and gigantic waterfalls, beautiful hikes into lush forests of bamboo trees and thick brush, many black sand beaches, and one secluded green sand beach. The island was small but beautiful. It rained a great deal on Kauai, and everything was in full bloom almost all year round. It was a great island for avid hikers. It was also considered the most romantic island for a couple in love to have a wedding and spend their honeymoon together. Kauai is a one-of-a-kind island.

Adam showed Ava and me around the island, and it was fun to see the beauty of Kauai. There were huge caverns that looked similar to the Grand Canyon, but it is the Waimea Canyon at the state park. The walls of the canyon were so colorful. There were breathtaking views of the deep canyons that go on for many miles with trails twisting and winding, and little billy goats on tiny ledges on the side of the canyon. We could hear the billy goats from a distance as their voices echoed off the canyon walls. I could see God's handiwork everywhere I looked. We saw great big sea turtles sunning themselves. We picked up sea shells along the shoreline as the sun beat down on the black sand. It was the perfect day! Adam had a random passerby take a photo of us three together with the spectacular mountains behind us. "Click," it was the perfect photo keepsake and a great weekend getaway with our Kauai friend.

I flew to the outer islands as much as possible. Island hopping for the weekend was always a nice treat. Maui was my favorite island to visit for so many reasons. I went to Maui many times by myself. I loved Lahaina which had so many fun activities to do. There were craft shows, gift shops, restaurants with great food to eat, and lots of entertainment. Lahaina was always a fun place to meet good people too! Every time I visited there, I always went to my favorite coffee shop where I would pick up a Chai Tea Latte. Then I would drive to Kaanapali, which was only minutes away from Lahaina. There was a long stretch of beautiful beach to walk on, the ocean was bright blue in which to take a dip, and there were numerous restaurants and shops to keep any tourist happy.

My very favorite thing to do in Kaanapali was visit the most unique hotel. This wasn't any ordinary hotel. It had the most beautiful pool! There was a long, rickety bridge to cross over the pool. Once I was on the other side of the bridge, a large waterfall splashed into the pool and gave the feeling of tranquility. I would jump in and feel the cold, brisk water hit my face. I swam under the waterfall which opened into a large underneath cavern. There was a small bar on a little island in the middle of this cavern. I would order a soft drink from the bartender and sit on the stool with my feet dangling in the water. After drinking my soda, I would swim under the waterfall again and see the bright blue sky above me. With the sun beating on my face, I would swim the back stroke and float in the water awhile before pulling myself out of the pool to lie on a beach chair to catch some rays.

Years before I had been in Maui with a boyfriend and I showed him spectacular views and amenities of my favorite hotel. We swam in the pool and under the waterfall, then sat on a stool at the secluded tiki hut sipping on coconut water right out the coconut. Then we jumped back into the pool and he followed me to an underwater cave that opened into a small three-foot-wide by ten-foot-tall area. It looked like It was a large hallow tree trunk. This area was called the "kissing cave." I liked that it was so secret! Not many people knew about it. Years later, the hotel added mesh to the door of the cave. I would suspect too many people found out about this secret cave and there was too much kissing going on with no supervision!

Driving back to Lahaina, I was hungry for lunch. I wanted to eat at "Cheeseburger in Paradise," so I headed that way. It was a sit-down burger joint with delicious food, especially their cheeseburger and fry combo. I saw a homeless man leaning against the wall close to the restaurant entrance. As he was kicking a stone on the sidewalk, I noticed he had his hands in his pockets and looked like he was down on his luck. I stopped in front of him, grabbed his arm, and said, "Come with me; let's eat lunch together." He looked surprised but followed me into the restaurant.

We sat at a table overlooking the beautiful ocean. I asked, "What's your name?" He answered, "Larry." I replied, "What's going on, Larry?" He responded, "This is nice and all that you want to treat me to lunch, but you don't have to." I smiled, "Of course I do. God told me to take you to lunch and I am not going to disobey God, so here we are." He stared at me for a moment. The waitress came over and asked what we were having. He ordered a bacon deluxe cheeseburger and a double helping of fries. I said I would have the same.

I looked Larry in the eyes and said, "God loves you! He loves you so much that He brought me in your path to share with you HOW MUCH He loves you." Larry started crying right there at the table! I thought he must have a rough life. My heart broke for him, and my emotions got the best of me. I started tearing up, but God reminded me at that moment to keep focused. I asked, "Larry, do you believe in God?" He replied,

"Yes," as tears fell down his cheeks. I said, "God wants you to know He is with you and you are not alone." He started crying even more. I prayed silently and asked God what to say. God said to me, *"Just wait."* I sat and waited. Larry told me his story about how he had a family, a house, and a nice car, but he had lost it all. He talked about how it felt to be homeless and lonely. Then he looked at me, and I really saw how bright blue his eyes were. He said, "I prayed this morning that God would bring me a friend and here you are." Tears continued to stream down his face. I tried to hold it together, but I teared up as well. I loved when God had me on these assignments where I could reach out to someone to share about the love of God. He said, "You are an angel, I just know it. I asked God to give me a friend, and here you are, having lunch with me and everything. How does that happen?" I replied, "With God, everything is possible!" He smiled and nodded in agreement as he said, "You got that right!" Our food came and we chit chatted. He seemed in better spirits after our initial talk, and I knew that God was touching his heart and giving him peace. I told Larry he was loved, and I prayed for him before I left.

So many people just need to know they are loved. God loves each and every one of us with an everlasting love. No matter who we are, God loves us ALL the same! If we could grasp the enormity of how much He loves us, we would fall down on our knees and cry out to Him in praise and worship.

For eight years, I lived on the outskirts of Waikiki, in a small, drab, cheap apartment, but it was mine and I loved it. My apartment was in the best location. I had a 7-11 across the street if I wanted an iced coffee or a pint of ice cream. Ala Moana Shopping Mall was the biggest mall in Honolulu, and it was directly across from my apartment. I lived half a block from the beach where I would swim and watch the best sunrises. I felt blessed living so close to the ocean and thanked God for the many blessings.

In the early mornings, I would sit on the rock wall at the beach and pray, letting God know I was thinking of Him. Then I would jump in the cold, brisk water for a quick swim before heading out to walk dogs in the early mornings. Now that work was plentiful, I continued to save a bit more money. I was tithing at church, paying the many bills that came in from my previous health problem, and I made sure I put away twenty dollars here and there to save for emergencies. I was never much of a saver, but I wanted to become more responsible with my money.

One morning, I walked over to the 7-11 store for my favorite breakfast, Spam Musubi. There was a homeless man standing out front. I asked what his name was, and he replied "Pepper." I asked if he wanted something to eat. He said, "Yes." I had him walk into 7-11 with me to choose what food and drink he wanted. We then went to the register where I paid for the food and drinks. We stood in front of the store together while he ate a bite of his ham sandwich. I asked him if he needed prayer. He replied, "Yes!" Pepper had a seven-year-old girl that lived with his girlfriend and he wanted to see her but had no ride to the other side of the island. I was leaving for work right then and couldn't take him, but I prayed that God would help him find someone to drive him to see his little girl. After I prayed for Pepper, he thanked me, and I went on my way. I had faith that God would answer my prayer. I saw Pepper once more and asked how his daughter was. He said he was moving back in with his girlfriend and would be with his daughter again! He looked so happy. I told him I would keep him in prayer. God had answered my prayer! He is always faithful!

I loved when God gave me the urge to buy a homeless person lunch. It gave me the opportunity to pray for someone and shine God's light in their life. I may not have known what that person was going through, but my thoughts were; what a difference a little hope and light can do for someone who has nothing!

One time in Kaanapali, Maui, I was walking up a stairway that led to a shopping mall. I noticed a homeless guy who was sitting close to the bushes in front of the mall area. I sat down right next to him and said, "God is watching over you." He smiled and said, "I know He loves me. I talk to Him all the time." I was so encouraged. We chatted for a while. He was such a nice person. Before I had to leave, he said, "I was feeling down this morning and asked God to bring someone by that would show me they care. Thank you, Becka, for caring." I got choked up. With tears in my eyes, I hugged him and left. I walked away feeling a bit overwhelmed, and when I sat in my car, I just started sobbing.

I said, *"Lord, I have everything, and he has nothing. Am I really making a difference?"* God responded, *"You made a difference to him."* I wiped my tears and said, *"Okay, Lord, what's next?"* I call those my "God-moments."

One beautiful spring day, I decided to do a thorough cleaning of my apartment. I did this every few months to clean, organize, and donate items I didn't need to a shelter. I was cleaning under the kitchen sink and scrubbing the white cabinet walls. I had half my body under the cabinet to reach the corner with the scrubber when the bleach smell stung my nose and made my eyes water. I didn't realize I had taken such a big whiff of the bleach solution. I looked up under the sink where the pipes were, and there were papers sticking out of a wedged piece of wood. It was a great hiding place for something naughty. I pulled hard on the papers, and magazines fell out. I just stared at these dirty magazines lying on the floor; it was

Playboy at its worst! I was disgusted! Whoever lived in the apartment before me must have hidden them there.

      I picked up a folded piece of paper that fell from the hiding spot, and sitting on the floor, I thought about opening it. It looked like a written letter. I was about to delve into someone's personal life, and I didn't know if I should or not. Curiosity won me over, and I couldn't help but open it. I recognized the neat and perfect handwriting. It was a note written to some lady. I sat there for a moment, and all the sudden I couldn't breathe... as I read to the bottom, my heart sunk! The name was signed "Richard." That's when it hit me; I had been to this very apartment before! I finally realized who lived there before me. It was my psycho ex-boyfriend, Richard! The *Playboys* sprawled pathetically on the floor. I was so disgusted and grossed out, I didn't even want to touch them! I grabbed my garbage can, threw the magazines in it, walked down to the big dumpster outside, and threw them all away. When I walked back into the apartment, I fell to my knees and prayed,

      "Lord, why would you bring me to this apartment? You could have led me to any apartment, why this one? Why didn't you tell me until now?" I cried in desperation. I was so upset.

      I thought about all the abuse in that relationship. Memories just came rushing back into my head. My ex had controlled and manipulated me in such a way, I felt I needed to stay with him out of fear. I thought about the times he physically beat me, strangled me, and had almost killed me! At that very moment, anger rushed over me! All the cruel things Richard had ever said and done to me, I couldn't forget any of it. I had gone on with my life and stuffed the memories down pretending I was fine, but I really wasn't. I had moved on with a new boyfriend and pretended it was all okay, but I never really healed from the painful memories. The bruises had dissipated, but my heart was scarred with pain from what he did to me.

I sat on my knees and with my face to the carpet, I prayed out loud and then waited for God to speak to me.

After a few moments, God said, *"Let it go, child. I can heal your pain."* I didn't know how to let it go. How do you let something like this go? This man was evil in my eyes, and I was so angry at him! God said, *"Let me be the judge. Forgive him. Your heart needs to heal."* I tried, but I didn't know how. For years I had carried this pain and anger I had toward this guy, but I knew I had to let it go. When I finally did forgive Richard, I was no longer angry, and I didn't even think twice about him. My heart started to heal, and I felt free! Praising God for healing!

Right after that incident, I asked the pastor of my church to anoint my apartment to cast any bad spirits out. I also needed peace of mind after this ordeal. The pastor came over with his son and anointed the apartment with oil as he read Psalm 91 from the Bible. He also prayed over me. I felt much better. It was now God's home, and nothing was going to come between God and me*! I love Psalm 91 which is the chapter for protection!*

I had a neighbor who lived right next door. Julia was a sweet, older Asian lady who loved the Lord with all her heart. I thought it was amazing that God had her living right next door! We became very close. A few times a week we would bring out chairs and a little table and sit and chat in the breezeway. We looked out over the many buildings in Waikiki and watched the "busyness" of life as we snacked on chips and cut-up apples and talked about what was going on in our lives. She was an insightful woman who encouraged me in my walk with the Lord. What an answer to prayer!

My first Christmas at the new apartment, I bought strands of colored lights and asked all my neighbors if they wouldn't mind if I put them on the railing outside. None of my neighbors seemed to mind. I loved Christmas time, and I wanted the apartment complex to look festive. I wrapped the entire railing with one-hundred-twenty-feet of colored lights that lit up the entire complex! I kept them up year-round, and they always made Julia and me smile at night when they were shining brightly. The tenants in nearby apartment buildings could see the lights as well. One neighbor who lived a few blocks away followed suit by putting red lights on their terrace and kept them up all year round! I would like to think my lighting had inspired the many neighbors around us. It reminded me how *God is always shining in dark places!*

Psalm 91:1-16 -- FOR PROTECTION
Whoever dwells in the shelter of the most High
will rest in the shadow of the Almighty.
I will say of the Lord, "He is my refuge and my fortress,
my God, in whom I trust."
Surely he will save you
from the fowler's snare
and from the deadly pestilence.
He will cover you with his feathers,
and under his wings you will find refuge;
his faithfulness will be your shield and rampart.
You will not fear the terror of night,
nor the arrow that flies by day,
nor the pestilence that stalks in the darkness,
nor the plague that destroys at midday.
A thousand may fall at your side,
ten thousand at your right hand,
but it will not come near you.
You will only observe with your eyes
and see the punishment of the wicked.
If you say, "The Lord is my refuge,"
and you make the most High your dwelling,
no harm will overtake you,
no disaster will come near your tent.
For He will command his angels concerning you
to guard you in all your ways;
they will lift you up in their hands,
so that you will not strike your foot against a stone.
You will tread on the lion and the cobra;
you will trample the great lion and the serpent.
"Because he loves me," says the Lord, "I will rescue him;
I will protect him, for he acknowledges My name.
He will call on me, and I will answer him;
I will be with him in trouble,
I will deliver him and honor him.
With long life I will satisfy him
and show him my salvation.

Chapter 22

My Pet-Sitting Business

The clients and pet names have been changed, as well as the movie star and show in which he played.

I moved to Hawaii in 1993 to be with my first boyfriend Ian. Ian and his friend Shane were co-owners of a salt water fish aquarium business. They picked the accounts they wanted, made their own hours, set their own prices, and they loved that their business was successful! Ian and Shane are the ones who truly inspired me to start my own business.

I thought what would I want to do in my own business? What was my passion? I loved dogs and cats! Sometimes I felt I loved them more than I loved people! Someday I hoped to have a houseful of animals. That would be my "happy place." However, at this time in my life, I lived in a place where I couldn't have any pets at all. I came up with the idea to start pet sitting because I wanted to be around animals all the time. The business would have no start-up costs! I could advertise for clients, build up my clientele, and be paid for watching their pets. It would be a dream come true. Once I thought of making it a business, I wanted it so badly that I started pet sitting that very week! Talk about motivation!

I lived close to a large dog park by Diamond Head, so I wrote on a 3x5 card that I was a pet sitter who was available to walk dogs daily. I posted it on the board, hoping someone would call me. A few days later a guy named Samuel called to say their family dog needed to be walked every morning, seven days a week, one hour a day. I made an appointment to meet Samuel. He worked for the owner of the home. I had a short interview, and then it was time to meet Benji who was a big, beautiful, male German Shepherd. I loved the dog instantly! How lucky was I to walk this dog every day? I gave my new client a price cheaper than the average pet sitter since I was new at the business and had no references. He said I could start Monday. I was so excited! My very first client!

First thing Monday morning, I was ready for my dog walk. My client lived on the backside of Diamond Head Crater which used to be an active volcano that had not erupted in one hundred fifty thousand years. Now, it was a hiking trail up to the summit, and at the highest peak of the volcano was an open view that stretched into the distance in all directions. The view was stunning – the mountains and ocean as well as how small the cars appeared like little ants moving along the road below! From the peak of the volcano, I would look down at the treacherous hike. It looked grueling to say the least, but it had to be hiked. I had been up and down this mountain many times with friends. It was good exercise, and the aerial view was fantastic and well worth it!

I took Benji up the backside of this mountain where I found many paths going every which way. I never even knew that there were trails on this side of the crater. Every morning I would pick Benji up for our walk. He would whine in excitement when he heard me drive up in my car, and then we would venture out to see where each path would lead us.

After a few days of walking Benji, I met his owner, Tim Baker. When I met him, I shook his hand and said, "Glad to meet you." He was surprised I was so nonchalant when greeting him. I could see from his house and many nice cars that he was a rich guy, but from our first meet, I could tell he was a down-to-earth kind of guy.

He said, "Do you know who I am?" I said, "Yes, Tim Baker." He said, "Maybe it's before your time, but I used to be a movie star. "I said, "Really? What show were you on?" He replied, "I used to be on that old 50's Show, you know the one, *'Mandy Crack Corn'*." I said, "Oh, nice, I have never heard of it. I don't watch T.V." He chuckled and told me to take good care of his dog. I promised I would as I headed out the door on a long walk with Benji.

After the dog walk, when I arrived back home, I called my mom. "Hey, Mom," I said, "I have my first pet sitting client. I started walking a German Shepherd." She said, "Oh, good." I said, "My client's name is Tim Baker or something like that." Suddenly my mom screamed into the phone, "TIM BAKER? YOU MET TIM BAKER????" I told my mom to calm down; he was just a guy. She said, "No, you don't understand! I grew up watching his shows. I love him!" I had to laugh. She wanted to know everything about him. "Is he as nice as everyone says he is?" she asked. "Yes, Mom," I replied. "When you met him, what did he say, what did you say, tell me everything!" She was so excited. I was laughing. I told her it was a brief conversation, and Benji was ready for his walk, so I left after our initial introduction. Mom said she would love to meet him someday, and she planned to do so.

During our walk, sometimes Benji and I would run into homeless people that lived on the back side of the mountain we liked to hike. Some of the people walked around naked, and that was a bit uncomfortable for me. I would usually turn around and go back down the mountain, escaping as fast as I could! Benji and I explored many trails and different areas of Diamond Head. I loved this job, and I couldn't believe I was being paid to walk this beautiful dog. It was a dream come true!

One time, Benji and I walked down a path that turned into a long, winding road. It was my first time venturing this desolate road, and I had no idea where it would lead. I had Benji off his leash. He always stayed close, so I never had to worry about him running after a wild animal. As we walked this narrow road, Benji had his nose in the air, and I told him he could smell a tree or two, just don't go too far. He started walking over to a tree to mark his territory when out of nowhere, three men walked down the road from the opposite end. When Benji saw the men, he came back to my side and stood there waiting for the men to come closer. One guy asked what I was doing on the road. I told him my dog and I were just out for a walk. I didn't have a good feeling about the three men. The guy who said something to me was looking at the other two as if he wanted them to do something, but they were watching the dog.

As Benji's fur stood up on his back, he walked a few steps toward them and stopped. I had never seen him act like this toward anyone before. His tail went up and I could tell his body went on alert. A chill ran down my spine. I thought we better hightail it out of there. The guy asked me another question as he slowly took a few steps toward me. I told him I was late for a meeting and had to go. I said, "Let's go, Benji." He quickly followed me back down the road. I am sure something bad could have happened if I didn't have Benji with me. I could tell he was ready to protect me. Believe me, I never went down that road again!

A few weeks later, I was walking Benji in a small cul-de-sac, and out of the corner of my eye, I saw a portion of a brown fence move and heard a thump. At first, I didn't think much of it. I kept walking but within seconds, I heard a loud noise, "BAM!" Out of the fence charged a large, stocky dog who in seconds clamped down on Benji's neck and hung on! We were standing in the street, and I screamed my head off. I had a piercing scream. I tried to pull the pit bull off Benji, but nothing worked. As Benji was crying, the dog tried to clamp harder onto Buck's jugular.

I continued to scream for help, and two guys came running over with a hose. One guy sprayed the pit bull in the face with water, but it didn't bother the dog at all while the other guy used pepper spray on the pit bull's eyes, but the dog again, wasn't even fazed. He would not let go of Benji's neck! I was terrified Benji would die right in front of my eyes. One guy dropped the hose and as soon as he grabbed the dog's collar, he pulled him backward. It didn't help. He then tried to pull the two dogs apart, but the pit would not let go. Benji looked weak and lifeless as he lay in the middle of the street and whimpered softly.

I cried and pleaded with the men, "PLEASE HELP HIM, I DON'T WANT HIM TO DIE!!" In a split second, when the dog went in to get a better grip on Benji's jugular, the man yanked back with all his might and pulled the pit bull's jaws off his neck! I ran to look Benji over. His neck was bleeding, but he stood up right away and otherwise looked okay. I thanked the guys and walked Benji back to the house. I ran inside the doorway yelling for Samuel to help me. I told him what happened and apologized profusely. Samuel grabbed his car keys, placed Benji in the backseat of the car, and headed to the vet.

I didn't know if Benji was going to be okay. This may have been the end of pet sitting my favorite dog! I felt horrible, but there was nothing I could do except wait and hear from Samuel when he returned home. A few hours later, Samuel called and said Benji was going to be fine. I was so relieved! The vet recommended Benji rest a few days with the antibiotics he was on, and then I could start walking him again on Monday. I was thankful to those two guys who helped. If it weren't for them, my client's dog would not have made it. That next Monday, I burst into the front door and ran to hug Benji. He was so excited to see me, but he didn't want me to fawn over him;

he just wanted to go on his walk! I had to laugh, he was such a boy! We left the house and went on our way.

I began building up my clientele in the Diamond Head area. I walked and fed a little white poodle for a week while the owners were gone on a trip. I had a lady who wanted me to watch her six cats while she was out of town, and my client Tim referred me to his good friend down the street who had two German Shepherds that I shampooed weekly. I kept busy, but I wanted more clients. I asked my mom to make flyers for me to pass out to different neighborhoods. She did a wonderful job on the flyers and It worked! People started calling me more and more for pet sitting, and soon a business was born!

I also had started advertising in glass cases that were set up around the island at different shopping malls. Businesses could put their card or brochure in the glass case, and people walking through the mall would see the advertisement. I selected my favorite areas to advertise in. It cost me just $5.00 a month for each case. It brought lots of business my way!

After my mom heard I walked Tim Baker's dog, she wanted to visit me. I'm sure having her only child in Hawaii was also a reason to come visit! My Aunt Isabella wanted to visit as well, so they both flew to Hawaii to see me. We had a wonderful time in Waikiki shopping at all the cute trinket stores, driving around the island, and seeing the beautiful beaches. We had so much fun together.

One day, I told my mom and aunt I wanted to show them a secluded beach. Aunt Isabella asked, "Where?" I said, "In the Diamond Head area." She replied, "But we can just go back to the hotel and hang out at the pool." I suggested, "Let's check out the beach, and then we can go back to the hotel." Isabella replied, "Let's stay by the pool. It's so much better than getting sand in nooks and crannies that shouldn't get sandy." I almost laughed at that image. I had planned a surprise for them, and my plan wasn't working. I told my aunt it would mean a great deal if she came with my mom and me. She agreed to come, and we were off toward the beach for a big surprise.

As I drove toward Diamond Head, I suddenly turned into a driveway Isabella asked, "Where are we? (I think secretly my mom knew what I was up to since I could be unpredictable and loved surprises.) When we jumped out of the car, I took two little plants from the trunk and handed them to Mom and Isabella. They asked, "What are these for?" I replied, "You are meeting Tim Baker today. The plants are for him." They were both thrilled and acted like two young teenagers at a rock concert about to meet the band!

The housekeeper opened the door and we walked into the kitchen and then she showed us into the living room. We waited a moment, and then Tim walked out and greeted us. He was such a gentleman. Mom and Isabella had their picture taken with Tim, and they spent their time talking to him and seeing his beautiful house. I was excited for them to meet Tim, but I was especially excited for my mom to meet Benji whom I walked every single day. This dog was my pride and joy! Years later, when my grandma and her sister came to visit, they were also able to meet Tim as well. They were thrilled. Tim was so sweet to meet many of my family members throughout the years, and it meant a great deal to me.

A year after I started pet sitting, I was extremely busy walking dogs. I needed to raise my prices just a few dollars for the clients I had since the very beginning because of inflation. My newest clients had a higher price to match what other pet sitters charged already. When I talked to Tim about the price hike, he said he would not pay me any more than what he was already paying me. I asked him to think about it over the weekend, and he told me to do the same. After the weekend, I asked him if he had changed his mind. He answered, "No." I had to say good bye to Benji even though I wasn't asking for much, just a few dollars. I had clients who were willing to pay me twice as much to watch their dogs. It was hard to find a trustworthy pet sitter, and my clients knew they could trust me. There were many times I wondered if I should have stayed, even though I only made a few dollars a day; but at the end of the day, this was a business I was building, and I couldn't give such a big discount.

I had another client who owned five cats that I adored! Each one of them had different personalities. There was Bray, who was very old and half blind but sweet as pie. He was very shy, but he loved snuggling and soon he became my favorite. There was Tia, a kitten that looked like an itty-bitty tiger. There was Spunky, who was very adventurous and spunky! She was a curious cat that liked to get into mischief. Her brother Roary, also a kitten, liked to jump on the bookcase and push books to the floor. He was a clown who was very playful and mischievous. He always made me smile, and I loved playing with him. Then last, the newest member of the family, was Stephen. He had a brain injury, and this lovely couple saved this kitten from dying next to a garbage can. He was well loved and taken care of. I would walk in the front door, and Stephen acted more like a dog. Even though he was mostly blind and wobbly when he walked, he would hear my voice and come running to the door to greet me. I would pick him up and hug him closely, kiss him and talk to him, and he would purr and purr. It was so loud, like billowing thunder from far away. He was the sweetest baby. He was my buddy who would follow me all around the house. Stephen and Bray became my two favorites in that family household. I know I shouldn't have favorites, but they were special! I still gave all the kitties love and attention. I always looked forward to watching the kitties. They were so much fun, and I loved them. The clients would be gone six whole weeks, and sometimes I would stay overnight to spend more time with the kitties. Some of the kitties would even sleep in bed with me! I loved it!

I plan on writing a book about Hawaii and my experience starting my own business pet sitting. I will be sharing more stories about beloved pets I watched over the years and what I have learned about business. I have been very blessed!

Traveling the World:

I'd love to travel the world someday

To sight see everywhere I went

I'd love the freedom of going anywhere

Without my family or friends.

I'd want to explore new land and water

And travel from state to state

I'd like to compare the different countries

And see which ones I rate.

Soon the future will be here

And I will have some stories to tell

I know someday I will travel the world

It's a dream I have right now

And when that day comes

where I have the traveling bug

I will journey the many roads in a VW bus.

-written in 1990 age 18

Chapter 23

Traveling to Europe

I left Hawaii and flew sixteen hours with many layovers to reach London, England. Walking off the plane, I couldn't believe I had made it. I had never taken a solo trip before, other than Las Vegas and the different Hawaiian Islands. This was the biggest, most courageous thing I had ever done! I didn't have any plans or know anyone in Europe. I didn't book a car, I didn't rent a hotel in advance, I didn't even map out where I would go or what I wanted to do. I was not afraid, and I had no doubt this was going to be a great solo trip. I was looking forward to exploring this romantic and exotic place! I was walking close to God, and I knew He was going to lead me where I needed to go.

The first thing I planned to do was find a hotel to stay near the airport. It was 10:30pm and unusually light outside. I walked around with a big duffel bag on my back as I went from hotel to hotel. Each one was booked up for the night. After being turned away from the third hotel at 11:30, I prayed, *"Okay, Lord, help me find a place to stay."* I had faith that He was going to put everything in place for me.

As I walked down a lonely, quiet street, I noticed a quaint, little building in an alleyway. I felt God tell me to go there. The door was locked, but someone was at the desk and came to open the door. The lady let me in and asked how she could help. I told her I was looking for a place to stay, but it seemed all the hotels were booked up. She told me they had no rooms available either. I asked what they did, and she told me it was a missionary house for youth. She said she would love to help, but only youth could stay there. I was thirty years old and not so youthful apparently. I said a silent prayer.

I asked, "Do you know a place I could stay?" She said, "No." Then I saw her thinking and felt God pressed something on her heart. She said, "There is a room, but it's more like a closet. It used to be a bedroom, but we keep storage in there now. If you don't mind the boxes piled up, there is a cot you could sleep on just for the night." I was so grateful. I thanked her, and she showed me to my room. It wasn't so bad. It was a 4X8 room with a cot and some boxes. It had a nice view of old, pretty buildings from the little window. I thanked God for the room and fell asleep. Early the next morning, God told me I would read the whole book of Job in the Bible while I was on my trip. The story of Job is a fascinating one to read about how Job had favor with God. I smiled knowing God was going to reveal something big to me. I just knew it! I could feel it!

I came downstairs for breakfast and met with the lady I talked to the night before. She said, "Good news, someone left this morning and we have a room for you to stay in." I was thrilled - that was a sign from God I was supposed to stay one more night! I loved this place. These missionaries were from all over the world. I talked with one guy from Africa who had a fascinating life as a missionary. He told me how God led him to London to win souls for Christ. That was so cool.

The missionary house had free internet. I promised my mom if I found an internet place, I would email to let her know I was okay. I emailed her that I was doing great. I also emailed a few of my close friends to tell them I was still alive. My friends had joked I might get myself lost never to be found again. After emailing, I ventured out to see a little bit of London. It is a beautiful place!

The very next morning I heard there was a popular hostel nearby that had openings. It wasn't far from the train station which I planned on taking to Paris in a few days. I met a girl just out of high school who was staying at that same hostel.

Paula was traveling the world solo, and she became an
inspiration to me. We were so excited to be in London and it
was fun to see the sights together. We walked for miles and
miles and looked at old buildings and churches. We saw Big Ben,
(also known as Elizabeth Tower), which is a beautiful, old,
brown building that had a big clock tower at the very top. We
wanted to go inside, but they had tall men dressed in red and
black with big guns hanging off their shoulders. We looked
through a tall, black fence and yelled at the soldier guy who was
standing just a few feet from the gate. We tried to distract him,
but he stood there like a statue. We told him jokes, said silly
things to him, and even said we would climb over the fence just
to see if this soldier would look at us, but he didn't move and
didn't even blink. I was impressed!

We became bored trying to distract the man and moved
on. We found an amusement center called Namco Funscape. It
has arcades, bumper cars, bowling, and all kinds of other
entertainment. We played games in a three-story game room
and had so much fun, especially when we found the bumper
cars. We had to go on that ride! We walked to the London Eye
which is like a giant Ferris wheel where we could see all over
London. The views were spectacular! The London Eye is
impressive at 443 feet high! After the games and rides, I told my
new friend I had to try London's pizza because I heard it was the
best in the world. We went to the boardwalk and found a little
pizza shop. I have to say, it was the best pizza I ever ate!
Walking through parks and down different streets in London,
we took pictures of practically everything! We clicked away with
pictures of old buildings, statues, and old-style telephone
booths. We took pictures of men dressed in Star Wars outfits.
We even stood in front of "The House of Parliament." It was
beautiful! I was fascinated with the old buildings in London!

I loved everything about London and walking through a park, I met a man that made a difference in my life. I wrote this story from my journal:

As I walked along a beaten path on a run-down sidewalk in London, I watched people who were walking by. There were men and women in business attire holding a briefcase or their filing papers, walking briskly to make their next meeting or appointment, and people enjoying their lunch hour as they took a break from a grueling day. There were beautiful couples in love holding hands and walking slowly, looking at the world through love-colored lenses and smiling like two Cheshire cats in a daze. There were so many kinds of people to watch on this lovely day. London is classy with its beautiful, old buildings and the city's upscale people with their British accents and welcoming personalities. I was truly falling in love with London and the people!

Coming from America, London is very different. I noticed that "right off the bat." I slowed my walking pace down to a sudden stop as I approached this lush, green park. I noticed a large flock of birds eating off the ground. When one bird flew up off the ground, all the rest of them followed. There were many benches along the path for people to sit and large English oak trees that filled out and hung their limbs low to give shade.

As I stood close to a bench, I noticed a man digging in a garbage can. He had a mess of brown hair that went every which way. He had a t-shirt on with stains all over it, a light jacket over the t-shirt to keep him warm, and jeans with holes in the knees. He had an old, brown army backpack with shabby, well-worn straps that looked like they would break at any moment. He was bending over the garbage can, and half his body would disappear inside it. I watched him as he pulled out a half-eaten sandwich. He stood up, took a bite of the sandwich, and put the rest of it in his scraggly, old backpack, perhaps saving the rest for later. He walked to the next garbage can, digging deeply for something tasty.

As I watched this homeless man, my heart sunk. It was as if the breath had been knocked out of me. I prayed silently, "Lord, I have so much in my life and he has nothing, please bless him." I was saddened by the situation. He started to walk toward me as he went from garbage can to garbage can. When he stood about five yards from me, I prayed again, "Lord, if he looks directly into my eyes, I will give him the change in my pocket." I had my hand in my pocket feeling the change that felt cold to the touch on this cool morning. As he was about to pass me by, he stopped a few feet from me and my eyes met his. I held his gaze for five seconds, but it felt more like five minutes. He had a very serious face. His wrinkled brow made me think of a scientist experimenting with chemicals as his mind raced with what to fuse together to make the perfect concoction. I stared at him and for a moment I was mesmerized by his beautiful, deep blue eyes. He stood there for a second, then threw up his hands, and yelled, "What? What? What?" I didn't notice anyone else around. It was just he and I standing there in our own little world. I took a few steps forward and grabbed his hand to put the change in it. I took a step back, smiled, and pointed to the heavens as if to say, "This money is from God."

I whispered, "God loves you." The homeless man stood there a moment looking at me, as if he were soaking in what I had just said. Our eyes met again as I saw a hint of a smile. His whole demeanor changed as he meandered over to the next garbage can and digging around inside, he found another half-eaten sandwich which he stuffed into his backpack. Then he found a quarter full bottle of wine.

He pulled the wine bottle out of the garbage can and brought it over to me as a peace offering. He smiled, and I could see his yellowed, crooked teeth that had probably not been brushed in years, but his smile made my heart skip a beat. I smiled *and laughed as I watched him. He laughed too as if laughter were contagious. I shook my head "no" to the wine. He walked away leaving the bottle of wine in the rubbish and checked the next garbage can. As he did, he looked up at me with a childish grin and my heart grew. I turned around to leave and I took a quick, final look behind me as I thought, "I will never forget this man and his sweet spirit."*

*Written from my journal July 2007

This is the moment when I realized it is the little things in life that make such a big impact in someone's life. A simple gesture, a kind word, encouragement, or a hug, such a simple concept, one that is needed in each of our daily lives.

This personal interaction with the homeless man, I also wrote as an online e-book called "Having Compassion."

After a few nights staying at the London hostel, I felt God tell me it was time to go to Paris. I loved London. I would have loved to stay longer because it was an amazing place, but when God says, *"Go,"* I go!

I took a train from the Waterloo to Paris. This train went under water in a huge tunnel. It traveled from London to Paris quickly. It wasn't like I had a view of the ocean with fish and sharks that would be swimming around, though that would have been fun to watch, but instead it was a closed tunnel that was pitch black. I couldn't see anything.

On the train, a guy chatted with me about Paris. He worked between London and Paris, so he took the Waterloo a few times a day. It was a 2 ½ hour ride. When the train stopped, he asked if I needed help finding a hotel. I told him I would be just fine. I knew God was on my side, and He would lead me to where I needed to go. I walked a few blocks looking for a hotel, but the ones I found were too pricey. I finally found one that was reasonable.

At the hotel, as I was walking up the curved stairway, half-way up the steps there was a door. I stopped. That was unusual. Out of curiosity, I opened the door to find a bathroom. It was an odd place to have a bathroom on a stairwell. The wall looked like they had punched a six-foot hole in it, put a toilet and sink out on a floating platform for guests to use, and then sealed up the walls and door frame. As I walked up the stairs further, I hoped there was a private bathroom in the hotel room. When I settled into my room, I was pleasantly surprised how cute it was, and I was relieved that it included a little bathroom. There was also a patio to sit outside where I could "people watch" below on the street. I was ready to go site-seeing. I was so excited to venture out and experience Paris. I was part French, after-all. I had been brushing up on my French, and I think I had it down.

My first stop was a coffee shop where I needed my caffeine fix. I was hoping they had Starbucks coffee. As I entered, I was enamored by the gigantic space for coffee drinkers. Ready to order, I walked over to the counter and this blonde, robust woman came out from the back closet. She asked what I wanted in French. I told her in English, "I would like a chocolate mocha latte, please." She stared me down for a moment, then threw up her hands, and started yelling in French what I could only guess was profanity! I just stared back. All the time I spent on learning French had just "gone out the window." A guy sitting at the counter turned to me and asked, "Are you American?" I answered, "Yes." I was relieved someone could speak English. I asked him, "What did she say?" He replied, "If you can't say your coffee order in French, then get out of my café." I laughed. The woman was still staring at me, waiting for something to happen, and then she flicked her finger toward the door and said something not so nice that made all the guys at the counter laugh, and then I walked out. It didn't offend me. I thought it was rather funny - a French woman just kicked me out of a coffee house! I walked to a gas station and bought a Starbucks drink there and went on with my day.

I bought a ticket for a four-hour bus tour around Paris for the next day. In the meantime, I walked around Paris for six whole hours. I wanted to see everything. I saw a "Peace and Love" sign on an old building, and I had to see what it was. I thought it may be a tie dye shop and joined cafe, but when I walked in, I was surprised to find it was a hostel. It was early morning, and when I stood in the entrance, a group of people were sitting down, eating at a long table, and they just stared at me. I said, "Hi." Someone standing at the kitchen counter gestured, "Come in and eat with us." I shrugged my shoulders and replied, "Okay." While I ate, the group of people talked about the fun things to do in France. There were some French people at the table, but mostly they were people from all over the world. I love hostels. I have met so many interesting people at places like this.

After breakfast, I picked up where I had left off. I walked around admiring all the old buildings, some which were covered in beautiful graffiti art. There were definitely talented graffiti artists in Paris! There was a river that went through Paris with boats going through the channel and apartment buildings with a terrace that overlooked the river. It was all so pretty and romantic. I took pictures of everything! The city was beautiful, and I was falling in love with Paris!

One day I met a French guy who could not speak a word of English. I thought his accent was so cute that I became mesmerized by it! He would speak in French, and I just smiled and had no idea what he said. I figured out what he was trying to say from his pointing at a coffee shop and gesturing to drink.

I nodded yes, and we went inside where he ordered me a hot chocolate and himself some coffee. Good thing he ordered and not me! I didn't want to be kicked out of this coffee shop too! After our little rendezvous with drinks, I thanked him and went on my way. I continued touring Paris and taking pictures as I was fascinated with all the wonderful sights. I walked for so many hours and took so many different turns sight-seeing, that I knew I was completely lost. It was a good thing I had the address of the hotel where I was staying. I asked someone how to find my way back to the hotel. It seemed to take forever to reach the hotel, but I enjoyed every minute of it.

It was late when I returned to the hotel to sleep. When I had planned this trip to Europe, I prayed God would use me to impact a life for God's kingdom. During this whole trip, I didn't feel God was using me to be a witness for Him. Before this solo trip to England and France, I had a feeling in my heart that I would impact someone's life for the better by sharing about God's love, and in that, I felt this trip would be the most epic traveling experience ever! At this point, however, I didn't feel I had made an impact sharing with someone about Jesus. I had one more full day in Paris before I was to fly to Minnesota to visit family, and I wanted to make this last day count. I prayed and pleaded with God to use me as His vessel on my last day in Paris! After my prayer, feeling exhausted from the long day, I crashed out.

The next day, I was ready for my four-hour tour on the "L' Open Tour!" The weather was nice as I waited for the double-decker bus where I hoped to meet someone that I could talk to about Jesus. The bus finally arrived, and I stepped inside to see steps that went to the second floor. I had always wanted to ride on a double-decker bus. I walked up to the second story where there was no roof. The view was incredible! I sat in the front of the bus where I could see in all directions. I met some nice people sitting next to me. We all gasped in amazement at the many sites. I saw the Eiffel Tower, Notre Dame, and even a glass pyramid that someone said had a shopping mall and food court inside! The bus never stopped at any of these places, but we were able to step off the bus briefly at a shopping mall to stretch our legs halfway through the tour.

After the quick break, everyone piled back into the bus where I sat right behind the bus driver on the main floor. I was getting tired because my feet hurt from walking all over the city the previous day. I began to think about this whole trip and realized I had experienced many fun things in such a small amount of time.

I talked to the driver whose name was Patrick. He was born and raised in Paris, and he spoke English well. I liked listening to his French accent. He was very proud of his hometown and loved to share knowledge of the history of Paris. He was fascinating to listen to with all the stories about France and Paris. He was a nice guy who loved answering any questions I had. I told Patrick I was on a solo trip with God, and we talked about religion and all the things that come with it. I told him that I am not in any specific religion, but that I had a relationship with God. I shared with him that I talk to God every day just as he and I were talking at that very moment, just like a friend. I shared with Patrick what God had done in my life and how I had an intimate relationship with Him through my prayer life. He was very receptive and wanted to know more about my relationship with God.

When we drove by Joan of Arc, I mentioned to Patrick that I would love to stand in front of the statue and have my picture taken. The statue was shining in real gold. Joan was up on a horse ready to lead her army to fight the English! It gave me chills just knowing the history and how God had led Joan to do great things to beat the English before she died at age nineteen. The statue was right there in the middle of a busy street, but it was breathtaking, and I so badly wanted to jump off the bus and see it up close! Patrick asked if I would want to tour around Paris with him after he was finished with work, and he promised he would show me Joan of Arc. It just so happened this was Patrick's last tour for the day, and he could take me there. I said I would love it!

After the bus tour was over, Patrick drove me to Notre Dame where we walked through the huge, beautiful church. Patrick knew a great deal of the church's history, and I loved hearing all he had to say. I was enamored by the beauty of the cathedral ceiling. We spent a great deal of time there. We saw the Eiffel Tower where people paid to walk up to the top of the tower to look out and see a great view of Paris. He showed me the Louvre Pyramid, a museum that was under the glass pyramid. Patrick and I had dinner at the food court as we watched all the activity around us. He showed me other places I had not seen on the bus tour as well. Then it was time to see the Joan of Arc statue. I was so excited and couldn't wait!

We crossed the busy street to stand on the sidewalk where Joan stood tall with her flag in arm, her sword at her side, and the horse with his left front leg up, both ready to fight. It was an awesome sight! Patrick took pictures of me with the statue and I teared up. I think I was emotional because this young teenage girl heard from God like I did, and she obeyed Him! She was obedient to everything He wanted her to do, and she changed people's lives! She changed history because she heard from God! I had been researching extensively about her story before my Europe trip, and here I was standing next to this statue in awe. Joan was someone to admire for sure. She died for her country and her God! Joan of Arc's story is an amazing account of bravery and courage!

After sightseeing with my new friend Patrick, I asked him to drop me off at Notre Dame, and I walked two hours back to my hotel. I didn't mind the walk because it gave me time to think and praise God for my day. I was very thankful that God guided me to this tour, and I was able to share with Patrick about God. After eight hours of touring all of Paris and finally walking back toward the hotel, a French man asked in broken English if I would have dinner with him. I said, "Yes." It was all so romantic, even though there was no kissing. After dinner, I went back to my hotel alone, prayed and thanked God for my day, and fell fast asleep.

The next morning, I woke up knowing I had to leave Paris and go back to London. I finished the whole book of Job and was saddened by what he experienced. I prayed, *"God, I don't understand the suffering Job had to go through,"* and God said, *"My Son Jesus suffered more for you than even Job went through."* I was humbled and thankful that God loved me so much that His Son died on a cross for me.

For God so loved the world, that He gave His only begotten Son, that whosoever believeth in Him should not perish, but have everlasting life. John 3:16

I took the Waterloo train back to London, found a hotel for the night, and then looked for a place on the boardwalk to eat lunch. After lunch, I had a lovely walk on the boardwalk. I saw two guys preaching on the street corner, and I went to talk to them. They brought up the story of Job, which we had a great discussion about, and the story of Moses as well. I asked if they would pray for my safe travel to Minnesota. The two men prayed for me, and they asked for my prayers for them. It was beautiful how we held hands and prayed for one another right on the boardwalk for all to see. I really felt the hand of God on us and was so blessed. They were very encouraging and gave me verses from the Bible for my travels. It was the perfect end to my lovely trip. I went back to the hotel to pack and get a good night's rest for my trip to Minnesota to see my family and friends before heading back home to Hawaii.

*Solo trip to Europe 2007

*I am working on a future book about my Europe trip more in journal form

A CHILD OF GOD

Do not forget to entertain strangers, for by so doing, some people have entertained angels without knowing it.

Hebrews 13:2

Chapter 24

Angels in My Life

There are so many people on Earth, too many to count, but what if some of them were angels that God gave an assignment to help those who are following God and need encouragement? I have actual accounts of meeting such people who I had no doubt in my mind were real angels that made an impact in my life.

I was driving to Waikiki to pet sit for a client of mine who had a cat that I adored. I was at a very long light, waiting for it to change from red to green when God pressed on my heart to look out the window. To my right, a lady was standing on the sidewalk staring at me. She looked homeless. She wasn't gawking at me, but I could see she was thinking about something. God said, *"Feed this woman."* I had a little Mazda Miata which was a quick, little sports car with two seats in it and no extra space. I looked around my car but didn't see any food.

She was still looking at me, and the light was about to change. I put my hand behind my seat where there was about a two-inch space and found a bag of dried fruit that I had forgotten about from days before. It's as if she knew the food was for her!

She put her hands on my car, leaned in the passenger side window, and said, "How are you?" She had a soft, loving voice, and I had a strange sense that I knew her. It made me stop and think for a moment if I had met her, but I knew I had never seen this woman before. She looked at me and I noticed she had the brightest blue eyes I had ever seen! They looked the color of heavenly blue. I said, "I am doing good." As I handed her the bag of dried fruit, she touched my arm, and I had chicken skin go all the way up my arm. (*Chicken skin* is the Hawaiian word for "goose bumps"). I instantly knew she was an angel as peace flushed over me. She held my arm and said, "God loves you and He is watching over you. He wants you to know that." The red light turned green and I thanked her as I drove off, but tears fell down my face. I had just been touched by an angel, and I realized God loved me so much that He sent an angel to tell me so! This has made an impact in my life to this very day. I will never forget those eyes or how it felt to hear how immense God's love for me is.

When I was only eleven years old, I had met a Christian couple and their daughter who changed my life forever. My mom had signed me up for a Kinship program in which a family - mom, dad, and child - would help a single-parent home by spending time with the child in need. This family came into my life at a time when I was at my worst. I was being sexually abused by men, I didn't get along with my mom, and my life was a mess. It was the perfect time to meet Jesus and watch how this family lived so differently than me.

Before this couple came along, as a child I had thought about suicide many times. In my mind, I had the perfect plan, and I could have made it happen at any time. I wasn't waiting for that perfect moment to die. I was just dying inside and didn't want to live anymore, and if it were going to be any more unbearable, I was going to "check out" and "leave it all behind." I was so numb to the world that it didn't even matter if I were to die. Anything would be better than being groped and molested by dirty, old men.

When I first met this Christian family, I didn't know what to expect. They didn't yell and scream or slam doors when they were mad or stop talking to each other for days. I paid close attention to every little detail of how they lived. When there was a problem, they talked about it, and were communicative. Yes, they had times that weren't all "peaches and cream," but they worked it out with each other. I didn't have that with my mom. I felt I was in a whole new world when I was spending time with this family. It was different from my home life. I learned so much about their Christian walk just by watching them.

I have some great memories with them. I remember one time when Jack and I were swimming in the Mississippi River. I had so much fun swimming in the river because the current would pull me every which way. It was usually cold and choppy, but on this day, the water was warm and steady, just flowing down the river in a nonchalant manner. We were trying to race each other to see which one of us was the faster swimmer, and when we were tired, we just floated on the surface and talked about nothing important.

As Jack talked, I wished he had been my dad. He was so nice, loving, and caring. He truly wanted to spend time with me like I had hoped my real father would have wanted. As we swam around, something bumped the whole right side of my leg. I whipped around thinking Jack was messing with me because he liked to joke around, but he wasn't even close to me. I was terrified! If that was a fish, it had to be huge! I panicked, and flailing my arms, I swam quickly toward shore. I told him, "I'm going in!" When Jack and I were up on shore, I told him I was never swimming in that water again, and I don't think I ever did. Jack laughed and laughed! He teased me for months afterward that I feared a little fish, but I knew that fish was BIG! Yet, I didn't mind him teasing me because it showed he cared.

On Sundays, Jack and his wife Sophia would take me to a Pentecostal mission church and I loved it. It's where I felt God's love the most and where I asked Jesus into my heart so that I would be saved! There was always food to eat after church, and I looked forward to that! They even fed the homeless and anyone else who would come in out of the cold. There were no judgements, just a heart after God to feed those in need! I made friends with the homeless and to this day, I have a softness in my heart for the less fortunate.

Life is hard, but it's our attitude and positive energy that makes the difference. We all have issues in life but climbing over the obstacles we face is the real test! We are all a work in progress, not one of us is perfect! No matter if we are rich or poor, homeless or have a roof over our head, God can work on us. He loves us all the same, which is why we should love others as God loves us. I am who I am today because God loves me, and I am thankful for what God has brought me through!

I always looked forward to my weekends with Jack and Sophia. I loved being outside and I especially enjoyed winter time! Jack and Sophia always had something fun planned on the weekends when I visited them. Sometimes they would have a group of children over at their house from the church. We would all build a snowman, have snowball fights, or go sledding or ice skating. In the summertime, we would go to a campground up north. Jack would take the boat out on the lake. There was plenty of fishing and listening to the Loons call each other. There were fun activities like canoeing and water skiing. My favorite thing to do was go inner tubing. I would hang on tightly to the inner tube behind the boat and hope not to fall off while he drove like a speed racer around the lake. Of course, I couldn't always hold on, especially when Jack would whip the boat around, and the inner tube would "fly through the air." Jack would laugh and laugh if one of the kids flew off the inner tube. There was much pain and many bruises, but it was always a fun time!

One cold winter day, we planned a day of sledding. Jack had a garage full of sleds, and a group of us piled into his van. He drove us to gigantic hills that were very popular for sledding. There had been a big snowfall the night before, and today was the day we would slide "the crud" out of this big hill. I picked my favorite sled, which I believed was one of the faster sleds because of how it was shaped. I picked a spot on one of the hills, I jumped on my sled, and there was no stopping me! I flew down that hill! I would zigzag and steer with my body weight, and I had the time of my life! I was zooming down the hills like a crazy girl as others would veer to get out of my way, but I was in a "zone." I was focused on speed and achieving a high from the adrenaline rush running through my veins. There were dips and pivots on the hills that made this especially fun. I had to grab on tightly to the sled, so I wouldn't fall off. I learned very quickly how to balance myself and keep steady to fly even faster down those hills and not crash.

After a few hours of sledding with the others and as I was climbing the hill to go again, I looked over to my right, and there was the "cherry on a sundae." It was the hill of all hills, ginormous and sleek. It was ready to be used and abused. Not one person was over there, but I had "an itch" for adventure and I wanted to "take this hill on." I looked at everyone having a good time sledding, and for a moment I had the feeling I shouldn't do it, but I wanted to conquer this hill.

I climbed to the top of the big hill and looked down. It was sleek and covered in sheer ice from top to bottom. I strategized on how I would slay this monster. There was a group of trees on the left of the hill, and if I made any mistakes, I would end up flying into the trees and hurting myself badly. The dips on this hill were much deeper than the other hills, and I thought twice about not even going, but only for a moment. I put the sled down, leveled it out, and pushed off. I flew down that hill faster than I had EVER flown down a hill before! The hill was very slippery, and I was trying to steer to the right so I wouldn't hit the trees, but as my sled moved just slightly, I hit one of the icy dips too hard and flew through the air. For a moment, I was flying, NO, like really flying! It was amazing how I "flew through the air," but then I came crashing down!

The next thing I knew, I woke up with Jack and the group of teens from church standing around just staring at me as I lay on the ground. I felt a bit groggy, and I remember Jack saying, "I saw you fly through the air and come crashing down, and I thought you were dead!" After a few moments, I had a burning sensation in my nose as if it were on fire. I sat up and touched my nose as I cried, "Ouch, my nose hurts!" Jack walked me back to the van, and I couldn't believe other than a few scratches, I only sustained a nose injury. I sat on the side step of the van and held my nose. I knew it was broken. Jack laughed and laughed, just because he laughed at all stupid things people did. I was not offended that he was laughing at me because I really did a stupid thing! He said, "I can laugh now that I know you are not dead." I didn't think it was THAT funny! I didn't go to the ER; instead, I went home to rest and put ice on my nose. The next morning, I woke up to a slanted, puffed up rhino nose!

Many years later in my thirties, I prayed and asked God if I should have my nose fixed. My crooked nose bothered me, and people would ask if I was Polish. I am not Polish! I was also compared to an actress that had a big nose and it bothered me being compared to her. Another thing that bothered me was losing my sense of smell. Something had to be done! I prayed, and God gave me a peace about having it fixed. That was a "YES." I needed more than one surgery on my nose because it was broken far worse than the doctor had anticipated. I had broken it a second time when a group of my friends and I had jumped off a bridge into freezing, cold water. I had hit a large log that was lodged on the side of the bridge. As I was pulled under the log and came out the other end, I had a burning sensation on my nose, knowing full well I had broken it again! So much for adventure! In the end, I am grateful to the doctor who corrected the injuries, and my senses are so much keener than ever before!

I may have been the toughest child for Jack and Sophia to take under their wing, but I am so grateful they were obedient to God and nurtured me in such a way that I was receptive to meet Jesus. I don't know where I would be today without Jesus or meeting this family. I watched how God worked in their lives, and I wanted that! Jack and Sophia are a great example of two people being led by God, pouring into many children's lives and making an impact in the world because God is in the middle of everything in their lives! They are angels in my life! They have no idea how much they have impacted my life and I am so thankful that when I was a child, they were there when I needed them the most.

"My Testimony," (Chapter 2) explains how this couple led me to meet Jesus and changed my life!

I have so many great stories of people passing through my life, giving me an encouraging word, or being there at just the right time I needed them. God does that! He puts special people in our path when we need someone the most. I call these "God-moments!"

Assuredly, I say to you, if you have faith as small as a mustard seed, you will say to this mountain, 'Move from here to there,' and it will move; and nothing will be impossible for you. Matthew 17:20

Chapter 25

Family is Everything

Back in 1941, Grandpa and Grandma met on a blind date set up by a friend. The date went well, and Grandpa courted Grandma and wooed her for many months until they married on October 15th, 1941. They were parents to six children, and many years later, my cousins and I came along.

When my mom became pregnant with me, Mom's two sisters were also pregnant. Not long after my two cousins and I were born, Mom's sisters again were pregnant, and Mom's brother's wife was pregnant, and soon there were so many babies crawling around everywhere at our family gatherings! I was the oldest out of all my cousins, and as I grew up, many of my fourteen cousins were at the family gatherings, which made it a whole lot of fun.

I have very fond memories of my grandpa and grandma. In 1957 they moved from Kasota to St. Peter in Minnesota and lived on a farm with many acres. I remember one time when I was very young, maybe three or four years old, Grandpa had me sit on the back of his dirt bike as he drove down the dirt road by the farm house. I had hung on tightly to Grandpa, but I fell off the back of the bike. Luckily, I was all bundled up in winter clothes and had fallen on a patch of snow. Grandpa just put me right back on that bike and told me to hang on tightly again, and off we went. I loved those short rides with him. Luckily Grandma didn't know, or she would have had his hide for doing a stunt like that.

I remember as I was growing up, my mom and I would go to Grandpa and Grandma's house every Christmas. We drove an hour-and-a-half from the Twin Cities to Mankato, Minnesota, to see family. We would go in any kind of weather - rain, sleet, snow, and even a mild blizzard! We always made sure we would see family each Christmas. It was my favorite time of year with family, a time of eating endless amounts of desserts. There were mounds of chocolates, brownies, cookies, Twinkie's, Hoho's, cakes, and half a dozen pies Grandma had baked to top it all off! There was always an array of food dishes sprawled out every which way on the kitchen table for us kids to snack on before dinner, and the dishes of delicious food we knew not to touch before the big feast!

It was a great time at Christmas with food, presents, fun, and laughter in the air. My aunts and uncles with all the children would show up at Grandma's house with a large bag of presents and a dish to share. A mound of presents would fill the whole space under the large Christmas tree, and whatever couldn't fit underneath, a mountain of presents would pile high against the corner wall climbing its way to the ceiling.

When everyone had shown up, one of the parents or Grandma would say, "OPEN THE PRESENTS!" and Christmas wrapping would fly every which way being torn up as all the children squealed and yelled excitedly at every present opened. No matter if we were getting an ugly Christmas sweater, socks with Rocky and Bullwinkle on them, the newest, popular Barbie doll or an electronic controlled car or truck that could be driven all over the messy floor of wrapping paper, no matter what we received, we loved all the presents! The best part of Christmas was knowing our tight-knit family was together for the holidays.

Spending time with family was important. Grandma made sure we were all together, especially for Christmas. By the end of the night, we had eaten as much as our stomachs could hold. Grandpa and Grandma as well as my mom and her siblings were all flopped on the couches and chairs, relaxing and talking to each other while the children played with their new toys and snacked on sweets. We all knew Christmas was so very special. Grandpa and Grandma really enjoyed having us at the house, and they loved us all so much. They would sit in their comfy chairs watching how much fun all the grandchildren were having, and that's what made them the happiest. They made every one of us feel very special, letting us know how much they loved us.

No matter what was going on in my life, I could count on my family! We were such a close-knit family. I was happiest at Christmas time in the midst of love, laughter, and fun with my cousins, but most importantly was the special bond I had with both Grandpa and Grandma. That is what I loved the most!

Growing up, I didn't know the meaning of Christmas. Sure, I had heard the story of Jesus being born, but I didn't know anything about Jesus when I was growing up. No one had explained Jesus in the manger or what Christmas was all about. I truly thought it was about family, food and presents. I didn't know it was a celebration of Jesus' birth. It wasn't until after I asked Jesus into my heart that it occurred to me that Christmas was more than just a day to open presents, eat lots of food, and spend time with family. Christmas was a celebration of Jesus' birth, when He came to Earth to take our sins upon the cross, and if we chose to accept Him into our hearts, we could live eternally with Him in heaven someday. The meaning of Christmas meant so much more to me after I met Jesus.

Grandpa and Grandma always had a large box full of extra presents for my birthday which landed right after Christmas and before New Year's Eve. I loved how they made me feel so special! My Grandpa and Grandma always seemed to spoil me. It was a perk of being a grandparent. I would see the box full of presents in the corner of the kitchen and knew they were for me. I couldn't wait to open them for my birthday.

Every year they made sure I had a pile of birthday presents, and most times they would celebrate my birthday on Christmas Day or right after Christmas. Family would be at the house with a great big birthday cake, plenty of delicious food, and everyone around the table singing "Happy Birthday" as I made a wish and blew out the candles.

On occasion we would visit Grandpa and Grandma at the cabin they owned at the lake. My grandparents owned one cabin, and my uncle owned the one right next door. Our family would meet there on the weekends in the summertime, especially to celebrate someone's birthday or any other special occasion Grandma could think of to bring the family together. The cousins and I always had so much fun at the cabin. In the early morning after waking up, we would run down the hill, onto the dock, then jump into the icy cold water, and swim all day long! It was my favorite thing to do at the cabin. I could swim all day, every day, and I would be in a happy bliss! I was a fish in water who loved to swim, and it was hard for my mom to even pull me out of the water when it was time to go home.

Grandpa wanted to make something fun for us children to play with at the lake. He had an idea. With the gigantic tree on the hill in front of the cabin, he found a big truck tire that he threw a rope around, tied it tightly, and tossed the other end of the rope around the thick tree limb high above. He then tied it up and there it was, this big swing hanging off this large tree on the hill. All the children wanted to swing on it, and sometimes there would be fights about who would use the swing next. That was the most popular thing to do at the cabin - swing on that old tire. Sometimes two of us would jump on the tire at the same time, and it would swing far and wide and twist around and around. We loved that old tire! One time, one of my cousins ran and jumped on the tire to make it swing far and wide, and the rope snapped! Then she fell tangled up in the tire. It was a bit comical!

There was a lot of swimming, camping outside on the hill, fishing off the dock, and playing on Grandpa's old pontoon that made the weekends even more fun and memorable. One time, my cousin was running on the dock acting silly and jumping around when she stepped on a certain board just right, and her foot fell through it. She was stuck there screaming, and we had to help pull her out of the dock. I couldn't help but laugh. I was a kid after all, and seeing her arms flailing about as she dropped into the dock seemed a bit funny.

Grandpa was amazing. He loved us children so much. At the cabin he would sit in his favorite lawn chair outside watching us play. He would call me over to him and have me sit on his lap and secretly hand me a dollar, which back in the 70's was A LOT of money for me. He would say, "Don't tell your mom I am giving you this. Go spend it on whatever you like." I would get all happy and giggly as I slipped it into my pocket and looked around to make sure no one saw. It was our secret just Grandpa and me! Sometimes Grandpa would say to me, "Did you know you are my favorite grandchild, but don't tell anyone. This will be our little secret." I would nod and smile and just soak in what he was saying. I was his favorite and it made me feel on top of the world. I felt special to him. He was the closest to a loving father figure I had in my life.

Many years later when I was a young adult, I visited Minnesota for my grandpa's funeral. As I was mourning his loss, I thought of the fond memories of him and mentioned to family sitting next to me that Grandpa used to tell me I was his favorite grandchild. A few of my cousins piped up and said, "Me too!" and I had a look of shock on my face as I said, "OHH!" We laughed and laughed. It was such a wonderful feeling that Grandpa could make all of us children feel so loved.

My favorite times were when all the cousins would camp overnight at the cabin. It was so fun! We would pile our sleeping bags inside the small tents with lots of pillows, our favorite books or toys, and flashlights. The boys would run around outside and try to scare us girls in the tents. We would scream and yell at them for trying to frighten us.

One time my Uncle Tyler, who was the youngest of my mom's siblings, was hanging out with all the cousins but me. I had always been ousted by him and it bugged me. I just wanted to be liked by him so badly. It was almost midnight and all the children were settling down to sleep when I asked him why we weren't as close as he was to my other cousins. He would play with them and everyone loved him, but he always liked to tease and torment me. He said, "I know how we can be friends." I asked, "How?" He said, "Down at the dock there is an alligator that hangs out in the water at midnight. If you run down the hill, run to the end of the dock, lean over and touch the water without being eaten by the alligator and run back up the hill, then you will prove to me we can be friends." I replied, "I can't do that, it's too dark and I don't want to be eaten by an alligator." I was almost in tears. He said, "Well, it's your choice. I guess we can't be friends," and he walked off. For a moment I thought maybe I could do it, but I was so scared. It was pitch black outside and I was already scared of the dark. I was just a child who believed uncle Tyler and his story about an alligator that hung out at the dock late at night. It terrified me. Back then, I was naïve, and I didn't know there were no alligators in Minnesota.

In the wintertime, Grandpa and I had our special times together. He would drive out on the lake, and we planned a day of ice fishing together. We walked to Grandpa's ice shack. It had three rickety wooden walls and a shaggy looking door that wouldn't completely shut. It looked like the outhouse at the cabin. Grandpa and I would walk in the door and the fishing shack had just enough room for us to sit on little stools over a small hole in the ice with a fishing pole hanging over it. Grandpa and I would sit there, adding bait to the line, and drop it deep into the icy cold water and then wait. He would turn on the small radio in the corner that was battery operated. We would be listening to some old country music as we intently looked at the line in anticipation for any movement. There was a small heater in the corner to keep us somewhat warm in the sub-freezing temperatures, and in my excitement, I didn't feel cold at all. I wanted to catch a fish in the worst way. Some days we would catch a bunch of fish and other days, there would barely be a nibble on the line. Sometimes we would be out there all day long, but I didn't care. It was the ability to withstand anything so that my grandpa and I could spend some quality time together. We chit chatted about nothing special, but to me it meant the world, and I loved our time together!

When my Grandparents and my Uncle Tyler moved to Arkansas, I stayed with them one summer. I was about eight or nine years old. They lived in a small community of houses surrounded by a thick forest. Grandpa told me once there was a big, black bear that liked to fiddle around digging for food in their garbage cans. I would have loved to see the bear, but I never did see him.

Uncle Tyler told me once that there were big, black snakes that climbed trees and fell on people walking by, but I never did see those snakes, though I must admit I always looked up in the big trees when I walked under them. I didn't want a snake falling on me! There were always squirrels running around, and sometimes I would see a raccoon or a deer walking through the yard. I loved nature and really took in the beauty surrounding me at Grandma's house.

Grandpa and Grandma lived in an old, brick two-story home where the upstairs was bright and comfortable. It was where Grandma always baked something delicious, and Grandpa would read the newspaper sitting in his favorite chair. He would have me sit by him as he told me stories about when he was younger. He would say, "When I was your age, I would walk miles and miles to get to school and I would go uphill, both ways." I would laugh and laugh. He was so funny. He loved to eat ice cream with me too, and he would sing this little tune all the time wherever he was, "I scream, you scream, we all scream for ice cream!" It always made me smile. I loved Grandpa so much!

For the time I stayed with my grandparents, I slept in the basement where it was dark and musty smelling. Now that I am older, if I walk through an old house and that same musty smell hits my nose, it brings back memories of my grandparents home.

Grandpa and Grandma had their bedroom upstairs, and so did my uncle Tyler. They had a cot for me to stay downstairs, and I loved having the big basement to myself. There were lots of nick knacks on metal shelves that made the place homey. My grandparents had a book shelf with many books to read and a big T.V. with a comfy couch to sit and watch old VHS movies on the VCR. Grandpa would be outside tinkering around with his tools and fixing things, and Grandma would be in the kitchen baking. She always had food or snacks out for us to eat. I loved spending time with my grandparents!

There were only about a dozen homes in the cul-de-sac where my grandparents lived, and I kept myself busy climbing trees or running through the forest. In the early mornings I would meet with the neighbors and talk to them while they were gardening or cleaning up their yard. Sometimes, I would catch one couple in the middle of breakfast, and they would invite me in to join them. They were so nice! They would tell me stories about wild animals that had visited their yard or how a stranger's car would break down on the road and they would invite the stranger in for dinner. They were that nice, just helping anyone and everyone they could. It's just the way people were in this small town.

One late afternoon, my uncle Tyler wanted to show me something in the forest, so I followed him a long way out in the middle of nowhere with huge trees that stretched to the sky. He showed me what he had been working on. He set up a fake graveyard with actual coffins on the ground with closed covers, and a few deep holes were dug in which to put the coffins. He created fake zombie-looking people that were propped up against a few of the trees. He had made many life-sized characters that looked real like Darth Vader and Chu Baka, so this coffin scene in the middle of the woods didn't surprise me. It was rather creative. My uncle was also a Sci-Fi writer and wrote many horror stories filled with dark evil lurking around every corner, so when he showed me the graveyard he had made, it didn't faze me one bit. He was very proud of the work that he had created.

It was almost dark by this time when I heard a noise behind me. As I looked in the direction of the noise, I noticed a cave about as tall as me just a few feet away! I could just see the outline of the trees hanging low over this cave. It made it look dark and eerie. I just stared into the pitch-black cave for a moment. After a few seconds my eyes adjusted, and I saw two large round eyes looking at me from inside the cave. I started screaming thinking it was a bear or some other big animal that wanted to eat me. I wished I had a flashlight, but I didn't. I blindly ran through the tall brush screaming and crying and hoping that an animal wasn't running after me planning to eat me. I was terrified and had no idea if I was running toward the house or running deeper into the forest. I just kept running! The tall, dry grass was brushing against my bare legs, and I could feel it catching on my skin and stinging my legs, but I didn't care. It wasn't going to stop me, and I just kept running!

Finally, after what seemed like an eternity, I saw lights in a clearing and the road to Grandma's house. I ran across the street and up the few steps to the front door. I flew open the door and stood in the doorway, my hair was a mess, my chest heaving in and out, and I was crying hysterically. Tyler burst out laughing. Grandma scowled at Tyler as she yelled, "What did you do?" and she glared at him. She opened her arms for me and I ran into them. She hugged me tightly. She told Tyler to get the first aid kit, and she patched up my scratched up, bloody legs. I never did find out what was in that cave, if it were my imagination, or if Tyler and his friends had pulled a prank to scare me. Tyler, however, looked quite smug that I was upset.

Uncle Tyler had some odd items sitting in the basement. He had different Halloween costumes. One of his favorites was a Darth Vader ensemble with the whole black face mask. He would breathe into a mouth piece which made him sound like Darth Vader. I was impressed. Uncle Tyler said I needed to be good, or he would send the real Darth Vader over to talk to me. I laughed because I knew Darth Vader was not real.

A few nights later, I was in a deep sleep and heard a buzzing noise but didn't think anything of it. Then I heard heavy breathing. I thought maybe it was a mosquito buzzing near my ear as it tickled, so I swatted at the air and rolled over to sleep again when I heard a deep-throated voice say, "Wake up, Becky, I am here to talk to you!" I rolled back over and with sleepy eyes, I saw a silhouette standing in front of me. It was Darth Vader in the flesh! I lay there a moment trying to figure out if I were dreaming or if this were real. Darth Vader walked toward me until he was standing practically over me. He was large and intimidating! In a gruff voice he said, "If you are not going to be good to your grandparents and your uncle Tyler, I will come back and take you away from your grandparents and you will never see them again." He touched my arm with his big, black glove, and that's when I realized I was fully awake. I pulled myself and my blanket back toward the corner of the wall. I was trying to crawl up the wall as far as I could to get away! I was terrified to see a real Darth Vader. I started crying and screaming for him to go away. After a moment he slowly backed away into the darkness and he was gone. I didn't sleep the rest of the night. My eyes were wide open looking into the blackness of the night. The next morning as daylight filtered through the room, I was still staring at the back wall where Darth Vader had disappeared. There I saw the Darth Vader costume hanging on the wall. I knew I didn't imagine it! I thought Darth Vader must have come to life because he had touched my arm. That's when I knew he was real. I went upstairs and ate my cereal at the table, not saying anything to Grandma about what happened the night before because she probably wouldn't believe me.

While staying that summer with Grandpa and Grandma, I sucked my thumb when I would go to bed. I'm not sure why I sucked my thumb while staying there, but when my uncle Tyler saw what I was doing, he would tease me relentlessly. I thought I probably deserved his teasing. He would laugh and badger me about being too old to suck my thumb, but I had been through a great deal in my life up to that point and knew he didn't understand.

One night when it was dark out and past my bedtime, my uncle told me a story that scared me stiff. Tyler said, "There is this giant who lives in the forest and in the middle of the night he quietly pulls the roof off each house looking for children who are thumb suckers. If he finds a thumb sucker, he grabs them out of their bed and chops their thumb off." I just sat there listening with fear in my eyes, scared to say anything. I went to bed with my thumb in my mouth and thought I may just wake up without it. I thought, how much do I need my thumb? I pulled my thumb out of my mouth and wrapped my blanket around me hoping I wouldn't meet this big giant who chops off thumbs. After a week, Uncle Tyler boasted to Grandma and Grandpa that he cured my thumb sucking problem. He was so proud of that.

About mid-summer at Grandma and Grandpa's place, I called my mom and asked if she could come pick me up, and so she did.

When I was older, Grandma shared a story with me about Grandpa. A long time ago he had buried $15,000 cash in their yard in Arkansas! It was funny to me. He stuck the cash in an old vegetable can, dug a hole in the ground, and buried it. For many years, Grandpa was glad to have that money put aside for any emergencies that might happen. Many years later, he went to dig up the can of money, but he couldn't remember exactly where he had buried it. He dug holes all over the yard, but he couldn't find the money anywhere. Grandma wasn't too happy about the holes in the yard or that he had lost all that money. Grandpa never did find that money he buried. To this day, I wonder if someone ever found that buried treasure.

Years later Grandma told me a heart-warming story about her favorite fish. Grandma had a fish, but he wasn't any old fish. He was a goldfish named Frankie:

"I have this fish. His name is Frankie," Grandma said. "He lives in this little glass bowl on my kitchen table," she said as she pointed to Frankie. "He loves to swim around and watch me as I walk through the kitchen. He is the funniest fish. I would sit at the kitchen table and drink my coffee, and he would just stare at me. He was my little friend."

She looked at the fish bowl and took a sip of her coffee as she went on with her story. "One day I walked into the kitchen and looked over at Frankie in his bowl, but for some reason, the bowl looked empty. I towered over him, but I didn't see him anywhere. He must have jumped out! I looked all over the kitchen table. I even looked on the floor. Surely if he had jumped out, he would be flopping around on the floor, but I couldn't find him anywhere. I was panicked because a fish can only go so long without water."

Grandma sat at the kitchen table and took another sip of her coffee as she said, "I looked in the sink and on the counter tops. It was a far-fetched thought that Frankie could jump so far, but I had to save my little fish. I looked high and low for him. I finally gave up on Frankie. I just couldn't figure out where he went. As I sat at the kitchen table, I picked up my coffee cup to take a sip, and as I did, two big eyes looked at me from inside my cup. It was my fish Frankie! I couldn't believe it! It was the darndest thing! I dropped my coffee cup and poor Frankie flopped around on the table, so I scooped him up and put him back in his bowl. I swear that fish looked mad at me, but wouldn't you believe, to this day, there he is, live and well. Good thing my coffee wasn't warm at all. He had quite the adventure that day."

Grandma sat there reminiscing and chuckled about Frankie the fish, and I laughed right along with her. It was the funniest story I had heard in a very long time!

Dear Reader: I have written a children's book about Frankie the Fish. An illustrator is working on the artwork. The book, "Grandma's Fish Frankie" will be published by Christmas 2018.

Chapter 26

Our Family Heritage: Stolt and Carpenter

This chapter is dedicated to my grandpa Raymond Harvey Stolt and grandma Evelyn Marie Stolt who are loved dearly now and forever. I would like to thank my uncle David Stolt, for his dedication and hard work to find our family history and information to help with this chapter. I also want to thank my mom and aunts for adding important information as well. It means a great deal to me, and I hope this brings our family closer together. Learning about family history is important for all of us.

My great-grandfather (Grandpa's father) was John C. Stolt, he was 100% German.

My great-grandmother (Grandpa's mother) was Augusta M. (Hopp) Stolt, she was 100% German.

On the paternal side of my family, my grandpa Raymond Harvey Stolt, of German descent, was born in 1917 in Nicollet, Minnesota. He was the son of John C. Stolt and Augusta M. Hopp, both were from families that immigrated from Germany. This side of Grandpa's family history revolved mostly around the rural Nicollet area in Minnesota back in the era when many families often did not travel more than twenty-five miles from their home.

My great-grandpa, Laverne Carpenter, was my grandma's father who was the one who had an interesting mix of nationalities in his bloodline: English, Dutch, French, and a small percentage of American Indian. Great-Grandpa worked at a hospital, and he was also a beekeeper. At one point, he had more than fifty bee hives in Kasota and sold both honey and bees' wax locally to help him earn a living for his family.

My great-grandma, Theresa Spokes, was my grandma's mother who was 100% German. She met and married Laverne Carpenter and ultimately settled in Kasota, Minnesota to raise their family.

On the maternal side of my family, my grandma, Evelyn Marie Carpenter, was born in 1922 in Alpha, Michigan. Evelyn's parents moved to Minnesota where Evelyn eventually met her future husband, Raymond, on a blind date. Grandma was German, English, Dutch, French and a small percentage of American Indian.

My grandpa Raymond Harvey Stolt, married my grandma Evelyn Marie Carpenter October 15, 1941. Their home resided in St. Peter, Minnesota. They had six children. The oldest to youngest were David Raymond Stolt, Irene Marie Stolt, Sylvia Louise Stolt, Judith Ann Stolt, Theresa Pauline Stolt, and Thomas Laverne Stolt.

Raymond Harvey Stolt (my grandpa) passed away in 1992. Evelyn Marie Stolt (my grandma) is now ninety-six years old.

My uncle David Raymond Stolt, married Leanne Kay Reitzel and had three children: Michael Stolt, Sarah Stolt, and Debbie Stolt. David and Leanne later divorced.

My aunt Irene Marie Stolt, married Raymond LePage and they had three children: Stephen LePage, Marcus LePage, and Angela LePage. Irene and Raymond later divorced. Marcus LePage passed away in 1995.

My aunt Sylvia Louise Stolt, married Gregory Koch and they had four children: Marie Koch, Jonathon Koch, Susan Koch, and Laura Koch. Sylvia and Gregory later divorced. Sylvia Koch passed away in 1997.

My mom Judith Ann Stolt, married Daniel Lee Janssen (my dad) and they had two children: Rebecca Janssen and Matthew Janssen. Judith and Daniel later divorced. Matthew Janssen passed away in 1971. Judith remarried in 1976 to Gregory Groves who adopted Rebecca who took his surname, Groves. Judith and Gregory later divorced.

My aunt Theresa Pauline Stolt, married John Smith and had three children: Christopher Smith, Stephanie Smith, and Andrew Smith. Theresa and John later divorced. Theresa remarried Chip Martyn, and they had a son Noah Martyn. Theresa and Chip later divorced.

My uncle Thomas Laverne Stolt, was not married and had no children. He passed away in 1994.

My grandpa was a medic in the United States Army Air Force. He was a corporal in the Army who served from February 9th, 1942 to January 8th, 1946. He had a unique job where he worked in mobile military hospitals as a surgical technician and an assistant surgeon in the Army operating rooms with an assortment of duties. He would prepare the sterile supplies, the instruments for surgery, as well as the anesthesia and oxygen equipment for patients.

Both Grandpa and Grandma worked at the St. Peter State Hospital as psychiatric technicians. Grandma worked there from August 1940 to January 1980. Grandpa worked there from March 1946 to April 1975. My grandparents did not have an easy job working with psychiatric mental patients, especially in the earlier years. Patients were violent and out of control and needed to be restrained, especially the males. As psychiatric care improved with better methods of control and medications, the environment improved for both employees and patients, but that wasn't until the later years.

Grandpa worked in an all-male ward called Upper Flat North. These were the toughest men that were hard to handle, and Grandpa had numerous challenges working with them. The ward he worked in was next to a ward called Upper Flat South, housing female mental patients. It was equally tough for staff to deal with these mentally unstable women. If things would get out of control in the women's ward and they needed extra help, they would call on my grandpa to come rushing to help with the patients. Eventually, Grandpa moved to the hospital ward where he worked with the criminally insane, the most dangerous men around. It was a scary place to work. These were the patients no one could deal with, so it was an extremely challenging job. These men had been murderers or rapists who had done the worst things you could imagine, and they would end up in this prison type facility. Grandpa retired from work in 1975.

Grandma worked in several wards, starting with the "sick room," where ill or dying patients were housed. From there she worked in many other wards over the years and finished out her career in a ward called Shantz Hall.

Not only had my grandpa been in the military, but also my uncle David Stolt had served as well. David was a medic in Vietnam from 1966 to 1967. I highly respect all those who have been in the military, and I especially want to thank my grandpa and my uncle David for serving our country in the military. Thank you to all who have served to protect our country! You are a hero in my book! I am a proud American!

For anyone in the immediate family who wants more in-depth family history and dates, let Uncle David or I know, and we will give you the information.

Do not be anxious about anything, but in prayer with repetition, make your requests known to God. Philippians 4:6

Chapter 27

Beach House Ministry

In September 2010, I married the love of my life! He is not only my soulmate, but we also have the best time together in whatever we do. Lonnie is a godly man who has been my better half and my best friend for many years. God has been in the middle of our marriage, and we love His leading in our lives. With a three-strand cord, God has bonded Lonnie and I together for a bigger purpose than just being a married couple. God has prepared us for a ministry we never even imagined! We were ready for whatever He had prepared for us because with God, all things are possible! He led us down a path that would teach us what "LOVE" and "Compassion" really means.

In January 2014 Lonnie and I were living in Minnesota when we visited friends in Hawaii. We loved to swim at the beach in Kahala where we were married almost four years before. The water was a light blue color, beautiful, and breathtaking. As we dived into the water, it was refreshing and cool. We floated around on the water looking toward the beach. There was an enormous 6,000 square-foot mansion set snugly between tall palm trees and a huge pool that filled the whole backyard. This mansion had been abandoned.

At one time, it must have been a fabulous place where the elite once lived. They probably had dinner parties almost every night, and the guests' children would play in the pool and throw a beach ball around. They may have had chauffeurs for the limo, a housekeeper or two, a chef, and a door man to answer the door, maybe even a servants' quarters for the help. Celebrities were probably showing up every hour for the party and looking for friends they knew and sipping on a glass of wine as they chatted it up with royalty. I could only imagine how it once was.

Lonnie gazed at the mansion, now dark, drab, and desolate. No one had lived there for many years. The structure was falling apart, and there were holes in the windows from rocks being thrown. There was an empty pool with rock boulders piled high and garden beds that had become a shrubbery of weeds. This run-down mansion was now one of many sad statistics of abandoned mansions in the area.

Lonnie paddled along the top of the water with his flippers, and as we swam the backstroke, we looked on in wonder at this once magnificent, beautiful home. He was deep in thought as he said, "Wouldn't it be great if we lived in this beach house, but not only lived in it, but had a ministry that we ran as well?" I loved this man of God who could look at an old, junky, rundown house and see a future of hope in rebuilding it and changing lives for Jesus! I said, "Yes, wouldn't that be amazing!" but in the back of my mind, I figured it would never happen. We had no money to live in a big beach house like this. Yet, God had plans in the making. Our dreams were about to come true.

Lonnie and I left the beach, and on our drive around the island, we thought about looking at places for rent, just for the fun of it. We had been tossing the idea around about moving to Hawaii, and we were curious about the cost of the average rental. We both prayed asking God if we moved to Hawaii, where would we live. Every town that we drove through, we just didn't feel God say anything, but when we drove to the west side of the island, in Waianae and Makaha, we felt a calling on our life. This neighborhood was where God wanted us to minister to people and share with them about Jesus! We both felt the calling at the exact same time and said, "This is it!" We had no doubt in our mind God called us to something bigger than us, and we were excited! Sometimes I am in awe how God would speak to both Lonnie and I to confirm something important in our lives.

We drove around Waianae where there wasn't much for rent, but when we drove into Makaha, a smaller town of approximately 8,000 people, we found a few places available for rent. I had always LOVED Makaha! It was a very memorable place for me. It was where I had camped many weekends and swam with large fish, turtles, stingray, and dolphins; and I had hiked trails deep into the cascading mountains where the views were breathtaking.

At the very end of the road in Makaha, there was a flat hiking trail that eventually led to a bird sanctuary where a person could only walk by foot to enter. Sometimes fisherman would drive their truck on this trail to a great fishing spot. They would hike down the side of the mountain to go fishing. I remember one time on a Hawaiian vacation, Lonnie and I had driven a rental jeep down this very thin trail where the ocean was just inches off a cliff on the left side and there was a gigantic mountain that went straight up into the sky on the right side. There was barely any room to drive on the road, but we had wanted an adventure, so we moved slowly forward watching for big boulders and careful not to fall off the steep cliff. When the trail cut back to nearly nothing because of erosion, Lonnie took the jeep practically sideways up the hillside to get back on the narrow path. As we were sideways, I looked over his shoulder to see the crashing waves against the rocks far below. I nearly had a heart attack! This was one of the scariest and craziest things I had ever done! I told Lonnie to stop the jeep, and while it was still sideways, I climbed out the window and walked back to the trail while he figured out how to get out of the jam he was in. He drove forward, then somehow turned the vehicle around, and when he drove back toward me, I jumped in the jeep and we drove on the narrow path back to the entrance. Ahh, one of my favorite crazy adventures in Makaha!

Back to the present. Lonnie and I drove around the back streets of Makaha where we parked in front of a house that had a rental sign, and we checked out the cottage that was for rent. It was a cute, small three-bedroom cottage. After walking through the place, I loved it and thought, "This is it!" When Lonnie and I went back to our friends' house with whom we were staying, we told them about the rental we found. Ironically, our friends had a house they were fixing up in Makaha to make into a ministry house and if we were interested, we could go see it.

The very next day we all drove to Makaha where we stopped in front of a huge 4,000 square-foot beach house. My jaw dropped open. THIS WAS OUR DREAM HOUSE!! Our friend, who was also a pastor, said they had a lot of work to do on the house, but once it was fixed up, we could move right in! As we walked into the foyer, I saw that this large house was completely gutted, but as we walked through each room, God showed me what it would look like once we moved in. He showed me people's lives changed and the difference we would make in this little community all for the glory of God. We walked out the back door and there it was... the ocean - right outside the door!

We looked out over the coral where the ocean was just massive! The waves were crashing on the huge coral, spraying water up into the air and splashing right in the yard. I WANTED THIS! I prayed silently and asked God if this was what He wanted for us. I couldn't believe how beautiful it was here! Even with the house gutted, God showed me what it would look like when it was finished! We would make it our sweet home. This would be a dream come true! Lonnie and I told our pastor we would have to pray about it. Secretly I hoped God would say yes to this ministry opportunity, not only to reach out to the community, but also to enjoy life right on the beach. We may never have this opportunity ever again.

When we returned to our friend's house, Lonnie and I walked to the beach in Waikiki where we discussed the pros and cons of renting this house for ministry. There seemed to be many more pros than cons. We sat on a bench close to the water, held each other's hands, and prayed, asking God what He thought. Then we waited for God's response. Almost immediately, we both had a rush of peace about the place. God said, *"Yes."*

We told the pastor we wanted the house, and he walked us through all that they had to do to fix up the house first. We shared with him that we would need six months to sell our belongings and home in Minnesota as well as say goodbye to our family and do the steps needed for quarantine for our puppy. We gave the pastor a large sum of money to hold the beach house for us, in good faith that when it was finished, we would be the couple to move in and run the ministry. Then Lonnie and I flew home to Minnesota.

Within six months, we sold everything we needed to sell. We prayed, asking God to take the reins and sell it all. We had a boat that needed repair which a friend took for cheap. We had a great old-style camper that fit on the back of Lonnie's truck. We used it quite often to camp on the weekends, and I was a little sad to see it go, but we made a few hundred dollars more than what we bought it for. We posted our home online and within seventy-two hours, it sold, not only selling quickly, but the man who bought it was so kind that he was willing to let us stay in the home for the remaining two months until our flight out to Hawaii. We received more money than we had purchased it for. With the extra funds, we fixed up the home and left most of the furniture including the large expensive T.V. We sold everything we had within that two months, and it felt good to start fresh! We had only a few large duffle bags and our puppy to fly to Hawaii. It was all a "God-thing." It was so easy for us to let go of all the material things, start over, and look forward to a new chapter in our lives that could save souls for Christ and encourage those around us who had lost hope.

A few nights before the flight, we hit a bump in the road that could put a halt to our plans. It was Saturday night and as I was cleaning the house and packing, I realized at 10:30 that the papers we needed for quarantine were still at the vet. I was supposed to pick them up Friday and completely forgot with all the busyness of moving. The vet wasn't open on Sundays and our flight out was 5:00 Monday morning. Our dog was coming with us, and we had already done six months of quarantine at our home, so when we reached Hawaii, we would only have to walk off the plane and have them sign a piece of paper for them to allow Bella into Hawaii. Without that quarantine paperwork from our vet, Bella would end up in the quarantine station where she would have to stay one-hundred-twenty days in a jail-like cell to make sure she didn't have rabies from the mainland. They were very strict with any shipments of animals or any domesticated pets. They had never had rabies in Hawaii, and the plan was not to ever have even one incident on any of the islands.

As the thought sunk in that I needed these papers for Bella, I dropped my mop and started crying. Lonnie looked at me and asked, "What happened?" I told him, "We don't have the quarantine papers!" I was almost hysterical thinking we would have to leave Bella behind or leave her in jail in Hawaii. Lonnie took my hands in his and he prayed, *"Lord, you know our circumstances. You guided our steps as we prepared our hearts for this very moment and the ministry in Hawaii. We know Lord, You are in the little things, like Bella coming with us. Please help us so we can fly to Hawaii and not have any issues with the paperwork for quarantine."*

After we prayed, I felt peace and started to calm down. I knew God would take care of this situation for us. Even though I didn't know how it would be fixed, I trusted God knew what He was doing.

Lonnie and I drove to the vet clinic to see if there was an after-hours phone number, and there was. We called the number, and the person on the other line suggested we go on Facebook to leave a message to see if we could get ahold of the vet that way. We wrote a message on their Facebook wall saying, "Please call us. It's an emergency." After we sent the message, I noticed the last Facebook post had been posted over two months earlier! I was devastated. No one had been on this page for months! It was 11:00pm and I wasn't going to sleep anytime soon, but then the phone rang! It was the vet calling. She said, "It just so happens that an employee jumped on the Facebook page and saw your post, then called me to ask if I knew the Joneses. Of course, I know the Joneses!" She said with a laugh. The vet continued, "I am leaving for a trip early tomorrow morning, but I can meet you at the clinic to give you the papers before I leave." We thanked her and hung up the phone. I was so relieved! What are the chances an employee saw the Facebook page, called the vet, and we were able to meet up for the papers before her trip and everything worked out as it should? It was a GOD-MOMENT and I was in awe and so thankful! Why do I ever worry about anything when God will take care of it all?

I love the verse that says, *Do not be anxious about anything, but in prayer with repetition, make your requests known to God. Philippians 4:6*

Finally, we were off to Hawaii to do what God had called us to do.

And He said to them, *Go into all the world and preach the gospel to all creation." Mark 16:15*

We had been praying for God to use us to make a difference in people's lives in Makaha. There were many homeless and hurting people in the area, and we wanted to change their lives and show them God's love. Our hearts were big, and hopes were even bigger! All glory to God! Our God is a big God and He can do miracles!

The flight to California was five hours long, but it was a turbulent one because of the wind, so it slowed the plane to the point that we almost missed our next flight. We had to make that second flight because the quarantine in Hawaii was only open until 3:00pm, and with Hawaiian time different from Minnesota time, if we missed the cut off, Bella would end up in quarantine jail for months. We prayed as we were walking off the first plane and suddenly heard our names over the loud speaker, "Jones, party of two, we are closing the doors soon!" We walked fast toward the walkway going to the next plane, but when we asked how far the plane was, an employee told us it was half a mile and we wouldn't make it in time.

We headed that way, praying as we went, when a lady in a golf cart whizzed right up to us and stopped. She asked, "Need a ride?" It was music to my ears! Lonnie said, "Yes, we are the Jones party they called over the loud speaker. We are going to miss our flight if we don't get to the gate soon." She said, "Hop on!" Lonnie hopped into the front seat with his bag and mine, and I jumped on the back seat holding Bella's carrier with her inside as the lady exclaimed, "Hang on, this will be the ride of your life!" She whizzed through a clump of people honking the horn like a crazy person, yelling, "MOVE, MOVE, WE NEED TO GET THROUGH!" She was driving like a maniac honking the horn and weaving to the right and left as Lonnie held my arm tightly, so I wouldn't fall off the back of the golf cart. Finally, we reached the terminal right when they were shutting the double doors. The lady on the cart yelled, "Here's the Jones party, I've got them, they are here, open that door!" The guy who almost had the doors closed, opened it, and as we tipped the gal and thanked her profusely as we ran toward the gate, I looked back, and she was gone. That's when I knew she was an angel! There were so many people swarming the area like bees that there was no way she could have driven away that fast! I thanked God quietly as we walked onto the plane and sat down. I felt like we had run the marathon, and we had won!

We flew to Hawaii and as we walked off the plane, the smell of Plumeria flowers hit my nose. I knew I was back home again. We stayed with our friends while the beach house was being fixed up. It was supposed to be completely done when we arrived in Hawaii, but it still needed a lot of work and we were disappointed to find out it wasn't finished like it was supposed to be when we arrived. We prayed and asked God if this was a ministry He wanted us to do, and God confirmed, YES!" Many months later with beautiful souls that helped volunteer to make this beach house livable for the Joneses, and with Lonnie's help, the house was finally complete, and we were able to move in.

Not soon after we settled in, God told us we would open the doors on a Sunday for church service. We weren't prepared, but we opened those doors anyway to be obedient to God.

That first Sunday was Palm Sunday and we hoped for a large turn-out. Lonnie and I had a T.V. in the main room where we had the pastor from our home church preaching a live sermon. We had unstacked many chairs in our living room for people to sit. A few people showed up to watch the sermon. I felt God was pleased. The next Sunday more people came! Every Sunday people were showing up. We knew God had a plan, and He was filling the seats. On average we had ten to twelve people in each service, and we never had a Sunday where no one showed up. People from all over the world would travel to Hawaii, stay in Makaha, and God would guide them to our house. Nothing was by chance. They would be walking by or driving by, and God would tell them to stop at our Sunday Service. We welcomed everyone and met so many wonderful people. I am thankful what God had done through this ministry. To this day, we have wonderful friends from everywhere around the world - brothers and sisters in Christ we pray for even to this day!

One of our close friends and a neighbor, Lilly, was definitely an angel in our life. When she spoke, she spread joy everywhere she went. I could tell her life was all about Jesus. She would talk about Jesus and as she smiled, her face just glowed, showing the love of Christ to all who listened. What a gift this woman had! I could tell she had a heart for God, a woman on a mission to reach others for Christ. She was a great encourager for us all. She had a God-given gift to invite her friends, and almost every Sunday she brought someone. Her many girlfriends would walk through the door with beautiful smiles, and they loved to "talk story" with us after the service. We met so many wonderful new friends because of Lilly.

One lovely family, who came to our services a few times while vacationing in Hawaii, were from Indiana. They became friends of ours very quickly. The very next year when they came to Hawaii again, they stayed at our beach house, and that next Sunday, their spirit-filled teen son sat in front of the congregation and played guitar and sang live worship for all of us. What a big blessing! We felt the Holy Spirit in worship, and we were in awe of God. God was moving in this ministry in so many ways, and it amazed us every single time!

Our good friend and neighbor Nathan showed up every Sunday with his mom! He brought his eighty-six-year-old mother in a wheelchair. She was a sweet woman who loved to sing, and she lived for Sunday mornings. All week long she would ask her son when church was, and she would count down the days until Sunday morning when she would get all dolled up to come to service to worship God. We played YouTube worship songs with words at the bottom of the screen to sing and praise God. Because we had one older lady hard of hearing and another one who was deaf, having words on the screen made all the difference in the world so they could sing along. Every Sunday right after the service and when worship ended, Ruby, Nathan's mom, would belt out a worship song with no music in the background. Her lovely voice would ring through the house as everyone stood around and listened, appreciating her passion for singing. Nathan's brothers, who lived down the street, even checked out the Sunday service to see what it was all about. Every single person who came to Sunday mornings made this a great experience for all, and God's blessings showered down on us. Praise God!

For Lonnie and me, we were learning as we went. We had no one to shepherd us or come along side us to show us what we needed to do, so we relied 100% on guidance from God, and He showed us the way! We prayed over our home for protection, over each chair the neighbors would sit in, and over each person who walked through that door. We were prayer warriors being obedient to what God had called us to do.

Word spread through the neighborhood about the pastor preaching on T.V. and the ministry at the Jones house. The children started coming to the service, even without their parents. They just showed up at the door on Sunday mornings and watched the long-drawn-out sermons with the adults. These children were young who didn't have a long attention span, yet they would sit through the hour-and-a-half sermon! It was amazing! Nathan was also a big part of helping with the ministry, and the children thought he was great! We thought so too! He had a pool the children loved to swim in, and after service they had cookies and juice, and then they would go jump in his pool next door. It was perfect. God was really working in the neighborhood!

Lonnie and I prayed about starting a children's service to teach them all about Jesus. These were children that had not heard anything about Jesus or knew about Him but did not have a relationship with Him. We had no idea what to do, but God said, *"Do it,"* and we opened our doors for the children's service. On average we had five to fifteen children for the service. We prayed and asked God for someone to help with the children's ministry since we were doing everything ourselves and between working outside the home and doing ministry, we had our hands full. Then God sent a wonderful young woman from California to help with the children. Praise God for answered prayer! Every Sunday those children would show up, and they were open to learning as much as they could about

God and Jesus. The children watched a cartoon centering on God, the Bible and Jesus, the Son of God. Then they sat at the tables and wrote a Bible scripture to memorize and then they would create fun arts and crafts. Afterward, they went outside for other games and activities. Relaxing in the hammocks was their favorite thing to do. Sometimes two or three children would lay in a hammock at one time. Our hearts grew for these children. For me personally, they taught me about strength, courage and perseverance in the face of danger. These children lived in a harsh environment, and yet they blossomed with beautiful hearts and souls into wonderful young girls and boys. I am so proud of each one of them!

Even though we didn't have anyone to shepherd or teach Lonnie and I how to run a ministry, God promised He would be there, and He was. We stepped out in faith, being obedient to what God wanted us to do, and trusted He would get us through, and He did. We had such a peace about the whole thing, and it worked out beautifully. We ran into a few obstacles because we lived in a neighborhood where our Sunday gatherings could not be called church, ministry, or anything related. It had to be called a "Bible study," which we didn't believe it was. We watched a sermon on the large T.V., sang worship songs afterward, and had snacks, juice, and fellowship to end the beautiful day. It was truly a ministry from God, all glory to Him, and we so badly wanted to call it just that, "A Ministry."

The initial promises the church said they would fulfill had fallen through from the beginning. Financially they weren't going to help at all, and we had counted on their assistance. We didn't have money ourselves, but God always came through for us when we needed the finances for the ministry. We prayed consistently to God about everything in our lives and He promised He would be there every step of the way on this journey and He was. We knew we could trust in Him. God had never broken a promise.

Trust in the Lord with all your heart, and lean not on your own understanding, in all your ways acknowledge Him, and he will direct your path. Proverbs 3:5&6

We persevered in ministry no matter what the cost. We both worked hard to live in the beach house that attracted people from all over the world. We opened our doors to anyone at any time to share the love of Jesus. We never realized how far God would take this ministry, and we were amazed. God taught us how to reach the people in the neighborhood, and in the end, God kept His promise. We lived on faith, and God met every single need we had!

Even my dog Bella wanted to be a part of the ministry. She acted like she had the most important part. She was a happy greeter when neighbors showed up for service. Every Sunday she faithfully waited at the front door for the children or adults to come. It was fun to see her sit at the door, and as soon as she saw someone, her tail would wag, she would jump up, and excitedly run outside to greet them. As service started, Bella would walk around and check on the children who would pet her as she walked by. Afterward, she would lie down on her dog bed and sleep through the rest of the sermon. After the sermon was over and everyone was eating chips or cookies or whatever we had on hand for snacks, Bella would eat up all the crumbs on the floor. As the last person left the house, usually by mid-afternoon, Bella would sit at the door and sadly watch people leave. Sundays were her favorite day of the week! Exhausted after an eventful day, she would sleep the day away.

So much has happened in the years we lived at the beach house. I had built from scratch a firepit with bricks and loved the look of the gray stones piled a few feet high in a perfect circle. Once in a great while the neighbors and some of the Sunday school children would come over, and we would all sit around the fire, roasting marshmallows or hotdogs. We really enjoyed those times. I loved just staring at the fire. It was relaxing to watch the flames dance higher and higher and listen to the ocean and see the billowing waves crashing on the rocks silhouetted in the background. What magnificent beauty. I had to thank God for the many blessings within this ministry at the beach house.

We loved where we lived, and some events that happened at the house were just downright entertaining. A few times a year, the tree trimmers would come to our home to trim the very tall palm trees and cut off all the coconuts that had grown on them. These skinny Hawaiian men would climb up the trees as if they were monkeys. They would reach the very top and start cutting down the coconuts from the tree as if it were the easiest thing to do. I couldn't believe how they climbed those trees! We loved the coconut parties afterwards! One person would bring a machete, chopping off the top of the coconut, put a straw in it for someone to drink, and then use a spoon to scrape the meat from the sides to eat. At the first coconut party, we had twenty-five children from the neighborhood waiting for a drink of fresh coconut water. When everyone had their fill of as much as they could drink and then eat the coconut meat off the sides, we would sit around relaxing in the backyard and watch the large waves crash into the yard. Sometimes the waves were so large that when it would crash, it shook the whole house. After the party finished, we would send home coconuts with all the children and adults and pass out extra coconuts to any neighbors that wanted to take them home.

We also had movie nights about once a month. We would prepare hotdogs and chips. Then there were mounds of popcorn to eat, and juice to drink. We had chairs and futons sprawled every which way for children to watch movies on the big screen. Adults would sit around the kitchen table and "talk story" or play games. Those parties went late into the evening, sometimes overnight. We always had twenty or more adults and children, and it was so much fun. After a movie, the children loved sitting outside in the hammocks and watching the ocean waves crash or they would chase each other around the oversized yard playing games.

In everything we did, Lonnie and I made sure that Jesus was the focal point praying to Him and giving Him all the glory for everything in our lives. At the end of the day, we would sit in the hammocks and watch the most stunning sunset with the ocean waves lapping at the coral in front of our place. It was the perfect end to the day. We always talked about what we are thankful for and reminded ourselves daily that God loved us so much and was guiding us in everything in our lives.

One Sunday, we felt God lead us to start communion, and we were obedient to what God wanted. We also started having regular potlucks every month, and everyone brought a dish to share. Sometimes many parents and children showed up, and other times it was very few. No matter what, we somehow always had plenty of food. We were thankful, knowing God was guiding us and blessing us. I was excited to see what was next!

On our first Thanksgiving at the beach house, we had a huge meal with two turkeys and all the fixings that filled up the entire bar in our kitchen. We invited friends and neighbors to join us. We were pleasantly surprised to see thirty people come! We felt blessed because we had invited anyone that walked up to our front door, including many homeless. God provided, and everyone had a good meal. Not one person went home hungry. God was faithful! Every Thanksgiving and Christmas we invited people from the neighborhood, and we always had a full house with friends, neighbors, parents with children, and the homeless. We welcomed everyone with open arms. We were blessed more than we could imagine. God is so good!

There are so many amazing blessings and miracles that happened in this ministry house. We are thankful for all the volunteers who put the house together for this very purpose, and we praise God and are thankful that He guided us daily and faithfully showed us what to do in this ministry. Lonnie had his pastoral license and married a beautiful couple who have become our close friends. He was also able to baptize a mother and daughter in Nathan's pool next door, and many people needing prayer, we saw God heal them! Even children asked for prayer, and we prayed for them right then and there. A few of the children even raised their hands to accept Jesus! It was a beautiful thing. This was God's ministry, and we were thankful that He gave us the chance to be a part of it. What an amazing journey and spiritual growth we had, all glory to God!

Years later, God called us in a different direction. We have always been obedient to what God has for us, but I will never forget how God spiritually grew and stretched me personally to unbelievable heights to make me who I am today, a better woman of God!

Chapter 28

All About Bella Mocha

My dog Is amazing! She is a five-year-old, tri-color King Charles Cavalier. Her fur is black and white. She has a black face with a brown and white freckled nose and brown eyebrow markings. Her belly is spackled with adorable black freckles. She loves the belly rubs I give her. She sprawls all four legs out wide waiting for a belly rub with no consideration for decency. No modesty at all! It is the funniest thing. She is smaller than the average Cavalier at ten pounds. Cavaliers are typically twenty to twenty-five pounds. She is my best friend who goes everywhere with me! She is beautiful and attracts so much attention everywhere she goes! Everyone adores her cute, little puppy face, and I am asked a lot of questions about her. The top six questions I receive are: "Is she a puppy? How old is she? Is this a good breed to have? Is she a Cocker Spaniel? Where did you get her? She is so quiet; did you need to train her to be like that?" I answer questions everywhere we go, but I don't mind. I like to educate people on the type of breed Bella is, and well, she just loves the attention!

Bella loves the beach and takes after me, being a beach girl! My husband Lonnie and I lived in Oahu, Hawaii, in a big house in Makaha, and the beach was just steps from our house. It was beautiful, and we enjoyed every minute of it!

Every day when I would tell Bella we were going to the beach, she would whine in excitement and run to the door waiting in anticipation for her leash to be strapped on. When the door opened, she would rush down the driveway to the street and on the path to the beach. I could say the word "beach," even when she was in a deep sleep, she would jump up and run to the door, ready to go. At the beach, I would let Bella off her leash, and then she would run and play with her doggie friends. She loved running the whole stretch of sand, and I would lag behind trying to keep up. Her and I would run along the ocean almost daily, with her paws flipping the hot sand up into the air, and her tongue hanging out the side of her mouth. Bella really enjoyed the beach life. She could run forever and never tire. She would be at the shoreline, and when a wave would push its way up the sand, she would run away from the turbulent water. If she ran too far ahead along the shoreline, I would make a noise, like a Hawaiian person would call another person. I would yell, "Hui!" (*Hui* in Hawaiian sounds like "Whoo-eee"). Bella would whip around in a circle with her floppy ears going every which way and her feet kicking up the sand under her, then she would run back to me. She was very attentive and always came when I called her.

For my husband and me, our favorite beach to watch sunsets was only a half mile from the house. There were huge boulders up against the shoreline, perfect for hiking as the waves crashed and sprayed water up into the air. What a beautiful sight! It was a large beach park. This was Bella's favorite park where she could chase the big, four-inch, black, ugly crabs that lurked in wet, dark places under the coral rock. Bella was fast and would chase the crabs, but she was not fast enough to catch any of them.

In the winter time, the waves were big on the west side of the island. At the beach by my house, sand had been pulled way out by the huge twenty-to-thirty-foot waves. It left massive coral rock exposed for all to see! The waves pushed up on the sand and lapped at the coral, then pulled back into the massive ocean again. It was my first winter in the beach house, and I wasn't used to such large waves. The endless beach of sand that

Bella and I ran every day was gone. It was something I would have to accept - the change in seasons.

One morning as Bella and I walked along the coral, she started hunting for large crabs. I stopped walking and watched the waves. I could almost predict when the waves were going to crash on the shore and pull back out again. Waves usually came in sets of three, so it would push in, then pull out, push in again, pull out, push in again, pull out again, and then take a brief break before it would do it all over again. Today, it was more turbulent than usual. Very choppy and unpredictable. I started walking on the hot sand and paid close attention to the waves, so they wouldn't push me down or pull me into the ocean. When the waves would pull back out, Bella would run ahead and look under any rock or coral shelf left empty of water as she searched for a large crab to chase. Ahead of us, there was a huge reef shelf. Sometimes waves would push large shells from the bottom of the ocean and they would end up on the beach or hidden in a coral shelf. I always liked to search for pretty shells on our walks. As we reached the large clump of coral close to the water, Bella ran around having so much fun looking for crabs. She stayed close to me as we waited for the waves to crash and roll on the shelf, then pull out and crash in again. At one moment, the water was just a trickle at our feet, and the waves were pulled back an unusually long time. I looked at this large, flat shelf and thought it would take us less than thirty seconds to cross this area. The wave was still pulled back and didn't seem to want to come in, so I took the chance and yelled to Bella, "Let's run!"

As we ran across the shelf, the water was calm, so we were barely wet. We were almost on the other side when I heard a rolling thunder. In a second's time, a large wave was coming our way! I looked at Bella who was about four feet in front of me chasing a crab and not paying any attention to an enormous wave that was only feet away. She looked up when the wave billowed right over her. The wave knocked me down as well, and as I picked myself up, I looked over the large amount of water surrounding me and couldn't see Bella anywhere! The waves were just rolling in, and they wouldn't stop! I knew the waves were pushing Bella down and not letting her up! The waves were so sporadic as they were pushing and pulling and going every which way! I didn't see Bella, and I was praying hard for God to save her!

God told me to reach my hand into the water, so I did. I felt her fur, but the water pulled her away. I knew I had only seconds before the wave was going to pull out again. Once that happened, Bella would be gone forever! I felt around, and Bella bumped into my hand, so I was able to grab her collar and pull her up. She choked and sputtered as I held her closely and walked up on the beach. It was a close call - my little girl almost died! Thankfully, she was fine, but from then on, Bella never went into the ocean again!

So many people have been pulled into the massive ocean because they didn't realize how powerful one little wave can be. All it takes is a small wave to push a person to the ground and then swiftly pull them out into the deep ocean. Someone can be safely standing on the sand but if a wave comes and pulls the sand out from under the person, they can fall, and the water can easily pull them out to sea! It can happen in a second's time. If they are caught in an under-current, sometimes it is too strong even for the best swimmer to return to shore. This situation may end with the person drifting out to sea, never to be found again. It happens more frequently than people think. I have seen rescue helicopters flying over the ocean at least two to three times a week by our home in Makaha! Many times, the rescuers never found the drowned victims.

Back to Bella! She had the run of the beach house and the yard. In the house, she loved to chase all the little "geckos" that would skitter across the walls or ceiling with their little sticky feet. They are green or brown lizards that the Hawaiians consider "good luck" if one were found in the home. Geckos looked like the little "Geico lizard" on the Geico commercial. Bella was obsessed with finding geckos, and early in the morning as soon as she ran outside, she looked around at every potted plant or rock in the yard to find any skittering lizard she could chase. They were fast, and Bella was never able to catch one, but it made her happy to chase them around. I liked the geckos because they ate bugs in our house or yard, and I liked hearing the chirping noise they made.

One day, I was leaning up against a palm tree in our yard. It had the perfect nook in the tree to lean on. I was talking to my neighbor Nathan when he pointed to the tree. When I slightly turned my head toward the tree to look, Bella was standing just a few inches from my face! I jumped back, not expecting her to be in my face, almost six feet off the ground! It was a good laugh Nathan and I had. Bella, scurrying up the tree, must have thought she was a squirrel! Once she climbed that first palm tree and saw a gecko scramble up the side, she chased that lizard even higher. I couldn't believe it! She was a tree-climbing dog! Maybe I could teach her to scramble to the very top of the coconut tree, knock down a few coconuts, and climb back down. Bella made tree-climbing a regular habit. When she saw anything move on the tree, she would chase whatever it was, an ant or bug, thinking maybe it was a gecko, but when it came to those fast-moving lizards, she would chase it all over as if it were a cat-and-mouse game! It was the funniest thing to watch!

One morning I woke up to find beach front property. We had a huge yard and beyond the rock wall, there was a large coral shelf with just a little bit of sand which was not an area to safely dive into the ocean. On this beautiful day, the beach was not only steps away, but smack dab right in front of our house with sand everywhere. The southern swell had pushed large mounds of sand right in front of our place, and it covered practically all the coral! I could walk right out there and swim. The beach was there for more than a week and we loved it! I couldn't believe we had such a spectacular view right from our yard.

That day, as Bella and I ran to the beach, she saw movement close to the lapping waves, and she quickly started chasing around a white crab. This crab was an unusual white with some coloring in his big claws. He was a large four-inch monster crab! I was fascinated by how he looked. I had seen many large black crabs, but never a white one quite like this. Bella was so excited about finding the crab that she jumped and pranced toward him while its claws reached up toward the sky to defend itself. Bella was rather cautious though, and I refereed the whole playful battle to make sure neither one of them hurt the other. As Bella ran at him, the crab would run at her! It was like a game of "chicken." They would both retract and run at each other again. A wave came up to pull the crab a few feet toward the ocean, which would have been the perfect time for the crab to bow out gracefully and go about his day. Bella watched the crab as their little game might have been come to an end, but that crab came running back up the sand embankment with claws up high. He was again ready for battle! Bella was so happy! She raced around him in circles which may have made them both a bit dizzy. The crab turned and turned making sure he faced Bella at every angle. Finally, they both stopped, and Bella went in for a sniff. With the crab's snappers up and ready for action, I warned Bella to back off. She retreated a bit, knowing my stern voice meant business.

Then I picked up the crab with my flip-flop and took it to a large rock that he could sit and contemplate life without defending himself against the dog. I told Bella we were going home. She followed me with her head down, like a child playing on the swings at the park having been told they were going home. Bella was pouting. As we were walking toward the house, she suddenly whipped around and ran back a few feet to where the crab was for one more game of "chicken!' I turned around and thought, "Well, she is on her own." Bella ran over to the crab, and I saw her face go down as if she were sniffing it. I thought, "Oh, boy, her nose is going to be pinched." I waited to hear her cry but heard nothing.

Bella then sauntered towards me with her head down and I noticed something rather large hanging off her long, fluffy ear. I couldn't make out what it was until she stood right in front of me. The crab dangled there helplessly, but he was not willing to give up the fight, so he hung on tightly. He had won! Luckily Bella wasn't hurt. The crab was hanging from her fur, but Bella looked at me with a look of annoyance like, "Please take this from me!" I laughed as I brushed the crab off her ear, then picked the crab up again with my flip flop to return him to the shallow water. The next small wave came and pulled the crab out into the water, so he could find coral to climb on. Bella was ready to go home. She was happy. She had her beach time filled with play and fun with her friend, the crab.

Moral of the story: When you are crabby, the world can come against you, but when you look at life through a positive light, things seem to fall into place better. Be optimistic.

*No animals were hurt in this story – I am serious! *

My husband and I were invited to a sandbar with friends. A sandbar is an area of sand way out in the ocean where it looks oddly displaced. It is a sand mass that is in the midst of deep water in which boats need to be aware, so they don't go aground. When the tide goes out, the sandbar is revealed, and when the tide comes in, the sandbar is completely covered where you would never know it was there.

One day our friends took us on their boat to the sandbar. The sandbar was already packed full of people, and boats were all over the place. We had come later in the morning which meant the ocean had covered the sand about four-inches high, yet all these people had set up their lawn chairs in the water and big umbrellas covered them to keep cool from the hot sun. Music was playing loudly, and some people were grilling out from their boats, while other people were dancing with a beer in their hand. It looked like one big party place!

It was our first time to the sandbar, and we were amazed this place even existed! In ankle-deep water, we brought out the chairs and pushed the umbrella deep into the sand to keep the sun off our faces. Then we sat down to relax. We passed out drinks and cheese and crackers for "pupus." ("*Pupu*" is a Hawaiian word for "appetizer") We had a great time together, one I will never forget. It was the perfect day!

We had brought Bella with us, but she was not too enthusiastic about the vast ocean all around us. Bella was not a fan of swimming or being in the ocean, yet she was a good sport about it and walked around in the water for a bit. However, most of the time she just sat in my lap looking around for dry land.

After so many hours, Bella had to pee. I tried coaxing her to do so in the ocean, but the water was up to her chest. Bella was not thrilled about the idea and would not go. I put my towel down in the boat and told her to pee on that, but she wouldn't do it. She needed dry land away from all this water. Bella was determined to hold it until we were on dry land. We stayed on the sandbar all day long. I thought for sure Bella would eventually give in and pee in the water, but she wouldn't. She looked miserable!

Finally, we were back on the dock. My husband took Bella off the boat to dry land, and she bolted like lightening to the parking lot area. As soon as she hit the asphalt, she squatted and started peeing as she walked. She peed and walked for a good long minute, and it looked like a thirty-foot stream. POOR THING! Next time, we would leave her home with the sitter!

This next story was terrifying for me! My neighbor heard screams from the beach, looked out the window, and this is his account of what he saw and heard:

"I heard someone screaming on the beach, I looked out the window, and saw two big dogs mauling a lady. It looked like one dog had gotten ahold of her throat and was yanking at her neck, and the other dog was biting at her feet. I came running out of the house, grabbed a shovel, and told my brother some lady is getting mauled on the beach. My brother said, 'Becka just went to the beach, that's probably her.' We both went running down the street to the beach path..."

Mark Abrell

The terrifying attack: Bella and I were walking on the beach when two loose pit bulls came running from the street and started chasing her around on the sand. The wild dogs were on either side of Bella, nipping at her sides and back legs as she ran. Bella was yipping in a high-pitched cry, and I thought for sure she was going to die right there in front of me! The dogs were playing with her just before they would grab her legs and tear her apart. I kept screaming her name, "Bella!!" I hoped she would run to me, but she was terrified and trying to run as far away from the big vicious dogs as she could. I prayed and asked God to save Bella.

It felt like forever before Bella ran toward me, but I am sure it was just seconds. I grabbed Bella and threw my body over her to save her! At the time, Bella was just a small, ten-pound Cavalier, and these big bullies were sixty-pound pits that could kill her in a second! A fisherman came over to hit the pit bulls with his fishing pole in hopes the dogs would leave, but it did nothing. One dog bit my feet trying to make me move so he could grab Bella's back end and pull her out from under me, while the other dog was inches away from my face. Bella's head was against my chest, and the pit bull closer to my face went in "for the kill." He was reaching toward my chest for Bella's head, and I had only seconds to react. I didn't even think! My hands were holding Bella, so she wouldn't crawl out from under me because then I would be defenseless to protect her! As this big dog's head came nearer to my face, I clamped down on his forehead as hard as I could with my teeth! I was so angry! This beast was NOT going to kill my dog! The dog was surprised, and he pulled back as he cried out. He was whining and pulling away, but I wouldn't let him go. He was so strong, and I was thinking if I kept biting down, he would pull my teeth right out of my mouth. I held on for as long as I could and then let him go and both dogs ran off!

I walked up the beach path carrying Bella and looking her over. Bella was a little shaken but seemed okay. I looked behind me to see that dog coming right at me again! I whipped my whole body around and took a step toward this monster, and I angrily screamed, "I WILL KILL YOU!" The dog turned around abruptly and hightailed it back down the beach. As I walked out to the street, my neighbors came running around the corner. Mark had a shovel in his hand and he was looking behind me for those dogs! He asked if I was okay. I asked Mark to look Bella over. I said, "Does she have any cuts? Is she bleeding anywhere?" He looked her over but didn't see anything. Bella could have been mauled to death, but she wasn't. I couldn't believe it!

Mark Abrell recalled: *"I really thought Becka was being mauled to death, but come to find out, she had bitten the dog and he was trying to get away. It was the sweetest revenge!"*

Mark took me back to his house to wash my bloodied feet. I had bite marks all over my feet and it was painful. I tried to avoid going to the ER. Hawaii was 100% rabies free, so I didn't have to worry about rabies. By the next morning, however, my feet were puffy and more painful than the day before. I went to the ER to have my feet cleaned, and I left there with antibiotics. The nurse had told me I shouldn't have put my life in danger for my dog, but I told her I would do it all over again. Anyone who has a dog that they love will tell you they would do anything to save their dog, just like a mother would give her life for her baby. I would do anything to save my dog Bella! Those stray dogs were not going to kill my dog!

To this day, neighbors still jokingly bring up the fact that I once bit a dog! It was rather comical after the fact. I am thankful that Bella survived, and even to this day, she loves all dogs, including large ones. She has no judgements and no fear of any of them. She loves them all. I still have scars on my feet from the bite wounds, and clear as day, it is still fresh in my mind what happened. After this incident, however, my bond with Bella has been closer than ever.

Bella is more than a dog to me. She is by my best friend who is by my side 24/7. When she was six months old, I had an anxiety attack. She ran up my chest, put her paws around my neck, placed her face on my face, and then pressed against me. At first, I had no idea what she was doing, but I felt better, and she kept pressing into my face, which made me burst into laughter. Then she jumped down and went back to playing with her toy. She had fixed me! I couldn't believe it!

Every time I had anxiety or trouble breathing or was overly stressed, Bella would do it again - run up my chest, wrap her paws around my neck, press her cute little face on my face, and wait for my problems to go away! I told some people what Bella had been doing, and they told me to research about Service dogs. As I researched, I realized Bella chose to be my service dog. She knew how to fix me, and she was so "in tune" with me that she could alert me even before I would have a panic-attack, so I had time to calm myself down. I made it official – I made her my service dog. She had an assigned number and badge, and I had a special vest for her when entering a grocery store. I put her to work. Bella went everywhere with me – shopping at grocery stores, hardware stores, gas stations, restaurants, or anywhere else I went. Bella knew to alert me when my anxiety would start. It was the beginning of having my life back!

I had made sure when Bella was a puppy that I would socialize her with other dogs right away. She loved to meet new people and play at the dog park, but when I put her service dog vest on to go anywhere, she knew it was time to work. She didn't seek attention from people and didn't even look at other service dogs in a store. She knew she must focus on my needs while the vest was on. It's like she became a totally different dog.

If I had an anxiety attack around a group of people, Bella knew how to calm me. Without Bella, I could not be in a social setting, and with her, I felt more normal and comfortable around strangers. I never had anxiety before that one relationship that sent me over the edge years before, and the anxiety had lingered for many years after. Only those who have had anxiety attacks would really understand what I have gone through. I would hope those who have been blessed not to have them, not judge those who do. Anxiety attacks are real, and they don't just go away. I have prayed numerous times and asked God to take this completely from me. I am a work in progress and God is a God of healing and He is FAITHFUL, AMEN.

-Bella stories in Hawaii 2014-2017

Say "I love you" more times than you are used to. Everyone wants to hear it and you never know if you lose that chance to ever say it again.

Chapter 29

"Happily Ever After"

I was standing in front of my mom's house with my wonderful new husband. We had just been married two weeks before. I moved from Hawaii to Minnesota to be with him, and here I was about to reveal to my mom that I was a married woman.

Lonnie had me wait by the car while he went around the house to the front door. He knocked on the door, and when my mom opened it, he told her he had a surprise from Becka for her birthday. She smiled and excitedly asked, "What is it?" Lonnie replied, "I will get the gift; it is in my car." Then Lonnie walked toward the car to come get me. He came walking around the corner with me in hand, and I said, "Surprise! Happy birthday, Mom!" She was so happy to see me and bolted out the front door to give me a great big hug. She asked, "You came here for my birthday? You are so sweet." I had just visited her months before for Mother's Day, so this was a huge surprise. Of course, she had no idea the bomb shell I was about to drop on her!

I told her, "We have another surprise for you." Lonnie and I walked into her house, and my mom and her husband Sebastian sat down so we could tell them the big news. I said, "Well, I just moved back to Minnesota." She replied, "Are you kidding me?" She knew how much I didn't like the freezing cold temperatures in the winter months. I had told her years before I would never live in Minnesota again, but God had bigger plans for me. I answered, "Yes, I really live here. I shipped my cats and everything!" Mom was so happy, finally her one and only child was home! I said, "There is more! Lonnie and I are married!!" She gasped excitedly, "WHAT!!??" As the blood drained from her face, mom looked as white as a sheet. She loved Lonnie. Lonnie and I had been dating a little while, and she always said good things about him. I went on, "Yep, we are married, and we only live twenty minutes away, so I can see you anytime I want." She was ecstatic and hugged me tightly. Then she gave Lonnie a great big hug and smiled at him as she said, "Thank you for bringing my daughter home. I am so happy for you two!" I knew it was the best birthday present I could have ever brought my mom. I don't think I could ever top that one!

I met my husband on an online dating website, Christian Mingle. I signed up on this site five years before I met him. It was one of those promotional deals, pay a one-time fee of $70.00 for a lifetime membership until you find your soulmate. At that time, I was looking for love and really wanted to be on the website, but I was broke and didn't have the money to sign up. I prayed about the fee and left it in God's hands. A week later, my car insurance sent me a refund check because somehow, I overpaid. The check from the insurance company came to exactly $70.00, the amount I needed to join the singles website! I signed up right away.

I fiddled around on the site with building my profile, posting a few pictures, and waiting for messages from guys. It was like crickets chirping. I got nothing. I would get a wink and smile every so often but that was it. I started talking in the mingle chat rooms and made some friends. These people weren't looking for dates. They just needed prayer and support from fellow brothers and sisters in Christ. I truly built good relationships with these people on the site and loved how God used them to pour into my life, and mine into theirs. If I asked for prayer, I would have a dozen prayers right then and there from people in the chat room. If they needed prayer, I would pray for them as well.

I wasn't looking for a long-distance relationship, and most of the men on this site were on the mainland, not in Hawaii. Some of the guys online were just creepy, and I had the feeling they weren't Christian at all but just prowling around on a Christian site to find a "good church girl." The few guys I did meet in Hawaii, we didn't connect at all. I was done dating. I completely focused on my business. I stayed friends with prayer warriors that were in the chat rooms, but other than that, I gave up on finding love altogether. At one point, I even told God it was just He and I for the rest of my life, and I really meant it.

Fast forward a few years. There was this guy from Minnesota who sent me a wink on my profile. I always received winks on Christian Mingle, and I didn't think much of it. I messaged this Minnesota man and asked him in what town he lived. He wrote back immediately to let me know the city. Ironically, he only lived twenty minutes from my mom! How funny! Every so often he would message me, and just to be nice, I would respond in a cordial way. One day, I checked a message from Lonnie, and he had a nice write up about himself. Oddly we had a great deal in common, other than the fact that we were both born in Minnesota. I abruptly told him I wasn't dating, especially long distance, and left it at that. He said we could be friends as he had other "prospects" in mind on the site. That made me feel better. We started talking by email (just as friends), and Lonnie began following me on my Twitter account. I thought, "What a stalker!" but in a good way.

After watching Lonnie's posts on Twitter, I discovered that he was truly a "man of God." I not only watched his posts, but also how he talked to others and started realizing how much he loved God with all his heart. He would say really nice things to me on twitter and it sparked my interest in him.

After a few months on Twitter, I asked if he was ever going to call me. He told me he had been wanting to call but didn't want to ask for my number and was relieved I had asked him. We started talking on the phone, and I felt such a connection to him. I loved the sound of his voice and could listen to it for hours, which is exactly what happened.

Every night after he was off work, he would call me, and we would talk five to six hours. We would talk about anything and everything. How was his day, how was my day, how was his children, what are they up to, what are his likes, what are my likes, what would he do in this scenario, what would I do? We could talk for hours and there was never silence. It was the craziest thing. I felt like I had known him forever.

I was planning a trip to Minnesota to see my mom for her birthday in September. I wanted to fly home and surprise her. I liked doing things like that. I told Lonnie I would like to see him when I visit. He said definitely! I looked online for a ticket to fly home in September, but the tickets were too expensive. I looked for an earlier date and found a cheaper flight in May. I would be home for Mother's Day, and that would be perfect!

When May came around, I flew to Minnesota and stayed with my mom and visited with Lonnie just about every day. We hit it off well, but I made it clear we were "just friends." He was fun to be around, and I couldn't believe how many of the same interests we had.

My mom, Sebastian, Lonnie and I went to a museum in St. Paul, Minnesota that was exhibiting the Dead Sea Scrolls. I had always wanted to see them, and here they were in the museum for only two weeks. Praise God! We were excited to see them together. I say it was not a date, but even to this day, my mom says Lonnie and I were definitely on a date!

The few weeks in Minnesota went fast, and I started liking Lonnie more than I anticipated. I flew back home to Hawaii and returned to my work and beach life. Lonnie and I made sure we talked every single night. Thank goodness for cell phones that have free long-distance calls!

In July, Lonnie took a few days off work and planned a weekend to visit me in Hawaii. He was a complete gentleman who stayed at a hotel in Waikiki close to my apartment. We spent all our waking hours together. We went hiking, swimming, driving around the island, and watching movies on the beach. We did so many fun things. It was a perfect time. At night I would go home, and the next morning, I would pick Lonnie up at the hotel to go about our day. Time went too fast. I learned so much about him, and I truly saw how God was everything to him. I started falling for Lonnie. When he left to fly home, I was missing him already.

Lonnie's version of the story:

"I knew she was 'the one for me' from the first time I talked to her on the phone. I prayed about it, and God told me He picked her for me. God told me not to confess this to her

because she would run. I just let God take the reins, and He would reveal to her what I already knew - that we were supposed to be together, and by the way, yes, it was a date!"

After Lonnie left, I had a serious conversation with God. As I knelt down, I was crying out to Him.

"Lord, did You pick this man for me?" I waited and didn't hear from Him. Tears were falling down my face. *"Lord, what is going on, please tell me what to do. I am falling for this man, but I thought it was just going to be You and me forever. What should I do? Please tell me what to do!"*

I waited for an answer. I was not going to stop praying until I heard from God on this! I questioned Him,

"Is this the one that I am supposed to be with? Please answer me!" After a few moments, God replied, *"This is the one I chose for you, but you have to choose if you want to be with him. You will make more of an impact in the world together than you will alone."*

I sat up, wiped my tears, and thought about what God shared with me. Lonnie was my best friend whom I truly loved. I wanted to make a difference in the world and why not make a difference together? I would love to make more of an impact in this world with God and Lonnie by my side.

The next day I called Lonnie to have a real heart-to-heart talk. He confessed he loved me, and we talked about marriage. From then on, God orchestrated everything. We set a date to marry. Lonnie was going on a mission's trip with his daughter, which was an amazing father-daughter time. Right after they returned, we would marry in September. Time flew by, and before I knew it, he flew out to Hawaii to marry me. He was a perfect gentleman who, again, stayed in a hotel the first few nights until we were married. I was so blown away about his respect and love for God. He made sure we didn't fall into sin before we were married! I loved this man of God!

The day before we married, we were up at 4:00am, drove to a hiking trail in Hawaii kai, and started hiking a long stretch of paved road up the side of the mountain. It was pitch black outside. Good thing we had flashlights! After forty-five minutes of hiking, we reached the top of the mountain when the sun started coming up over the ocean. I looked at Lonnie and his shirt was soaking wet. It was a hot, very humid morning, and he wasn't used to the heat, humidity, or the intense hiking. I had been up this mountain many times, but this particular morning, I felt different.

Lonnie and I looked out over the water and saw stunning colors hit the sky. Through the sunlight poured pinks, blues, and purples so vividly spread over the horizon - it was breathtaking. A large, dark cloud pouring down rain was out over the water but moving closer to where we stood on the edge of a cliff.

I looked at Lonnie, amazed at the beauty in the sky. I said, "Look at God's creation, isn't this beautiful?" He responded, "Yes," as he looked directly at me and then gazed into my eyes. A moment later, he was down on one knee asking me to marry him. I asked, "What are you doing?" I was surprised he was asking since we would marry early the next morning. He said, "I have to make it official; it's the right thing to do." He wouldn't get up off the ground until I said, "Yes," so I replied, "YES, OF COURSE!" He was so happy and stood up to give me a great big hug and kiss.

As we looked out over the water, a large black cloud had stopped about 300 feet from us. It just hovered over the ocean pouring down rain. It looked amazing with all the mixed colors and the sun coming up over the horizon. I thanked God for the perfect morning and the proposal. A few more hikers showed up for the stunning sunrise. Lonnie and I started our long hike down the mountain. It went fast for me! I was on cloud nine! I was engaged and about to be married! I was so excited! I couldn't believe it. It was a dream come true!

Right away, we went to Ala Moana Shopping Center to pick out wedding rings. I liked a three-heart gold ring that cost only $99.00, and Lonnie found a nice gold band to match that cost about the same. It was perfect for us, and we were smitten.

We didn't plan to go traditional with a large expensive wedding - a bushy white dress for me or an expensive black tuxedo for Lonnie and no paid photographer to take our pictures. We decided on a simple wedding. We shopped at the international marketplace in Waikiki for our matching outfits. I had a beautiful Hawaiian print dress, and Lonnie had a matching shirt with tan khaki shorts. We decided on instant cameras that our friends could snap shots of us as we were to be married.

Before the ceremony, I was at my favorite nail salon where I told the lady to rush because I would be getting married in half an hour! I had no cares in the world. I had overflowing peace blanket me as God told me this was going to be the perfect day for Lonnie and me.

Finally, on the beach, both of us barefoot and holding hands, we were overly excited and ready for what came next. The waves crashed on the shore, and I looked at the stunning view in front of us. It was so beautiful! Only the pastor, his wife, and our two close friends were there to share in our ceremony.

Everything was perfect! The pastor, Bible in hand, shared with us what "TRUE LOVE" meant. He shared how our commitment to marriage is forever, and as we said our vows, we became one. With God in the middle of our marriage, we are a three-strand cord which stays strong and can withstand anything. It was a short but sweet ceremony. We said our vows, kissed longingly, then looked at each other and immediately hand in hand, ran into the ocean! As the pastor's jaw dropped open, Lonnie and I baptized one another, washing away our pasts and starting our new lives together. We didn't plan on running into the ocean to baptize each other. As we said our vows, however, God revealed to both of us at the same time, that is what we would do. Officially married, and after the baptism, we went to celebrate and had a great day out on the town.

The next day, Lonnie helped me pack boxes and ship them to his place in Minnesota. I sold furniture and gave many things away; then we flew with my cats to Minnesota. I settled in well at Lonnie's apartment, and we started our new married life together. Lonnie had previously been married for seventeen years, and he had two beautiful children who were eighteen and nineteen years old. One was in college, and the other was finding her way in life. God gave me an immense love for Lonnie's children, and I loved them from the moment I met them. I had never been married, so this was all new to me, but I was so happy for this new life I had with my new family.

Because of my past, however, I brought baggage into my marriage. I had been hurt by men all my life, and I was insecure and scared Lonnie would abandon me because men always left. I had to rely completely on God, and my prayer life was full of questions and insecurities. God was there every second of every day when I needed Him to pull me through something hard in my life. God molded me and sculpted me into a woman of God (Proverbs 31 woman). Lonnie had prayed for me so much that I think calluses were on his knees from praying. Such a faithful man of God, and because of his faith, I became a confident woman in our marriage.

The first year of marriage is usually the hardest, but for us, it really wasn't. It just felt like it was *"meant to be."* Before our marriage, I was a very independent woman that had lived on her own for far too long. For years, I did my own thing without anyone telling me what to do, so there were some adjustments, not that he was telling me what to do, but having to take care of someone else made me grow in ways I never thought I would. I was learning as I went.

I truly saw how Lonnie looked to God for answers in his prayer life. Lonnie's relationship with God was genuine. I realized in this marriage we had a three-strand chord with God in the middle which made the marriage stronger than a two-strand cord. That was when I found security in my marriage and knew this man would never leave me no matter what. God matched us up for reasons I did not know, and He knew that my weaknesses were Lonnie's strong point. We are both far from perfect, as anyone in a marriage is far from perfect, but with God in the middle of the marriage, it was perfect for me.

MEANT TO BE

I wrote this poem in 2003 when I prayed God find my perfect "match" for me.

Dear Lord,
I come before You as a withered flower
with all my imperfections
humbled and inspired by You, Lord.
I can do no wrong
when You fill my soul
with peace and song.
I pray You bring someone
special into my life
who is thoughtful, warm, funny and a delight
someone who is sensitive and kind
a cuddly best friend I can count on
and someone who has a deep love for You, God.
I pray he knows at our first meet
we are to be together forever
God, You plant the seed.
Lord, I pray for the one I marry
that he has a strong structure for family
that he is on fire for You, God
and believes family time is more
important than material goods and making money.
I pray You bless my future honey abundantly
and ask You to keep him safe for me
through any travels he may be doing.
Until then, fill his heart with joy and laughter
and mold him into someone whom I can look after
In Jesus' name I pray, Amen.

What a testimony to me that God is in everything!
Poem written in 2003
I met my husband in 2010
Lonnie fits the poem's description perfectly
because God is a great matchmaker!

I can honestly say Lonnie and I are happily married. We have been married for eight years and growing stronger every day. I have learned key points to a healthy, strong marriage:

1. Always forgive, always
2. Communicate about everything
3. Respect one another
4. Be slow to anger
5. Don't hide sin; confess it to your spouse
6. When you disagree about something, always say you are sorry, even if you are right
7. Don't ever go to bed angry with one another. Talk it out before your head hits the pillow
8. You are both individuals with different background. You can agree to disagree and still be okay

*Years before I met Lonnie online, I had a signature on my email that read:

'I want to be so close to God that when the man of my dreams walks into my life, he has to go through God to get to me.'

In Lonnie's words:

"I saw the quote and took that challenge. I prayed and asked God how do I win this woman over. God replied, 'With love and patience.' I won her heart and asked her to marry me, and I am so glad I did."

Dear single reader; I share this from my heart: Anyone who has a close relationship with God who wants to marry, know that God is the best matchmaker and that in His timing, He will find the right match for you. Don't be discouraged. God has the right person for you.

This chapter in the Bible inspired us. We make sure we tell each other "I LOVE YOU" every single day and more than once a day. It's important we share our love for each other in many different ways. God poured His heart out in this love chapter:

LOVE:

Love is patient

Love is kind

It does not envy

It does not boast

It is not proud

It is not rude

It is not self-seeking

It is not easily angered

It keeps no record of wrongs

Love does not delight in evil but rejoices with the truth

It always protects

Always trusts

Always hopes

Always perseveres

Love never fails.

1 Corinthians 13: 4-8

*I will be writing a book about love and marriage in the future.

A CHILD OF GOD

About the Author

Becka L. Jones has always been and always will be a writer at heart. She loves to put her pen to paper not only to write stories, but also to express herself through poetry. She has been writing poems and stories since she was fifteen years old and has accumulated ten folders full of stories and two notebooks full of poems. As a teen, Becka published four poems in different anthology books. She has written many poems for a high school newspaper and many other submissions for booklets full of poems from students. She also has the gift of writing encouraging letters and cards for friends and family. She is passionate about bringing stories to life in books for her readers as well. Becka plans to write many books in upcoming years. Her focus in 2018/2019 will be writing humorous and encouraging books for small children and teens.

Becka was born in Minnesota, moved to Hawaii, then married a man from Minnesota, bringing her "full circle" back to her roots. She now resides in Texas with her husband and two adorable dogs, Bella Mocha and Finn, who are King Charles Cavaliers. Becka is living the dream... writing!

How to Contact the Author:

Email: bringingstoriestolife@yahoo.com

Facebook: Facebook/bringingstoriestolife77

Twitter: @Oceanbutterfly7

Website: https://oceanbutterflylove.wixsite.com/mybooks

E-book on Amazon: Having Compassion
E-book and physical book: Meant to Be

Coming Soon: Grandma's Fish Frankie (Children's book)

NOTES

NOTES